$12 25

# Deconstructing Harold Hill

| DATE DUE | |
|---|---|
| MAY 1 3 2000 | |
| FEB 5 2002 | |
| | |
| | |
| | |
| | |
| | |
| | |
| | |
| | |
| | |
| | |
| | |
| | |

# Also by Scott Miller

*From Assassins to West Side Story:*
*The Director's Guide to Musical Theatre*

# Deconstructing Harold Hill

*An Insider's Guide to Musical Theatre*

Scott Miller

HEINEMANN ■ Portsmouth, NH

**Heinemann**
A division of Reed Elsevier Inc.
361 Hanover Street
Portsmouth, NH 03801–3912
www.heinemanndrama.com

*Offices and agents throughout the world*

Acknowledgments for borrowed material continue on page 190.

CIP is on file with the Library of Congress.
ISBN: 0-325-00166-9

*Editor:* Lisa A. Barnett
*Production:* Vicki Kasabian
*Cover design:* Jenny Jensen Greenleaf
*Author photo:* Jennifer Silverberg
*Manufacturing:* Deanna Richardson

Printed in the United States of America on acid-free paper

03  02  01  00  99  DA  1  2  3  4  5

*This book is dedicated to Brian Tibbets,*
*for being the perfect collaborator,*
*for helping me do the best work of my career,*
*and for always inspiring me to greater heights*
*and deeper thoughts*

# Contents

# Acknowledgments

Thanks go to my editor, Lisa A. Barnett, for giving me a chance to write about my greatest love—not once but twice; to Steve Spiegel and Jim Merillat at Music Theatre International for helping so much and for genuinely caring about the art form; to Alison Helmer and Deborah Sharn for being wonderful to work with and genuinely inspiring; to Johanna Schloss and Tracy Collins for their valuable input; and to my infinitely resourceful friends on the Sondheim Internet discussion list, who always challenge me in the best way and who knew who Texas Guinan was and what a peck horn was, too.

# Overture

**W**hy are all the most imaginative, most daring new productions of classic American musicals directed by foreign directors? Why aren't Americans doing work like this? There have been British director Sam Mendes' amazing work on Stephen Sondheim's *Company* and Kander and Ebb's *Cabaret*, British director Nicholas Hytner's brilliantly revisionist staging of *Carousel*, Australian director Christopher Renshaw's smart and sexy new *King and I*, British director Trevor Nunn's revelatory new *Oklahoma!*, and others. True, American directors are doing revivals and "revisals" (greatly rewritten revivals) of great American musicals, but Des McAnuff's Broadway revival of *How to Succeed* lost all the show's bite and half its humor, and Walter Bobbie's *Chicago* lost much of the show's social satire and the dangerous sexuality that made the original so brilliant.

And don't even get me started on the recent New York revivals of *Company, Once Upon a Mattress, The Sound of Music, Grease*, or *Damn Yankees*. The only worthwhile revival in recent memory directed by an American was Hal Prince's *Show Boat*.

All of us—directors, actors, designers, and yes, even audiences—have a serious obligation to the musical theatre, this uniquely American art form that we love so dearly. We have an obligation to keep it not only alive, but also fresh, exciting, and invigorated. We have an obligation to demand intelligent, thoughtful productions. We have an obligation to refuse to do a particular show a particular way merely because that's how it's always been done. We have an obligation to approach every show, whether it's brand-new or fifty years old, with the same seriousness of purpose, the same sense of wonder and joy and fun, and the same courage to risk.

I directed a production of *Camelot* recently and it shocked and amazed many people in the audience. We didn't rewrite anything, we didn't add anything, and we didn't change the period. We just put back into it the sexuality and violence that have been there all along but had been forgotten or ignored for too many years. Our "innovative" approach was to read the script and try to put on stage all the complexity and human drama we found there. "The Lusty Month of May" was finally lusty again, after nearly forty years. "Fie on Goodness" was violent again. Arthur was played in the first scene as (*gasp!*) the twenty-five-year-old he is, all the critically acclaimed performances by fifty-year-old actors notwithstanding. Guenevere was played in the first scene as a seventeen-year-old because that's how old *she* is. And most astonishing of all, they both *changed* over the thirteen years that the show covers. In short, the basic rules of working on a play were applied to this classic musical and the result was astounding to many people who saw it.

But it shouldn't have been.

Why don't we apply the same rules to working on *Camelot* that we do to working on *Death of a Salesman* or *Sweet Bird of Youth*? Why do we care less about character growth, about subtext, about over-arching themes when we're working on a musical?

Part of the problem is time. Most professional theatres put together a show in one to two weeks. A community theatre may take four to five weeks. But the practical concerns of a musical—learning the score, choreographing dance numbers, bringing the orchestra in, and other things—take time away from the basic dramatic work of the director and actors. They just don't have the time to talk about characters that they have when they're working on a nonmusical, which is technically less complex and less demanding. How can you discuss Arthur and Guenevere's different childhoods, Guenevere's rebelliousness in response to her sheltered upbringing, the social conditions in England in the 1200s, or the philosophical flaws in Arthur's plans when you have to worry about choral arrangements, balancing the sound between the orchestra and the actors, making sure the dancers can move in their period costumes, and designing the more complex sets and lighting that many musicals demand?

But what's the solution? Most theatre companies can't afford to double their rehearsal time for a musical. Certainly directors and actors could come into the process better prepared and more open to new and unusual choices. Too often, musical theatre in America seems to implicitly condone or even endorse a lack of creativity in its artists. Ultimately, only the audiences can change that by voting with their pocketbooks. But since Broadway is still considered by many to be the center of musical theatre in America and the yardstick for quality, and since Broadway is still a commercial enterprise aimed more at tourists than at serious theatregoers, change may be slow in coming. When truly brilliant works like Adam Guettel's *Floyd Collins*, William Finn's *A New Brain*, and Jason Robert Brown and Alfred Uhry's *Parade* can't sustain a long run in New York, perhaps it's time for us to stop looking to Broadway as a role model for our work.

On the other hand, we can't go to the other extreme either. We can't make our work different merely for the sake of being different. We can't set *Jesus Christ Superstar* in a mental asylum just because nobody's tried that before. We have to make intelligent choices. We have to serve the material and the creators' intentions. That doesn't mean we have to do it the way the creators did it. That means only that we have to try our damnedest to figure out what the show's creators were trying to say and what effect they were trying to make on their audience, and then we have to try to achieve those same goals with the tools we have. What made *Company* exciting in 1970 is not the same thing that made it exciting in 1996, and that's why Sam Mendes' production was so very different from the original while still being utterly true to Stephen Sondheim and George Furth's intentions.

Likewise, there are times when it's not only okay but appropriate to do a musical the way it's been done before—because that may be the best way to serve the material. The important point is that *all* the choices must be made for a reason, with thoughtfulness and intelligence. It's not bad to make some of the same choices that were made fifty years ago, as long as the director and actors have made an active, informed choice to do that, as long as they know *why* they're doing it.

Musical theatre is finally being taken seriously in America. Universities offer degrees in musical theatre. Books are being published by the dozens about musical theatre. And with the help of the Internet, up-and-coming musical theatre artists are being better educated than ever before, as they find themselves in daily or weekly discussions with professional directors, actors, and writers from across the country and around the world. And yet, despite all that, we still allot the same amount of time to put on a musical with twenty sets, a cast of thirty, and an orchestra of sixteen that we allot to put on a one-set, four-character nonmusical drama. Why can't we see how ridiculous that is?

This book is an attempt to point out how rich, complex, and endlessly fascinating great musicals are, how much they deserve our fullest attention, respect, and efforts. It is an attempt to make clear the fact that *The Music Man, The King and I,* and *Ragtime* are brilliant, surprising, serious works of theatre, no less than *King Lear, Waiting for Godot,* or *Angels in America.* I'm one of those heretics that thinks that *West Side Story* is a better, more dramatically satisfying theatre piece than *Romeo and Juliet.* Surely that point can be argued, but no longer does *West Side Story* lose merely because it's a musical. The opinions I express in this book are strong ones (as you'll soon see) but there's nothing wrong with disagreeing with me. My only goal is to provoke and stimulate thoughts and discussions about these musicals in particular and about musical theatre and its endless possibilities in general. As far as I'm concerned, the only crime is in not exploring all that these amazing works of art have to offer.

# Camelot

Book and lyrics by Alan Jay Lerner
Music by Frederic Loewe
Based on The Once and Future King by T. H. White
Originally directed on Broadway by Moss Hart
Licensed by Tams-Witmark Music Library

T hough it is certainly flawed in some ways, *Camelot* is a magnificent work of the musical theatre and has become a true classic since it opened on Broadway in 1960. The critics were divided over *Camelot,* and though it ran two years and a respectable 873 performances, it couldn't compare to Lerner and Loewe's previous masterpiece, *My Fair Lady,* which ran for a staggering 2,717 performances. In fact, even though *Camelot* opened four-and-a-half years later, it closed only three months after *My Fair Lady* closed. Comparisons between the two were inevitable. Not only were they written by the same team and directed by the same director, they both starred Julie Andrews in the female lead and Robert Coote in the comic male lead, and both had sets designed by Oliver Smith and choreography by Hanya Holm. On top of that, they also both dealt with love triangles involving an older man, a young woman, and a young man (something also found in the film version of Lerner and Loewe's *Paint Your Wagon*), and they both featured a scene midway through Act I in which the ensemble watched an offstage equestrian event—the horse race in *My Fair Lady* and the jousts in *Camelot.*

*Camelot* had a very difficult development process. Before it had opened, director Moss Hart had had a heart attack and lyricist Alan Jay Lerner had developed ulcers and had been put on medication for depression. Costume designer Adrian died in the middle of the design process. Richard Burton and Robert Goulet both got sick during previews, a chorus girl ran a needle through her foot, the costume mistress' husband died, and the master electrician was hospitalized. Moss Hart died a year after the show opened, and composer Frederick Loewe never wrote another stage musical. But there were other troubles.

## A Lot of There There

Perhaps the show's main problem was trying to tell a story that was just too big for a single Broadway musical. Its first public performance ran four-and-a-half hours. They had to cut out the equivalent of a full musical. By the time all the cuts were made, the show was missing the two most important things in the story—the development of Arthur and Guenevere's relationship and the development of Guenevere and Lancelot's relationship. Audiences had to make the leap from no relationship to a full-blown relationship in both cases. But *Camelot* is more than just a tragic love story. Alan Jay Lerner wrote that at its core it contains the aspirations of mankind, and despite its shortcomings, *that's* what keeps the show from crumbling. And there's also an underlying subtext of great violence and unfettered sexuality that gives the show a very rich texture.

The critics complained that the show's creators tried to hide the material's inadequacies with expensive sets and costumes in its original production. But today, relatively free from the memory of the original, perhaps the trick to capturing all that is genuinely wonderful and provocative about *Camelot* is *not* to hide the book and score behind sets and costumes, but instead to meet the material head on, engage it, conquer it, and make it work. It can work. In fact, Alan Jay Lerner tells a story of the last rehearsal before the first New York preview. Lerner thought it would be good to run the show once on a bare stage with no sets or costumes. He writes in his autobiography, "Free of the trimmings and trappings, the company was unprepared for the rediscovery of intimacy and intention. When I think of *Camelot* today, it is that performance that remains most vividly in my mind."

Those who see *Camelot* as just an old-fashioned, romantic musical spectacle aren't looking very closely (or they've seen only shallow productions of the show). *Camelot* has a story and characters with a complexity and a depth that has been lost or ignored over the years. Going back to the source, *The Once and Future King*, you can see richer, deeper characters than we usually see in contemporary productions, characters the original production no doubt explored fully but that have been forgotten and simplified over time. *Camelot* is no fairy tale. It's a fiery, tragic, thought-provoking fable that somehow manages to work in a healthy dose of laughs between its layers of darkness. Like all the greatest works of the theatre, *Camelot* is underwritten—many things are left unsaid and unexpressed, just as they are in real life. Like the musicals of Stephen Sondheim, not everything is explained, not every emotion is laid out for us. And that's what makes it such thrilling theatre. As actors and directors—and audiences—we have to explore *why* Arthur ignores the signs around him, what is missing in Arthur and Guenevere's marriage, what Guenevere needs that Arthur can't give her and that Lance can, and how Lance can balance his obsessive love for Arthur and his passionate love for Guenevere. This is a show about passions—Arthur's passion for the philosophy of law and for changing the world, Guenevere's passion for life and romance and sex, Lancelot's passion for Arthur's dream and for Guenevere's love. *Camelot* is a muscular, aggressive, confrontational story, one that lives not in the world of musical comedy, but instead in the dark, violent, sexual world of Arthur and his knights of the Round Table.

Still, the show's greatest underlying flaw is that the two acts seem to be in two different styles. Act I seems to be almost a romantic comedy, full of laughs and larger-than-life characters, while Act II seems to be a reality-based romantic tragedy. One solution, of course, is to treat the first act more seriously, to find the sexuality and violence in it, to make it darker, to play all the wonderful subtext of these complex characters, and to look for laughs (dark though they may be) in the second act. Alan Jay Lerner found another solution in writing the screenplay. He began with the final battle and flashed back to the beginning, thereby setting up the final tragedy early on, letting the first act play in the shadow of the tragedy to come.

## White Knights

*The Once and Future King,* published in 1958, is the collective volume of four books written by T. H. White, loosely based on Sir Thomas Malory's *Le Morte d'Arthur* (*The Death of Arthur,* c. 1469). *The Once and Future King* includes *The Sword in the Stone, The Witch in the Wood* (later retitled *The Queen of Air and Darkness*), *The Ill-Made Knight,* and *The Candle in the Wind.* The fifth book, *The Book of Merlyn,* was supposed to be included in *The Once and Future King,* but White's publisher refused because of its aggressively antiwar politics. The first book, *The Sword in the Stone,* tells the story of Arthur's childhood (when he was nicknamed The Wart) up until the time he became king. Disney made an animated version of it in 1963. *The Witch in the Wood* tells about Queen Morgause and her sons, who later join the Round Table. Morgause is Arthur's half-sister, and she and Arthur conceived Mordred. This book is only partly related to the rest of the Arthur story. *The Ill-Made Knight* tells the story of Lancelot and his affair with Queen Guenevere. *The Candle in the Wind* tells of Mordred's arrival at Camelot and the fallout from Lancelot and Guenevere's affair, and it ends with Arthur knighting a young boy in the field the night before his last battle. *The Book of Merlyn* tells the full story of that battle, during which Merlyn returns to remind Arthur of important lessons from his childhood.

*Camelot* opened on Broadway in 1960, and it focuses mainly on the stories of *The Ill-Made Knight* and *The Candle in the Wind.* Even at nearly three hours, it leaves out a great deal and changes some details, but it's generally fairly faithful to the book. It's interesting to read *The Once and Future King* to better understand the characters and events in *Camelot,* but there are times when the book is at odds with the musical.

The story of *Camelot* takes place from 1200 until the late 1400s. T. H. White takes almost 300 years of actual history and compresses it into Arthur's single lifetime. This is roughly the same period as the Crusades and Robin Hood; England was in ruins, physically, spiritually, and economically. There were dozens of kings all fighting each other, hacking up peasants, and taking one another's lands. Arthur put an end to that. Though Camelot is a fictional place, historian John Leland has tentatively traced the legend back to the real-world Cadbury Castle. Excavations at the site in 1966–1970 confirmed that this large hill fort, with 1,200 yards of perimeter surrounding an eighteen-acre enclosure and rising about 250 feet above the surrounding countryside, was occupied in the Arthurian era by a powerful leader and his followers.

The Arthur Legend deals with love, loyalty, idealism, war and peace, perfection, and the ultimate in good versus evil. That's a tall order for a novel, but it's a *very* tall order for a musical. Arthur thinks he can live in an ideal world, that good intentions are enough. He doesn't realize that a fantasy world doesn't last very long, that the real world will always invade (here, in the person of Mordred). The seemingly schizoid structure of the show reflects Arthur's great mistake.

Most of Act I promises romance and chivalry and a Happily Ever After, but in Act II, the real world collides with Arthur's ideal and we see that no one can live in an ideal world. It's the same structure we see in *Into the Woods, The Fantasticks, Sunday in the Park with George, A Little Night Music,* and other musicals. And critics have complained about these shows as well. But one could argue that this approach is entirely legitimate and delivers a powerful message.

## Love Sucks

It's interesting to look at *Camelot* in the context of Lerner and Loewe's other musicals. The theme of impossible or nearly impossible love is a theme they returned to over and over throughout their collaboration. In their first hit, *Brigadoon,* the leading lady lived in a town that appears only once every hundred years, and the leading man is an outsider. If he stays in Brigadoon, he can never leave. If she leaves, the miracle will end for the whole town. It seems they can't ever be together. Of course, *Brigadoon* being an old-fashioned musical, a last-minute change of heart saves the day and they do end up together. In the stage version of *Paint Your Wagon,* the impossible love is an interracial relationship in 1850s California. In the film version of *Paint Your Wagon,* the impossible love is a three-way marriage that gets *very* difficult until one of the husbands finally leaves. In *My Fair Lady,* the leading man is a hard-core woman-hater who finds himself falling in love but won't admit it. And there's also a major age difference between the two leads. In *Gigi,* the age difference takes center stage, as an older man finds himself falling in love with a young girl he watched grow up. He only sees her as a child until the last-minute revelation. And in *Camelot,* the impossible love is a romantic triangle, in which each player loves the other two deeply. It involves an adulterous affair that threatens to destroy Camelot.

It seems one or both of the collaborators must have been obsessed with the seemingly insurmountable obstacles to romantic happiness. One clue to this obsession may be found in Alan Jay Lerner's difficulty in sustaining a relationship of his own. Not only did he constantly stray from Fritz Loewe professionally, while Loewe (who also had lots of trouble with women) remained completely "faithful" to Lerner, but Lerner also went through eight marriages in his lifetime. Perhaps both Lerner and Loewe were looking for answers as fervently as their characters were. Whatever the reasons, we can be grateful for

Lerner and Loewe's romantic difficulties because they inspired some of the most interesting dramatic situations ever written for the musical stage up until that time.

## The Wart

King Arthur is one of the most unconventional leading characters to appear in a musical before 1964 (the end of the "Golden Era" of musicals). He is a man of words, not actions, a man who is mostly passive, who allows Lancelot to steal Guenevere instead of fighting for her. This was not usual musical comedy fare in 1960. The challenge with Arthur and with *Camelot* is that Arthur continually makes mistakes, pretty much every step of the way. It's hard to keep caring about a man like that. Lerner and Loewe's solution was to imbue him with such innocence, such decency, and such a sense of wonder that the audience couldn't help but fall in love with him.

It's important to remember that Arthur is only twenty-five when he meets Guenevere, who is then only seventeen. They are both young and innocent. It's important that Arthur is a charming, restless boy. He's scared of getting married. He climbs trees. He pouts when Merlyn scolds him. Many directors ignore this because Arthur is always cast with an older actor. Richard Burton was thirty-five in the original production, and Richard Harris was the same age when he made the film version. And Harris was still playing Arthur for decades after that. We must see Arthur as a boy in order for his transformation to make sense to us, and in order for his downfall to make sense. Merlyn leaves Arthur before he's ready. He's not a mature man yet, and he is doomed to learn many lessons the hard way. Merlyn has taught him many things but he hasn't taught him how to think. As we see several times in the show, thinking remains a major effort for Arthur.

It's also interesting that Arthur seems to know *only* what Merlyn taught him. He doesn't seem to continue learning. It's as if his learning ended when Merlyn was taken away by the nymph Nimué, and that body of knowledge has to last him the rest of his life. All through the show, he constantly tries to remember back to things Merlyn told him. But this also illustrates how much Merlyn taught him, so many things that might not have registered on ten-year-old Arthur's brain because he saw no practical applications, but now, out in the real world, he sees the applications and strains to remember the lessons.

Arthur is only thirty when Lancelot arrives, while both Lance and Guenevere are then only twenty-two. Yet Arthur is still younger than his years. When the idea of the Round Table occurs to him, he leaps into it with a passion and enthusiasm and an obsessiveness that demonstrates his immaturity. In fact, his passion for the Table is so great, so all-consuming that Guenevere does not get the attention she wants—and she's not all that mature at this point either. From details in the book and the musical, we can speculate that Arthur is probably not giving Guenevere much sex, his passions far too wrapped up in his Round Table and in his desire to refashion the world into his idea of justice and goodness and righteousness. He does love her, wants to pay attention to her, wants her to share in this wonderful adventure, but his Table has seized both his imagination and his passion.

In the novel, White writes that Arthur had been "afflicted" as a boy by a tutor of genius, and that in his efforts to create a world of peace, he found himself up to his elbows in blood. We can only wonder how he would have ended up had Merlyn not been taken away. Arthur's head is always swimming with ideas but not practical knowledge or common sense. His three major problems come from not thinking ahead, not examining all possible consequences, and being preoccupied with being civilized in the abstract, with no thought as to how that might work in the real world. He knows his knights are fighting, are restless, are dissatisfied, but still insists that the Round Table remain an ideal. So eventually his knights rebel. He knows what's happening between Lance and Guenevere yet does nothing to prevent it or even to help them prevent it. He knows Mordred is trying to destroy him and his court but does nothing about it.

All well-drawn characters change over the course of their story, and most of them learn something. We see this process more plainly in Arthur than in most characters. He goes from boyhood innocence to a relative comfort in his crown and dedication to a philosophy, then to the pain of the complexities of mature love, and finally to the misery of the fallout from his blind idealism and his delayed arrival at full maturity. Interestingly, audiences always assume that Arthur's downfall is caused by Guenevere and Lancelot's adultery. But in reality, it is caused by *Arthur's* adultery. Had he not slept with his half-sister Morgause all those years ago (he wasn't married yet but she was), he would not have sired Mordred, who would ultimately destroy him. Arthur's punishment for not living up to his own ideals is the destruction of

Camelot. Both he and Lance have impossible ideals that they try—and fail—to live up to. They are more alike than they seem.

Arthur's Round Table is a flawed idea from the beginning. He sees a world where Might is Right, where the knights can do as they please because they have the money, the power, and the armor. If they feel like raping a woman, they can do it with impunity. Arthur decides that's not right, so he dedicates himself to changing things, to using Might *for* Right, in other words, using the knights strength and power to impose biblical morality on the population. But that can't work. Morality cannot be established through force. Politicians in our contemporary world have tried to impose morality through the force of legislation for years, but it always fails. You can't force people to be moral because morality comes from inside; moral behavior is only an expression of morality, not morality itself. In addition, Arthur thought that he could harness and rechannel the knights' aggression, their burning desire to fight and use force, but he couldn't. Once order was established, there was nothing left to fight for, yet the knights still wanted to fight (as illustrated quite humorously in the song "Fie on Goodness"). When Mordred appears and suggests a rebellion, many of the knights are fairly itching for battle and they join him without hesitation. Arthur finally sees his mistake and he says in the novel, "I have sown the whirlwind and I shall reap the storm." Arthur also ignores the fact that the knights' ability to do as they please was a privilege of being highborn, one they cherished. Why would they willingly give that up? When Arthur suggests that the knights stop chopping up peasants and foot soldiers and instead battle those knights who won't join the Table, his knights are understandably upset. By fighting only other knights, the danger of being hurt or killed is far greater. In the film version of *Camelot,* one of the knights says, "What's the sense of being born into the upper class when you can get killed like the lower class?"

At the core of the story, *Camelot* is about order versus chaos. There is social chaos and immorality all around Arthur (and in fact, throughout the Western world) as the story begins, and Guenevere, Lancelot, and the rest of the court represent this. Every song in Act I is about this, directly or indirectly. Arthur wants to control all this chaos, to harness all this energy and direct it toward good. But the sad truth is that he's not up to the job. As we see quite plainly, he can't control Guenevere, Lance, Mordred, or the knights. Even Pellinore rejects the new civil law. All the sex and violence swirling around in

*Camelot* is significant because it demonstrates Arthur's failure to realize his ideal, and it foreshadows his ultimate defeat at the end. Even today, it's a lesson for us—passions can't be controlled and morality can't be legislated. Human beings have some instincts and needs that always overcome reason and law. Arthur is battling the forces of nature itself, and nature will not be contained or controlled.

## Pirate Jenny

Guenevere is also an unconventional musical leading lady. She's a tease, a bit arrogant, very (perhaps overly?) sexual, and she ultimately betrays her leading man. Like Arthur, Guenevere also goes through a full, complex, fascinating transformation over the course of the show. We first see her as a child, only seventeen when she arrives at Camelot, only twenty-two when Lance arrives. She's been sheltered and pampered for her first seventeen years, taught how to be a queen, taught how to be a "proper lady." But she's never had an outlet for the rebellion and adventuring that a strong young woman desires. Her first excursion into the real world is to Camelot for an arranged marriage. We see in "The Simple Joys of Maidenhood" her immaturity, her lust for violence, her naivete about the ways of the world. She wants adventure but she has absolutely no concept of what she's wishing for.

A close look at the lyric of "Simple Joys of Maidenhood" tells us so much about Guenevere. Alan Jay Lerner has packed so much information into this song, all the while surprising us with punch line after punch line. Guenevere starts the song by calling St. Genevieve, apparently her personal patron saint. But Guenevere has to *remind* the saint of who she is. We can only assume that this means Guenevere doesn't pray very often. Yet only a couple lines later, she's purporting to be so devout—obviously a lie. She also says she's always been a "lamb," but we'll soon see that's not true either. She lets her anger take over and she rages at St. Genevieve, complaining about the details of her current situation, and finally—and hilariously—threatening to find another saint to pray to. But then Guenevere decides maybe that's a bad tack to take. If she wants rescue, she'd better be nicer to her patron saint. So she goes on to catalog the "conventional, ordinary, garden variety joys of maidenhood" that she's been robbed of. And what are those simple, ordinary perks of being a maiden? A knight committing suicide over her. Two knights battling over her and one of them being killed. A war being waged over her, and of course, the unstated but obvious death and blood-shed that accompanies war. And finally, the best perk she imagines is not only men killing each other over her, but men killing their own relatives over her. She has a lust for violence and for bloodshed. She is actually insulted because Arthur won't attack and rape her. But her lust for violence will come back to haunt her. In "Simple Joys of Maidenhood," she sings

> Shall I not be on a pedestal,
> Worshipped and competed for?
> Not be carried off, or better still,
> Cause a little war?

She sees war as romantic. She's delighted when Arthur tells her war would have broken out if they had not married. But at the end of the show, her wish comes true, with deadly results. In "Guenevere," the chorus sings:

> Guenevere, Guenevere
> In that dim, mournful year,
> Saw the men she held most dear
> Go to war for Guenevere.

She got her war. It brings to mind the old adage, "Be careful what you wish for, or you will surely get it."

Guenevere is also more oversexed than your average musical the-atre ingenue. Too often directors and actors overlook her very sexual behavior. They've spent years hearing Julie Andrews' delicate, lady-like singing on the original cast album and they ignore the actual evi-dence in the script and score. They want to be reverent with her char-acter because she's a queen and because ultimately she becomes a tragic figure, and perhaps also because they see Camelot as a "classic."

But even a cursory look at "The Lusty Month of May" shows the real Guenevere. The title of the song says it all. This song is an explicit celebration of sex, of unbridled, wicked, improper, unwholesome, shocking sexual acts. Guenevere thinks every girl wants her boyfriend to be a cad, that self-control is a bore, that going morally astray is blissful. The fragrance she smells wafting through the air is the smell of sex, make no mistake, that "dear forbidden fruit." But what does this tell us? That Guenevere and Arthur are hopelessly mismatched.

In the novel, White says, "She had felt respect for [Arthur], with gratitude, kindness, love, and a sense of protection. She had felt more than
this and you might say that she had felt everything but the passion of
romance." Can we be surprised when she eventually has an affair?
Can Arthur be surprised? Or does he just close his eyes to this problem? But Arthur needs Guenevere before he can be the king he needs
to be. It isn't until he meets her that he feels kingly, that he at last
wants to be a king. She is the muse he needed.

But Guenevere can be quite bitchy from time to time. In her initial comments to Lancelot when she meets him, she's sarcastic and insulting. Is that proper behavior for the Queen of England to someone
the King brings to court? And even though she knows how much
Arthur thinks of Lancelot, she keeps criticizing Lance over and over.
She doesn't even attempt to be kind to him, to try to understand him,
to help him feel welcome. In a sense, she's performing for the knights
and ladies around her, entertaining them with her thinly veiled jibes
at Lance. Later on, she helps build sentiment against him in the court
by gossiping with the knights and ladies. She gives three knights her
kerchief to carry against Lancelot in the jousts. And it's with this act
that she tries to make her childhood fantasies come true. At last she
sees an opportunity for her dreams of knights fighting over her to
come true. There will not only be battles; there may well be blood-
shed. She knows Arthur will never deliver those fantasies. He thinks
fighting is immoral unless it is to promote righteousness. Not only is
Arthur not the lover she had hoped for, he's also not the warrior she
dreamed of. They are mismatched in every conceivable way.

Yet, when the jousts happen, when her fantasies are at last made
reality, the result is tragedy. Lionel is killed by Lancelot. Finally, the
death of which she dreamed has come to pass, and she suddenly realizes what she's done. She has indirectly killed a man, and not just
any man, but a friend of hers, one of her favorite knights. And then—
the obligatory moment, that moment in any story toward which
everything before it leads and from which everything after it follows,
the moment that the story cannot exist without. Lancelot steps forward, bends down, prays, and brings Lionel back to life. We see for the
first time that his claims of purity, his claims that he can perform mir-
acles are actually true. When he rises, his eyes lock onto Guenevere's,
and we realize in an instant that they have fallen in love. Perhaps Guenevere already found him physically attractive (in the novel, Lance is
ugly, but in the musical, he's very handsome), but he's accomplished

two things. First, he has saved her from her folly; he has brought back to life the knight her immature schemes had killed. Second, he has fought for her and he has won. He is the greatest knight in the court, probably in all Europe, and she sees now that he loves her, no doubt with the same passion with which he loves Arthur and the Table. How can she resist? As Queen, she *should* resist, but she won't. And later we will see the difference between Lance and Arthur. Whereas Arthur's love for this Table outshines his love for Guenevere, Lance clearly loves Guenevere more (or at least as much).

It's interesting to notice how Guenevere's music gets more complex, melodically and harmonically, over the course of the show as she matures, as she becomes a more complex individual, and finds herself in progressively more complex situations. "Simple Joys of Maidenhood" is the song of a girl. "I Loved You Once in Silence" is the song of a woman.

## Ill-Made Nights

If Arthur and Guenevere are unusual leading characters, so is Lancelot. He's arrogant (although he really is everything he claims), cold, off-putting, and destructive. And who is the leading man—Arthur or Lancelot? Lancelot is usually cast as the more handsome of the two, and he's the one who gets the explicit romance (whether there is romance between Guenevere and Arthur is questionable), but that romance ends in tragedy, and at the expense of Arthur's dreams. Even in Act II, the story is really centered on Arthur, though Lance possesses all the usual traits of the leading man. So who are we rooting for? Is it possible to root for all three of them?

In the first scene of the show, Arthur says that protecting Guenevere would "satisfy the prayers of the most fanatic cavalier alive." He has no idea how right he is. Lancelot is indeed the most fanatic cavalier alive and being with Guenevere is clearly the answer to his prayers. When Lancelot arrives at Camelot, he is only twenty-two. He seems awfully arrogant, but we soon see that every claim he makes is true. He really is that strong, that pure, that miraculous. It's not that he's arrogant; it's just that he's completely lacking in social graces. He's never learned how to interact with people. He's spent every waking moment of his young life training his mind and body in hopes of joining Arthur and his court. The only person he ever interacted with is his Uncle Dap, who trained him. Like Arthur, Lancelot is obsessively single-minded, and his enthusiasm sometimes borders on frightening. In the novel he fully descends into madness twice and White suggests that his tendency toward madness is inherited. The obsessive single-mindedness that makes him the best knight in the world also makes him crazy. In the novel, Lance and his father visit Camelot when Lance is a young boy. Arthur tells him that he's putting together the Round Table with the best knights in the world and invites Lance to come back when he's older. From that moment on, Lance thinks of nothing but Arthur and his plans—which makes it all the more tragic that Arthur's dreams are eventually destroyed by Lance's hand.

The novel tells us a great deal about Lance. The third book of the collection (the one on which *Camelot* is based) focuses far more on Lance than on Arthur. Even the title, "The Ill-Made Knight" refers to Lance (in the novel he's physically "ill-made," not handsome). Lance believes that he is inherently bad and sinful (again, "ill-made"), which is why he works so hard at being good and pure. (Although, how impressive is it that he's so pure? He's never encountered temptation in any form until he meets Guenevere. It's easy to be pure when nothing tempts us.) Lance believes that he's at a distinct disadvantage to begin with. Interestingly, despite his claims of moral purity, it doesn't take long for Lance to commit several of the Seven Deadly Sins. When he arrives, he's already guilty of Pride. Soon, he's also guilty of Lust and Covetousness. Later on, he's guilty of Anger on several occasions. That's better than half the Seven Deadly Sins right there.

The other interesting thing about Lancelot in the novel is that his story is chock full of homoeroticism. According to many literary scholars, T. H. White was gay, so it may not be surprising in the 1940s and 1950s that he worked a homoerotic subtext into his story rather than addressing it directly. It's possible that it wasn't even conscious. Most of this has been excised from the musical, but there are traces still there. In *The Once and Future King*, White writes that when, as a young boy, Lancelot meets Arthur for the first time, "He had already fallen in love with Arthur on the night of the wedding feast and he carried with him in his heart to France a picture of that bright northern king at supper, flushed and glorious from his wars." Later in the book Lancelot is jealous of Arthur's love of Guenevere—"to have broken his body for the older man's ideal, only to find this mincing wife stepping in at the end of it to snatch away his love at no cost at all. Lancelot was jealous of Guenevere and he was ashamed of himself for being so." Lancelot "thought of [Guenevere] only as the person who had robbed him [of Arthur's love], and since robbers are deceitful, designing, and heartless people, he thought of her as these." After arriving at Camelot, Lancelot goes off on a year of quests, and quite a few of his adventures in the novel involve knights who are naked, and rarely for any discernible reason. None of this is in the musical, but his obsessive love for Arthur is expressed when they meet, and there is a great deal of tension between Lance and Guenevere when they meet. The dialogue shows explicitly only Guenevere's dislike of Lancelot, but Lance's jealousy of Guenevere can easily be played within the dialogue as it is, and one could argue that was probably Lerner's intention from the beginning. And this more intense, two-way hostility makes their eventual love affair all the more interesting.

Lance's jealousy of Guenevere is illustrated in the musical when they first meet (after the song "Lusty Month of May" in Act I, scene 5). Lance has trained all his life, become the best knight in the world, and traveled to England, all to be Arthur's partner, his right-hand man and commander-in-chief, in this new order of chivalry. But when Arthur takes Lance to meet Guenevere, Lance sees that Arthur has already been discussing all these plans with his *wife*, of all people. In Lance's eyes, Guenevere has already taken the place in Arthur's plans that Lance intended to occupy, that of confidante and cocreator. Lance is immediately jealous of Guenevere and sets about showing Arthur—and not all that subtly—that Guenevere is not up to the task, that Lancelot is far better suited for the job. And of course, the implication that she's not capable of understanding the complexities of the subject rankles Guenevere and she takes an instant dislike to Lancelot. What Lance doesn't know is that Guenevere isn't all that interested in Arthur's plans to begin with and has no intention of being his partner in that area. But Guenevere makes it very clear that Arthur is hers, not Lance's. They are essentially playing tug-of-war over Arthur, an interesting precursor to the romantic triangle later on.

I'm not arguing that Lancelot is gay. He's not. But he does fall in love with Arthur. It's not sexual in the least but it is romantic. It's a real-world phenomenon that most men would never admit to, but sometimes the connection between two men is so intense, so powerful, so intimate, that even though they may be heterosexual, they fall in love. As it is in this story, that love eventually gets overshadowed by the love for a woman, but that doesn't make it any less real. Lancelot thinks of no one but Arthur (until he meets Guenevere). He devotes all his attention, energy, and activity to Arthur. He pretty much dedicates his life to Arthur and Arthur's dream. He wants to be with Arthur all the time. When he's not with him, he talks about him. He's experiencing a teenager's first love, minus the sex. It has come late to Lance, but we already know that his emotional development is seriously arrested (or at least delayed) until he gets to Camelot. It's hero worship to be sure, but it's more than that. It's real love. And that makes his betrayal even more difficult and also more dramatic.

## Threeway

The romantic triangle at the heart of *Camelot* is fascinating. Unlike most romantic triangles, each of the three needs something from the other two. In a way, Arthur and Guenevere's marriage is incomplete until Lance arrives; it is only with the three of them that each one can be happy. Arthur certainly gets support from Guenevere when he's rambling on about the Round Table, Might for Right, and his new system of justice, but she's not really all that excited about his ideas. After all, she loves their world the way it is. She was born a princess, so for her the world has always been ideal. But Arthur was born an orphan and as a child, he believed he was never to be any more than squire to his stepbrother Kay. He didn't become king until he was sixteen, and even then, he didn't really *feel* like a king. He sees the world from the point of view of the peasants. He sees all the injustice and squalor, and now that he has power, he wants desperately to right all those wrongs. Guenevere just can't understand why Arthur would want to change things. She loves him and for that reason, she listens and offers encouraging words, but her heart's not in it. She'd rather be talking about knights battling over beautiful women, abductions of virgins, and brave knights dying for love. Both Arthur and Guenevere need what Lancelot will bring to Camelot. Arthur needs a companion who's just as excited about his ideas as he is, someone who will equal Arthur's enthusiasm and even offer ideas of his own. And Guenevere needs Lance's romanticism. She needs him to be hopelessly, madly in love with her. She needs passion in her love, and Arthur doesn't provide that. Early in the play when Arthur comes up with the idea of the Round Table, Guenevere just isn't all that excited about it, and we see right there that though they love and respect each other, though they're both happy, there is something missing in their marriage. They don't care about the same things. Arthur needs an intellectual partner in his philosophical endeavors and Guenevere needs a lover. It's significant that Guenevere is always talking and singing about sex, yet Arthur never even mentions the topic. We see that Guenevere is not getting from her marriage what she's always wanted, and we expect that soon she may well go looking for what she's missing. It's subtle foreshadowing, but it's important.

Interestingly, just as Arthur and Guenevere both need Lance, he needs what both of them can provide. Unlike Arthur, the cause is not enough for him. He has never been loved, and when Guenevere falls in love with him, it changes his life. As much as he loves Arthur's ideas, he loves Guenevere more. He needs Arthur to challenge him to be the best knight he can be, but he also needs someone to love him, to hold him, and to tell him he's worth loving.

## Mixing It Up

In the novel, Mordred is described as slightly crooked, one shoulder higher than the other. He's compared to Richard III. As many authors have done throughout history, White has given Mordred a twisted body to mirror his twisted soul, and more significantly, a twisted body born of an immoral coupling between Arthur and his half-sister Morgause. Mordred is the instrument of Arthur's destruction by Arthur's own deeds. Mordred is also the person who will no longer allow Arthur to pretend he doesn't see the adultery happening right under his nose. Mordred challenges Arthur's new system of justice. Once the affair is revealed, Arthur must either burn Guenevere at the stake or he must abandon (and thereby destroy) the system of justice he worked so carefully to construct. If Arthur can step in and overrule judge or jury, what real value does the system have? As we could have expected, Arthur chooses his ideals over his wife, just as Mordred knew he would.

King Pellinore is a character created by T. H. White. He doesn't exist in any earlier versions of the Arthur legend. He acts as a kind of father figure to Arthur and, in a way, as a replacement for Merlyn, who was also a father figure. But Pellinore can't really take Merlyn's place because Pellinore isn't a teacher. He's more friend than teacher. He's what Merlyn might be without his wisdom or magic. Frequently, directors cast the same actor as both Merlyn and Pellinore since Merlyn disappears after the second scene. And though it's usually done for purely practical reasons, it makes a lot of sense thematically as well.

Pellinore's other purpose is comic relief and to poke fun at the strict and sometimes pointless traditions of medieval customs and rules of knight errantry. There is a danger in making him too much of a cartoon character, which would be at odds with the show's tone. An extreme portrayal of Pellinore might fit in Act I, but he wouldn't fit in Act II. Also, most of Pellinore's quirks and peculiarities are much funnier if they're played straight. If the actor playing Pellinore "comments" on his character, if he's *telling* the audience Pelly is hilarious, he won't be half as funny. But if Pelly has no idea how funny he is, the comedy will be stronger, realer, and funnier. It's a tough role to play well.

The three main knights, Dinadan, Lionel, and Sagramore represent the rest of Camelot's population, or at least the rest of the court. They also serve as Guenevere's companions, almost boyfriends, to keep her company when Arthur's off working on his Round Table. The movie version has a scene with the four of them getting drunk together. Perhaps they are Guenevere's sexual outlet before Lance arrives.

## The Music of the Knights

*Camelot's* score is extremely well built. It progresses from light, innocent songs, to dark, sophisticated, minor-key songs over the course of the show, as both the love triangle and the idea of the Round Table move from idealism to decay. The first two songs, "I Wonder What the King Is Doing Tonight," and "The Simple Joys of Maidenhood," introduce our main characters, Arthur and Guenevere. These are their songs of innocence and immaturity. Even this early in the show, Arthur and Guenevere are connected musically. The end of "I Wonder What the King Is Doing Tonight" ends with a run of chords moving up chromatically, illustrating the panic Arthur is feeling. With no intervening dialogue, "Simple Joys of Maidenhood" begins, and its introduction mirrors the end of the previous song, another run of chords moving up chromatically, again illustrating the panic racing through Guenevere's heart as she runs through the forest. It's a wonderful little connection between these two people who will soon be married, a musical device probably not even consciously registered by the audience, but it provides dramatic and musical unity to the scene, and shows Guenevere and Arthur as kindred spirits, both scared and panicked, both in need of a friend, both in need of rescue—physical rescue for Guenevere and spiritual rescue for Arthur.

The title song, "Camelot," follows and acts throughout the show as a theme for Arthur's love of Camelot, its majesty and transcendent power. Arthur sings it to Guenevere and convinces her to stay in Camelot. The bugle call motif (an upward major triad) that accompanies the word "Camelot" shows up over and over again, throughout the show, sometimes as the sound of heralds' trumpets.

Lancelot opens "C'est Moi," his signature song, with the "Camelot" bugle call motif to establish the idea that he, like Arthur, has a great love and reverence for Camelot and its ideals. Once he's introduced himself, the music changes. The first verse begins and we see that it is a list song, enumerating the various deeds that Lancelot thinks a knight should be able to accomplish. At first, these tasks seem difficult but not impossible—climbing a wall, killing a dragon, swimming in a suit of armor. But halfway through the verse, we see the humor creep through, starting with the comic word, "unwinceable." We soon see that this is a song of unmitigated gall, and the further we get into the song, the more outrageous his claims become and the funnier it gets. That he was chosen by angels, that had he been in Eden, he would not have been seduced by Eve is so extreme that it becomes comic. In fact, we will learn later in the show that he is quite *easily* seduced, that he has wildly overstated the case for his purity. We laugh at him here the way Guenevere and the court will laugh at him when they meet him. The first verse covers physical prowess, and the second verse covers spiritual and moral purity.

"Simple Joys of Maidenhood" has established Guenevere's preoccupation with both sex and her curious attraction to violence. Midway through Act I, "The Lusty Month of May" confirms her sexual appetite, and we see that it has grown considerably since she's been with Arthur, perhaps because Arthur is less physical than she would like. The next song, "Then You May Take Me to the Fair," returns to her penchant for violence. As mentioned above, in this song, Guenevere arranges to make her earlier fantasies finally come true, unfortunately with tragic results. Though this song is important for several dramatic reasons, the song is optional and many companies don't include it in their effort to keep the show's running time down. But not using this song will rob Guenevere of some serious emotional resonance in the jousts scene when Lionel is killed. If Lionel's death is not her fault, then it's not as tragic for her and Lance's miracle is no longer a rescue for her.

"How to Handle a Woman" is next and we see that, unlike Guenevere, Arthur has matured. He takes his relationship seriously. But Merlyn was wrong—loving Guenevere will not be enough to "handle" her. Letting her do whatever she wants will prove to be dangerous. We see several times in the show that Merlyn is hardly a reliable authority on love and marriage. He tells Arthur that love and marriage have nothing to do with each other. He tells Arthur not to worry about figuring out what a woman is thinking since women don't think very often. "How to Handle a Woman" is such a beautiful song and its sentiment so romantic that we don't notice how misguided its advice is. After the jousts, we see in "Before I Gaze at You Again" that Guenevere is finally beginning to mature emotionally as well. She's beginning to see the complexity of love.

The music under Arthur's speech at the end of the first act is beautifully constructed. As he begins, he describes how much he loves Guenevere and Lance, while underneath we hear "How to Handle a Woman," the song in which he decided that the way to survive this storm was through love. His anger shows for a moment, but he stops himself. He tells himself that he doesn't get the luxury of irrational feelings. He is a king and must behave as one, and underneath, the music changes to "I Wonder What the King Is Doing Tonight," the song that described how difficult it is for Arthur to be the king, how frightening, how confusing. As he vows to act like a king, to be strong, to not fall victim to jealousy and doubts, the music turns to a march version of "I Wonder What the King . . ." and he turns his doubts into strength (at least for now). It's significant that Lerner and Loewe chose to end the first act not with a song, but with a spoken soliloquy, an extremely unusual choice (although they hedged their bet by thoroughly underscoring the speech). To set that speech to music would have taken Wagnerian-sized music and much more time, in a show in which time is already at a premium. Also, remembering that Richard Burton created the role of Arthur, it becomes less surprising that they would make this choice, secure in the knowledge that Burton could bring the proper weight to this moment.

The second act begins with "If Ever I Would Leave You," the song that marks Lance's maturing. He has progressed lyrically from "C'est Moi," which is entirely about him (even the title, which translates as "It Is I"), to this romantic song more about Guenevere. He has grown up (at least partially) and no longer thinks only of himself. Like Arthur and Guenevere, he now understands the complexity and pain of love.

"The Seven Deadly Virtues" is the first of the comic songs in Act II, though it is very dark. It's interesting that most people think of *Camelot*'s first act as lighter and its second act as much darker, but when you look at the score, each act has three comic songs. It's true that the comic numbers in the second act have a somewhat darker subtext, but let's not forget that "Simple Joys of Maidenhood" is about violence and death and "Lusty Month of May" is about unchecked sexual promiscuity. The acts are more balanced than they seem, at least musically. Though we laugh at the lyric of "The Seven Deadly Virtues," we know that Mordred will be a destructive force in Camelot. He doesn't operate by the same rules as the rest of society—especially this newly civilized society. He is a true sociopath. "What Do the Simple Folk Do" is the second comic number in Act II, but it's really a very sad song. Guenevere and Arthur are both deeply troubled. They try to lift their spirits by whistling, by singing, by dancing, but nothing cheers them. It's a funny song on one level, but the humor is undercut by the result of their efforts. At the end, they're still sad. And the rest of the act is just going to get heavier.

There is a neat connection between "I Wonder What the King Is Doing Tonight" and "Simple Folk." In the first song, Arthur wonders out loud if everyone in Camelot is wondering what he's doing on the eve of his wedding, if they're all "peering up at the castle with a question mark in each eye." He decides, yes, that's exactly what they're doing, which of course only makes his sense of victimization seem worse. Later, in Act II, at the end of "Simple Folk," Guenevere asks for the fourth time what the simple folk do when they're sad, and Arthur remembers back to the night he met Guenevere and he comes up with the answer—they sit around and wonder what the royal folks are doing. It's a small moment, but a revealing one. Of course, he also knows how simple folk spend their time because for his first fifteen years, he *was* simple folk himself, unlike Guenevere.

There is a song written for the scene in Morgan Le Fay's forest called "The Persuasion," in which Mordred tries to seduce Morgan Le Fay with candy. But the song is quite long in an already too-long musical, and it's just not a very good song. No one ever includes it in performance, but it's in the published score and the rental materials.

The next song is "Fie on Goodness," the nastiest of the comedy numbers in the show. The knights are restless. The erosion of the ideals of the Round Table is beginning to be evident. In this song, the knights bemoan the fact that they can no longer kill and rape. It is even

more violent than "Simple Joys of Maidenhood" (which isn't easy).
And because it's instigated by Mordred, we know that this explosion
of anger and frustration can only lead to trouble. Guenevere's comedy numbers are about disregarding the rules of good conduct. Mordred's first song is about how unpleasant virtue is. And now, the
knights themselves, supposedly the keepers of right and goodness,
say explicitly that "goodness" is bad. Can we wonder why Camelot
falls? Again, this song is optional when a company produces *Camelot.*
But without this song, we miss an important point—that Arthur's
plan was fatally flawed from the beginning, and that Mordred only
exploits the unrest that already exists. Mordred doesn't have to *create*
unrest among the knights; Arthur has already done that unwittingly
by creating impossible standards of conduct and by making Lancelot
his favorite among the knights.

As Lance and Guenevere's last romantic scene begins, we hear "If
Ever I Would Leave You" underneath, Lance's musical declaration that
he could never ever leave her. They don't know that in a few minutes
Mordred and the knights will burst in and Lance will have to leave
her. It's also interesting that when Lance mentions Arthur, the music
stops. The music of their love is interrupted. In this same scene, "I
Loved You Once in Silence," Guenevere's last song, makes an important point. Guenevere, Lance, and Arthur were all miserable while
Guenevere and Lance's love was unspoken, but now that they have
acted on it, they are all twice as miserable. Their actions will surely
destroy all Arthur's dreams. Only now that it's too late has Guenevere
finally reached full emotional maturity.

One of the flaws in the score is that two of the show's songs, "The
Jousts" and "Guenevere," describe offstage action, a universal no-no
for any play or musical. Or course it's unavoidable in *Camelot,* since a
real, live joust wouldn't fit on most stages and neither would a battle
involving hundreds of men on horseback. But these songs violate another cardinal rule of musicals—the Ten-Minute Rule. You can do
anything you want in a musical, stylistically, structurally, or otherwise, as long as you do it within the first ten minutes, to establish the
evening's rules for the audience. These two songs would have worked
better had the show opened with a narrative piece, perhaps some sort
of prologue sung by the knights, establishing the fact that there would
be narration from time to time in the show. But "Guenevere" works
as well as it does because it incorporates some actual dramatic interaction between Arthur, Mordred, and Dinadan.

And "Guenevere" returns to one of the major themes of the show, that violence is inevitable, that despite our greatest efforts, violence is part of being human. Arthur's attempt to civilize the knights was doomed from the start. Arthur's decision to fight Mordred's evil by being fair and just was foolish. Mordred says to Arthur, "How did you think you could survive without being as ruthless as I?" and Mordred is right. Arthur lives in a time of violence. His wife lusts for violence. He has won and kept his kingdom with bloodshed. His proclamation announcing his new peaceful order of chivalry threatens "death or reformation," in other words, either knights join the round table or they will be killed. How can he hope to build a peaceful world this way?

As the show comes to a close, we first hear the heralds blowing a battle call to the "Camelot" bugle call motif. The motif that has represented the majesty of Camelot now precedes the battle that will destroy it, and we are reminded of all that Camelot could have been. As Arthur says good-bye to Guenevere on the battlefield, the music underneath is "Before I Gaze at You Again," Guenevere's song of sadness, longing, and the denial of love. She did love Arthur and now she must leave him. She will never see him again.

Arthur has lost his wife, his best friend, his Round Table, and may soon lose his life. It is a tragedy worthy of King Lear. But then Tom of Warwick (pronounced War-ick) appears. (This character is named Tom as a kind of insider's joke, a subtle tribute to Sir Thomas Malory, the author of Le Morte D'Arthur, who was born in Warwickshire, England.) And in an instant, Arthur's fate changes. He can live on, and more important, Camelot and the Round Table can live on, because this boy will return to England and keep the story alive. Arthur has always regretted that he did not sire a son to ascend the throne and carry on the ideals of the Round Table. He hoped that even Mordred might finally find his way and carry on his legacy. But here, just before dawn, on the battlefield where he will probably lose his life, Arthur finally finds a surrogate son in this peasant boy who has stowed away on the ship to France. Finally Arthur has his heir who will allow the Round Table and all its ideals to live. All Arthur has created will not be in vain. His dream will live on. Men may die, but ideas do not. As Arthur talks to Tom about the Round Table, the underscoring changes to the melody of the knighting ceremony music. Not only does this connection make sense at that moment, but it also serves as short-term foreshadowing. A few moments later, Arthur will decide to knight Tom there in the field. It's almost as if the music is showing us that Arthur's thoughts of the Round Table remind him of the knights he's invested, which in turn give him the idea to knight Tom. The music gives us a glimpse into Arthur's thought processes.

To the melody of the song "Camelot," Arthur's hope is resurrected and he tells Tom to return home to keep the memory of Camelot and its great achievements alive. The ensemble is heard behind Arthur's dialogue singing the "Camelot" motif. Finally, in glorious four-part a cappella, the company sings those famous words:

> *Don't let it be forgot*
> *That once there was a spot,*
> *For one brief shining moment,*
> *That was known as Camelot.*

And the finale ends with one last quote of the bugle call.

## Other Resources

The script for *Camelot* may be out of print, but many libraries will have a copy. The full score and vocal selections are widely available, as is the videotape of the film. HBO broadcast the 1981 Broadway revival with Richard Harris, and though it's not available commercially, many collectors have it. (Richard Burton was originally set to do it, and this would have been close to having the original performance, but due to illness, Harris took over.) There is a videotape available called *The Best of Broadway,* including clips of performances from Broadway shows that appeared on the Ed Sullivan Show. The tape includes Richard Burton and Julie Andrews doing "What Do the Simple Folk Do?" *The Once and Future King* and *The Book of Merlyn* are also widely available. It might also be fun to rent and watch Disney's *The Sword in the Stone* and John Boorman's 1981 film *Excalibur* (which is based on *Le Morte d'Arthur*). Reading Sir Thomas Malory's and Alfred Lord Tennyson's versions of the Arthur legend is interesting, but they are so different from White's tale that it's not very helpful practically speaking.

# 2 Chicago

*Book by Fred Ebb and Bob Fosse*
*Music by John Kander*
*Lyrics by Fred Ebb*
*Originally directed and choreographed by Bob Fosse*
*Licensed by Samuel French, Inc.*

Bob Fosse assembled his cast for *Chicago* in 1975, and during the very first week of rehearsals he was rushed to the hospital for pains in his chest. He had almost had a heart attack and needed open heart surgery, which was not nearly as common then as it now. The producers decided they'd have to postpone the show. Miraculously, they managed to keep the cast together until Fosse could go back to work. But though his taste had always tended toward the dark side—lyricist Fred Ebb referred to him as the Prince of Darkness—it had now gotten darker. Before the open heart surgery, the darkness had been a kind of caricature; now it was real. Fosse had seen death and it had changed him. And it changed *Chicago.*

Like Oliver Stone's 1994 film *Natural Born Killers, Chicago* takes the form of that which it criticizes. A scathing satire of how show business and the media make celebrities out of criminals—and thereby make crime attractive—the story is told through a succession of vaudeville acts. Fosse was saying, okay, you've been lied to long enough—we're gonna pull back the curtain and let you see what's really going on. Like much of Bob Fosse's other, later work, *Chicago* is a show overflowing with raw sexuality, creating a world that is shocking, frightening, intentionally offensive. When *Chicago* opened in 1975, there had not been a musical of such depravity and savage satire since Brecht and Weill's *Threepenny Opera.* Bob Fosse made theatre pieces about the decadence of our world, the lies and conceits and compromises, the deals with the devil we all make, and as in *Sweet Charity, Pippin,* and Fosse's film version of *Cabaret, Chicago* is a show which makes the audience uncomfortable. This was the third time Fosse would use the false glamour of show business—the lie at its core—as a metaphor for life. He did it first with the film of *Cabaret* (1971), then with *Pippin* (1972), and he'd return to this idea, pushing it to its furthest extreme, with the autobiographical film *All That Jazz* (1980). He attacked hypocrisy wherever he saw it, even in his own work. He knew the world of *Chicago,* in which killers are made into stars, isn't far at all from the real world.

The primary premise of *Chicago* is that the world of crooked lawyers and a public who craves violence is as frightening in its own way as the crimes themselves. Fosse, John Kander, and Fred Ebb created a show with an attitude that never softened. Unlike other musicals about show business, this one never tempers its cynicism with compassion. Like the works of German writer/director Bertolt Brecht, it breaks the fourth wall and addresses the audience; indeed, because the entire show is written as vaudeville acts, the audience actually becomes a part of the show (as they were with *Cabaret*). In fact, the more we enjoy the show, the more we like Velma, Roxie, and the other "Merry Murderesses" in the Cook County Jail, the more we prove the show's point. We find decadence entertaining, seductive, tantalizing. The audience is actually a character in the piece. Like *Assassins* and *Sweeney Todd,* this show points the finger of blame at us, and we're having too much fun to notice.

Though Fosse always said *Chicago* was his reaction to Watergate, it is perhaps more relevant now than ever before. The media continues to make celebrities of criminals, while the public rebels against attempts at legislating morality; it was alcohol in the 1920s, but today it's sexuality, prayer in school, drugs, and marriage. Also, with the advent of the Court TV cable network, and the media circus surrounding the trials of O. J. Simpson, Lorena Bobbitt, the Menendez brothers, and others, we've seen the media make a mockery of our judicial system. With the right lawyer, enough money, the right clothes, and a modicum of acting ability, anyone can be acquitted in our society today. At the end of *Chicago,* the two murderesses thank the American people—the audience—for their belief in their innocence as they throw flowers at the audience. We know they're not innocent, but by enjoying their performances, we acquit them. Never one to be subtle,

Fosse goes for the jugular. Velma says, "You know, a lot of people have lost faith in America . . . But we are living examples of what a wonderful country this is." Ouch.

## The Road to *Chicago*

The original nonmusical play, *Chicago,* was written in 1926 by Chicago Tribune reporter Maurine Dallas Watkins, based on an actual 1924 murder case. In 1942, a film version was made called *Roxie Hart,* with Ginger Rogers in the title role. Sometime in the 1950s actress and dancer Gwen Verdon saw the movie on television and thought it would make a great musical. But Watkins, the playwright, would not release the rights to the play. It wasn't until Watkins died, in 1969, that Verdon finally got the rights from the playwright's estate.

Verdon convinced Fosse to do the show, and they brought it to the songwriting team of Fred Ebb and John Kander, who Fosse had worked with on the film version of *Cabaret.* It was Ebb's idea to tell the story in the language of vaudeville not only to establish the period but also to create the metaphor of show business as life, a metaphor Fosse had become obsessed with. (In fact the show's title has a double meaning because there was an actual vaudeville theatre called The Chicago.) With Verdon playing Roxie, they cast Chita Rivera as Velma Kelly, Jerry Orbach as Billy Flynn, and Barney Martin as Amos Hart.

Though Fosse had always had a very dark side that expressed itself in his work (see the movie of *Cabaret* or a good production of *Pippin*), that dark side was now getting significantly darker because of his brush with death. During the song "Razzle Dazzle" Fosse staged couples simulating sex on both sides of the stage while the lawyer Billy Flynn sang about flimflamming the court and the public—in other words, we're getting screwed. Eventually, Fosse was convinced that was too dark and he restaged the song. Despite some out-of-town troubles the show came to New York in good shape, and it opened in 1975. The show garnered eleven Tony nominations but lost all of them to *A Chorus Line.*

Fosse's dancer-girlfriend and sometime muse, Ann Reinking, stepped into *Chicago* late in its Broadway run, before going on in 1978 to wow Broadway in Fosse's antimusical *Dancin'.* She also appeared pretty much playing herself in Fosse's autobiographical film, *All That Jazz* (in which you can see a fictionalized account of all the events surrounding *Chicago* and the bypass operation).

In 1992, Reinking choreographed *Chicago* for the Civic Light Opera of Long Beach with Juliet Prowse and Bebe Neuwirth. A few years later, the Encores! Series in New York asked Reinking and director/performer Walter Bobbie to stage a concert reading of *Chicago*. It was so well received that it was transferred in 1996, with only minor changes, into a Broadway house for a regular run. Reinking used Fosse's dance vocabulary for the choreography but took a different, much lighter approach to the material. The cast included Bebe Neuwirth, Reinking, James Naughton, and Joel Grey. But in this newer version, the show was taken out of its period context and much of Fosse's nastiness and brutal but legitimate cynicism was rejected in favor of a more lighthearted feel. The show suffered for it.

## Concept Musicals

*Concept musical* is a term used too much and with too little precision. It has as many definitions as there are people using it. Shows as diverse as *Company, Hair,* and *Pacific Overtures* have all been called concept musicals. Most shows people call concept musicals are musicals built on a central concept or issue instead of a linear story, musicals that have a story but whose central concept is more important than the story, musical character studies with no plot (like *A Chorus Line*), or musicals that just don't fit into any other category.

The concept musical's development, from *Love Life* in 1948 to *Wise Guys* in 2000, has been a complicated one, and its evolution has taken a very meandering route. Kurt Weill and Alan Jay Lerner (on the shoulders of Bertolt Brecht) took a giant step in 1948 by discarding every device of linear storytelling with *Love Life,* and provided the model for the commentary songs to come in *Cabaret, Company, Pippin,* and *Assassins.* Eighteen years later, *Cabaret* (1966) with a score by Kander and Ebb, and direction by Hal Prince, partially followed the lead *Love Life* had set, providing the model for the narrator/devil figure in *Pippin* and the use of limbo in *Follies* and *Assassins.* Two years later, *Hair* (1968) set the precedent for the plotless musicals like *A Chorus Line* and *Working.* Stephen Sondheim and Hal Prince's *Company* (1970) did not follow *Hair* but instead followed closely the model created by *Love Life* and greatly refined it, solving many of its problems, and becoming a commercial and critical success. The next year, *Follies* (1971), with Michael Bennett joining the Sondheim-Prince team, followed *Company's* lead but focused on deeper character development and provided a genuine resolution at the end of the show. In 1972, Bob Fosse began his experiments with high-concept design and staging with the film version of *Cabaret* and the Broadway production of *Pippin,* which took the narrator/host figure from *Cabaret* and further integrated him into the story. In 1975, *A Chorus Line* improved upon the model set by *Hair* by adding a unifying dramatic situation (an audition), while *Chicago* continued Fosse's experiments with plot-driven concept musicals. As he had done with *Pippin* and the film of *Cabaret,* Fosse escaped the problem of balancing form and content; with *Pippin, Cabaret,* and *Chicago,* form became content. Show business was a metaphor for life, and so the show as a whole, the very fact that an audience was in a theatre watching a performance, became a self-referential metaphor in and of itself.

After *Chicago,* Sondheim and Prince continued the form's evolution with the Kabuki-inspired *Pacific Overtures* in 1976, this time with book writer John Weidman. Two years later, Stephen Schwartz's *Working* tried to imitate *A Chorus Line* but failed. In 1990, Sondheim and Weidman (without Prince) created the ultimate concept musical *Assassins.* In 1992, Kander, Ebb, and Prince came back together for *Kiss of the Spider Woman,* which continued Fosse's work with form as content. Sondheim and Weidman followed several years later with *Wise Guys,* another concept musical following in the footsteps of *Chicago,* using vaudeville as the language of the piece.

## Prohibition

*Chicago* is set in the late 1920s, a time of public rebellion (mostly against prohibition, but against other legislated morality as well) and tremendous lawlessness. The 1996 Broadway revival of *Chicago* jettisoned the period setting, but when it did, it lost the irony of how much America today is like America in the '20s, and it lost the show's central metaphor of the story being told through the language of vaudeville, which was at its peak at that time. In 1920, the U.S. Constitution was amended to make alcohol illegal. Throughout the 1920s a significant portion of the public defied the law at every opportunity. The "speakeasies" of that time period were secret clubs hidden behind innocent-looking storefronts, through false walls, and with the right card, knock, or password, you could enter and buy alcohol and sex. In 1929, it was estimated that there were between 35,000 and 100,000 speakeasies in New York City alone. And some legitimate restaurants and nightclubs might, if you knew the right person, slip some bootleg liquor into your tea or coffee.

In Manhattan, a divorcée named Texas Guinan ran some of the most notorious and outrageous speakeasies. By 1928, she had had four out of five of her roving clubs raided and closed, but a fifth was still going strong. Perched atop a piano, Guinan entertained her patrons with dirty jokes and emceed performances by singers and dancers from 11:00 P.M. until 7:00 A.M. She became famous for her battle cry, "Curfew shall not ring tonight!" as she greeted her customers with a police whistle and a derisive, "Hello, Suckers!" (just like Velma does at the top of Act II of *Chicago*). And she wasn't kidding—at Guinan's club a bottle of bootleg scotch or champagne cost twenty-five dollars or more, equivalent to a week's salary for many people. Cover charges ranged from five dollars to twenty-five dollars, and even plain water was two dollars a pitcher.

Liquor for the speakeasies was smuggled into the country from Canada and from the open seas. Ships carrying illegal liquor would anchor just outside the U.S. in international waters, and "rumrunners" in speedboats would carry the cargo to the mainland under the cover of night. (Joseph P. Kennedy Sr. was one such rumrunner.) Unfortunately, by the late 1920s, organized crime had taken control of the highly profitable liquor trade (approximately two billion dollars in sales per year) and in many major cities, murder and other crime skyrocketed. Finally in 1933, prohibition was repealed.

## Vaudeville

The story of *Chicago* is told in the language of vaudeville, with almost every song in the style of a specific vaudeville performer or tradition. *Chicago*'s central premise, that crime and lawlessness are glamourized by our culture and can too easily become popular entertainment, is communicated through the most popular entertainment form of the time: vaudeville. In 1919, there were about nine hundred operating vaudeville houses in America, but by 1931, there was only one left— the Palace in New York City. *Chicago* is set in the late '20s, not long before vaudeville died. The idea of Roxie and Velma becoming vaudeville stars because of their crimes was only a slight exaggeration of reality. Anyone who was famous—for any reason—could be a vaudeville star. Charles Lindbergh turned down an offer of $100,000 a week to appear on vaudeville. Evangelist Amy Semple McPherson accepted $5,000 a week to appear on vaudeville and she bombed. Temperance crusader Cary Nation appeared on vaudeville in sketches showing her destroying saloons, and she handed out souvenir axes to the audience. Both Babe Ruth and Helen Keller appeared in vaudeville.

Vaudeville emerged at the end of the nineteenth century from beer gardens, honky-tonks, variety shows, and British-style music halls. The specialty and novelty acts that populated the vaudeville stage came from minstrel shows, burlesque, and the feature specialties of the hippodrome (the largest theatre in New York). Vaudeville took everything from every corner of popular entertainment and crammed it all into one brand-new entertainment form. Some of the stars of this new form included Emma Trentini and Schumann-Heink from grand opera; Sarah Bernhardt, Mrs. Patrick Campbell, and Lillian Langtry from serious drama; acrobats, aerialists, wire walkers, and animal acts from the circus; musicians from the legitimate music community; physical comedians from the European pantomimes; and banjo players and blackface comics from minstrel shows. There were also hundreds of specialty acts, including trick cyclists, magicians, rope spinners and whip snappers, jugglers and equilibrists, dancers, monologists, ventriloquists, novelty musical acts, sister teams, dialect comedians, piano teams, and comedy sketch artists.

This form was just called "variety" until the 1890s, when producer George Lederer first used the label "vaudeville." Then B. F. Keith built a chain of palatial theatres designed especially for vaudeville shows. The new form was developed by impresarios like Tony Pastor, F. F. Proctor, Percy Williams, Oscar Hammerstein (the famous lyricist's grandfather), Harry Davis, and William Morris. And vaudeville thrived from 1900 to 1925. After 1925 vaudeville gradually faded until about 1929–30, when radio, talking pictures, and the depression destroyed it.

### Chicago as Vaudeville

Fosse knew vaudeville intimately. Though he wasn't born until 1927, when he came of age as a performer in his teens, the people he learned from were all vaudeville veterans, and many of the performers he shared the stage with in the sleazy burlesque theatres he worked were old, washed-up vaudevillians. He danced old vaudeville numbers himself. He knew this world. And perhaps it's his teen years in those burlesque houses that created in him a profound distrust of show business, even though it was his chosen profession. He hated it even as he worshipped at its shrines. Before the song "Razzle Dazzle" in Act II, Billy Flynn says to Roxie, "These trials—the whole world—all show business." And he's right, after all. The trials, his and Roxie's whole world, is all a musical called *Chicago,* and even beyond that, they're all vaudeville acts. They are literally just show business. And yet, they're also far too real.

Almost every song in the show is modeled on an actual vaudeville act or star. In "All That Jazz," Velma is playing Texas Guinan, inviting the audience in to drink and have a good time. She is our host for the evening. "Funny Honey" starts out being an imitation of torch-song queen Helen Morgan's song "Bill" from *Show Boat,* a song about an ordinary man, who's nothing special, but she loves him anyway. She even sits atop a piano, like Helen Morgan often did. But then Kander and Ebb turn "Bill" on its ear, as Amos finds out just who the murder victim is and rats Roxie out. As Roxie gets drunker and drunker, as Amos finally tells the cop how it really happened, the lyric changes its tone and it ends with her calling Amos "That scummy, crummy dummy hubby of mine." A perfect Fosse moment.

The "Cell Block Tango" is a tribute to the ethnic dances that were sprinkled throughout a vaudeville bill, but with a murderous twist. When Matron Mama Morton enters, with a big ring and a fur stole, she's playing one of the biggest stars of vaudeville, Sophie Tucker, and she sings "When You're Good to Mama," a conscious parody of Sophie Tucker's equally racy "You've Got to See Mama Every Night." Later, as Roxie metaphorically tap-dances around Amos, lying through her teeth, trying to get him to pay for her lawyer, four male dancers enter and do a literal tap dance throughout the scene, in tribute to the hundreds of tap-dance specialty vaudeville numbers.

Billy's "All I Care About Is Love" is in imitation of band leader Ted Lewis, who would begin his act by saying "Is everybody here? Is everybody ready?" As Billy sings the song, he strips, while chorus girls dance around him with giant feathered fans, à la the famous fan dancer Sally Rand. Rand would dance nude with two giant feathered fans, strategically choreographed to keep her covered, with just quick glimpses of flesh to tantalize the audience. She was, needless to say, a big hit.

Mary Sunshine and her hilariously optimistically "A Little Bit of Good in Everyone" is a direct imitation of Julian Eltinge, an extremely famous turn-of-the-century drag queen and vaudeville star, and Bert Savoy, his less classy successor. "We Both Reached for the Gun" recalls vaudeville's requisite ventriloquist specialty acts. "I Can't Do It Alone" recalls sister acts and acrobatic specialty acts.

Velma continues her role as Texas Guinan as she opens the second act with Guinan's famous line, "Hello Suckers!" "Me and My Baby" is sung in the style of Eddie Cantor, even down to his signature costume, too-short pants, white socks, and bow tie. "Mr. Cellophane" is a conscious imitation of Bert Williams, the well-known black vaudeville and Ziegfeld Follies star, and his famous song "Nobody," right down to Williams' oversized clothes and white gloves.

"When Velma Takes the Stand" and the entire courtroom scene is an imitation of the many courtroom comedy sketches, a staple of vaudeville and burlesque. "Nowadays" and Velma and Roxie's dance number "Hot Honey Rag" are tributes to Ted Lewis and his band. Lewis was a jazz clarinet player and bandleader, known for his battered top hat and his cheerily forlorn songs.

## Velma

Velma is the link in *Chicago* between the story and the structure of the show. She is a former vaudeville performer in the story as well as acting as a kind of host. She takes on the role of host at the beginning of each act by quoting famous lines from Texas Guinan. She killed her own vaudeville act by killing her sister, paralleling the death of vaudeville itself in the late 1920s when the story is set. She's the only one who performs a vaudeville-style song, knowing that that's what she's doing. She knows, in "I Can't Do It Alone," that she's doing a vaudeville act. None of the other characters know that they're doing vaudeville acts; that's merely the style of storytelling the authors chose. Her song "When Velma Takes the Stand," is also a song about performing. Roxie is a housewife, Billy Flynn is a lawyer, Mary Sunshine is a reporter, but Velma is a vaudeville performer. And by positioning her as our hostess, starting out each act not only quoting Texas Guinan but also singing the first song of each act, Fosse eases us into the convention of all the songs being full-front, "performed" vaudeville-style numbers.

# Mr. Cellophane

Amos is the only character in *Chicago* whose motives are entirely pure, never selfish. He's the only character who learns something, who changes. He's also the only one who really loses ultimately. Perhaps he can be seen as the show's moral center in some way. He represents us, the American people, who keep losing while O. J. and the Menendez Brothers win—because we let them, because, when all is said and done, we're really the suckers. We allow them, even encourage them, to get away with their crimes, and yet who knows which of us will be the next victim of a murderer who hires a high profile lawyer and goes free?

Amos is an average guy, not very good-looking, not very smart. Roxie says about him "that whole is a whole lot greater than the sum of his parts." In other words, he's rotten in bed; his "parts" don't work all that well. But we see Roxie's real feelings for Amos in "Roxie"— she does care about him ("you could love a guy like that"). But does she love him? She obviously isn't attracted to him, but is she in love with him? What was their earlier married life like? After years of dating bootleggers and gangsters, Amos was "safe" and "sweet," but for a girl like Roxie, who dreams of fame and fortune, safe and sweet only last so long. She got bored so she started screwing around with Fred Casely. And yet even though Amos is hurt and humiliated, he still comes up with the money for her defense. When he thinks she's having a baby, he immediately agrees to take her back. He just wants an ordinary, happy, domestic life. But that's not what Roxie wants, and once she gets her freedom, it's doubtful she'll ever return to Amos. He's "Mr. Cellophane," a guy so ordinary, no one—not even Roxie— notices him. And Fosse is telling us that nice guys don't always win in the real world; sometimes nice guys get dumped on, and the Billy Flynns of the world get it all.

## Crime and Punishment as Entertainment

The lyric to "Nowadays" shows us Fosse's conflicting feelings about show biz—it's dirty and sleazy, and yet it's exciting ("there's life everywhere . . ."). Notice that in "Nowadays" the announcer says his theatre is the home of "family entertainment" as he introduces "Chicago's killer dillers." Here we find yet another commentary on today's entertainment industry, as dozens of special-interest groups complain that movies and television are corrupting our youth. The show's "family entertainment," the presentation of two murderesses as stars, is the equivalent of the ultraviolent movies and TV shows like "When Animals Attack" and "World's Worst Police Chases."

Fosse's message is that publicity subverts justice. Courtrooms have become circuses as cameras in courtrooms have created a whole new breed of celebrity lawyers who perform for the television audience while they're presenting their case. Roxie is acquitted because of the media, the right clothes, good acting on the stand, a crooked lawyer, and a fake pregnancy, not because she's innocent. Fosse feels no sympathy for this heroine. As Roxie and Velma thank the American people "who made it all possible by believing in our innocence," they throw flowers at the audience. *Chicago* is about the blurred line between good and evil in America, even more prevalent today than in 1975, and the show biz in everything (especially the judicial system). Fosse told one *Pippin* cast member that *Chicago* was an analogy for the Manson murders. Today, *Chicago* is an even more biting commentary on other, equally grisly cases, mothers who kill their children, young men who kill their parents, wives who mutilate their husbands, men who stab their ex-wives to death. Falseness and lies thrive in America. In the song "Roxie," she says "not that the truth really matters. . . ." Americans have a talent for shifting the blame. Roxie says it's "because none of us got enough love in our childhood."

## Sex

As with most of Fosse's work, sex lies at the heart of *Chicago*. Along with the public's rebellion against prohibition, there was a rebellion against the strict morality of the previous century. After World War I, sexuality was much freer and more open, at least in the big cities, than it had ever been before. Homosexuality was accepted (as evidenced by the numerous lesbian references in "When You're Good to Mama"). Adultery became nearly respectable. Divorce became more widespread. Cross-dressing became less "naughty." Julian Eltinge and other drag queens became big stars in vaudeville and in the various Broadway revues, as represented in the show by Mary Sunshine.

*Chicago* would not work if the other gender roles were reversed, because men are the ones in control in the 1920s—it's the switching of traditional gender roles of control that makes "Cell Block Tango," Billy's striptease, and the rest of the show funny. Yet Billy Flynn still has the ultimate control (and Mary Sunshine, who's really a guy). Mary Sunshine is about reversing gender roles, and to an extent, so is Amos. He's the sensitive one, the domestic one, the victim of the adultery, not the perpetrator, while Roxie is the one out looking for greener pastures.

## Cleaning Up *Chicago*

If you "clean up" this show in order to make it more palatable to your audience, you lose one of the primary premises of the show—that the world of crooked lawyers and a public who loves violence is as frightening in its own way as the crimes themselves. Fosse, Kander, and Ebb created a show with a hard-boiled attitude. Certainly anyone who produces the show owes the creators no less than adherence to their original vision of the show. If this is a musical that might be offensive to your audience, it would be better not to do it than to do a castrated version. And despite the commercial success of the 1996 revival, stripping the show of its 1920s period, of its references to vaudeville stars, also robs it of its soul. What's funny about the show is that it pretends it's about the 1920s and yet it's really about today. If you ignore the period, as the revival did, the show becomes only about today, and you lose the important message that things haven't changed, that America hasn't cleaned up its act, that this time of lawlessness and gangsters in the '20s looks pretty tame compared to today's world. And that's one of the show's main themes. It would be like taking *Cabaret* out of 1930s Berlin.

## Other Resources

You can buy copies of the script through Samuel French, Inc., who licenses the show, or through theatre bookstores, like the Drama Book Shop in New York. Vocal selections are available commercially, but the full score is only available when you produce the show. The original cast album is available on CD. The 1996 revival cast album is good and contains two tracks not on the original, but it just doesn't have the bite the original has. There are three books about Bob Fosse that discuss *Chicago,* Martin Gottfried's *All His Jazz: The Life and Death of Bob*

*Fosse* (Bantam Books, New York, 1990), Kevin Boyd Grubb's *Razzle Dazzle* (St. Martin's Press, New York, 1989), and Margery Beddow's *Bob Fosse's Broadway* (Heinemann, Portsmouth, NH, 1996). There are also two great documentaries, if you can find them, a PBS Great Performances episode called *Kander & Ebb* and a documentary called *Steam Heat,* both of which include footage from *Chicago.*

# 3 The King and I

*Book and lyrics by Oscar Hammerstein II*
*Music by Richard Rodgers*
*Based on the film* Anna and the King of Siam *by*
  *Sally Benson and Talbot Jennings and the novel*
  Anna and the King of Siam *by Margaret Landon*
*Originally directed on Broadway by John van Druten*
  *(and Oscar Hammerstein, uncredited)*
*Choreography and musical staging by Jerome Robbins*
*Licensed by Rodgers and Hammerstein Theatre Library*

Today, at the end of the millennium, many of the leaders and intellectuals of mainland China are wondering how their country can continue to modernize, to compete with the Western nations, while still maintaining their cultural identity and traditions. Many wonder if it is even possible. Shanghai, for instance, is a city split between the cultural pride and traditions of China and the developments and economic pressures of the West. All of China faces difficulties in this area, as young Chinese covet designer consumer goods from the West and the yuppie lifestyle they see portrayed on American television, while the older generation worries about the decay of traditional morality and ethics. This friction between East and West has resulted in a generation and culture gap in China far wider than anything America has ever faced. But this is not a new problem in Asia. In fact, this is exactly the problem King Mongkut of Siam faced in the 1860s—how could he join the company of civilized nations, become respected and competitive among them, without losing the rich history and culture of his beloved Siam, without alienating his people, who were not prepared to discard their simple but treasured way of life.

In the 1860s, Anna Leonowens, a widowed British schoolteacher, was hired by King Mongkut to come to his country and teach his wives and children the English language and Western culture. She wrote of her experiences in a two-volume memoir. Later, Margaret Landon turned Anna's story into a novel called *Anna and the King of Siam*. A film version was made starring Irene Dunne and Rex Harrison as the King. British stage star Gertrude Lawrence saw the film and decided the story would make a great musical, with her as Anna. Rodgers and Hammerstein, after some initial objections, agreed to write the show, now called *The King and I*. Though Lawrence was supposed to be the lead, Yul Brynner became an immediate star playing the King when the show opened on Broadway in 1951. A film version of the musical was made starring Brynner, Deborah Kerr, and Rita Moreno. The stage version won five Tonys, including Best Musical, Best Actress (Lawrence), and Best Supporting Actor (Brynner). The film won six Oscars, including Best Actor for Brynner. By the time Brynner died of lung cancer (he made the film with only one lung), he had played the role of the King on stage 4,625 times. There was even, very briefly (a few months in 1972), a television series based on the story, called *Anna and the King*, starring Yul Brynner, Samantha Eggar, and Keye Luke.

*The King and I* has been revived in New York in 1956, 1963, 1964, 1967, 1977 (with Brynner), 1985 (for Brynner's farewell performance after a long tour), and 1996. The 1996 revival, directed by Australian Christopher Renshaw and starring Donna Murphy and Lou Diamond Phillips, was a radical reexamination of this show that was intelligent, sexy, and for many people, a genuine revelation. Renshaw had directed the show in Australia with Hayley Mills when Mary Rodgers and others from the Rodgers and Hammerstein organization saw it and asked him to bring it to New York. This production garnered seven Tony nominations, and won four Tonys, including Best Revival of a Musical and Best Actress in a Musical.

Like other Rodgers and Hammerstein musicals, *The King and I* is a classic and that had become its greatest handicap. American directors and actors bring too much baggage and too much reverence to the piece, too many recollections of past productions and of the movie, of pop singers' overly soulful renditions of the "hit tunes." As with *Carousel*, it took a foreign director and the 1996 Broadway revival to find again (or perhaps for the first time) the substance, intelligence, and sexuality of this incredible work. Never before had a musical been built around two more complex, more passionate, more intellectually fascinating characters (even Julie Jordan and Billy Bigelow, in *Carousel,* didn't have this complexity). Yet because of the time in which the show was originally created and because of our overfamiliarity with the story, these two characters had become sanitized, one-dimensional combatants, period-piece Rock 'em Sock 'em Robots, their sexual tension almost nonexistent.

When Rodgers and Hammerstein wrote and produced the show in 1951, their writing was too far ahead of the moralistic and artistic limitations of contemporary musical theatre. Though musicals could by then tackle weighty subjects (thanks largely to R & H), the conventions and traditions of musical comedy, the inadequate training of musical comedy performers, and the moral climate of the country still got in the way. Actors still *performed* songs rather than *acting* them (which wouldn't change until the early 1960s), even in serious musicals. Songs still needed choreography even when there might be nothing to dance about ("Getting to Know You," for example). Actors and directors hadn't yet figured out that all the principles of serious drama could (and should) be applied to serious musical theatre. And though Rodgers and Hammerstein had broken the restrictions of subject matter allowable in a musical, they hadn't really broken free of the structural conventions, needing a secondary couple, needing an explicit romantic love story, needing dance. Still, for too many American theatre artists, this show and others still rest uncomfortably in the time frame in which they were written, and though musical theatre has moved forward, the advances aren't always applied to these older shows. As we must with *Show Boat, Carousel,* and other older, serious musicals, we have to approach *The King and I* as if it were a brand-new show, forgetting all preconceived notions we may have.

## R-E-S-P-E-C-T

Hammerstein was a passionate and very vocal critic of racism in any form (as evidenced by the song "You've Got to Be Carefully Taught" in *South Pacific*). So it was surely unintentional that Hammerstein's book and lyrics are somewhat condescending toward the culture and people of Siam (now Thailand). The Siamese were laughed at throughout the show, with no acknowledgment of the racism, arrogance, and dismissal of Siamese traditions by the intrusive Westerners. Forty years later, director Christopher Renshaw came at the story from a different perspective. He had actually lived in Thailand for a while and genuinely understood and respected the Thai traditions and culture. He insisted that the costumes, set decorations, and other visual elements be as close to authentic as possible. He also began the show with a Thai prayer ceremony to establish for the audience the seriousness with which this culture would be treated. He even cut one song that seemed condescending to the Siamese, "Western People Funny."

Renshaw also made a significant change to the King's death scene. Instead of setting it off to the side or in back as usual (which was supposed to show that the King is no longer the center of power, having passed that on to the crown prince), Renshaw placed the King down front. Renshaw explained in several interviews when the revival opened that the Thai people believe everyone has two souls. One of those souls is the *kwan,* a person's sense of self, his confidence, his self-respect. They believe that you can lose your kwan through the top of your head, which is why they all wear their hair in top knots (and why the King should *never* be played bald), to keep the kwan in. When the King has finally lost his self-confidence, largely through Anna's doing, he has lost his kwan and therefore he dies. That's why Lady Thiang and the Kralahome try so hard to get Anna to stop her attacks on the King's beliefs and traditions; they worry about him losing his kwan. His death scene is extremely significant and consistent with Thai beliefs, and Renshaw didn't think it should be minimized. In a way, the King has sacrificed himself so that his country may move forward; but also, in a way, Anna has killed him.

Despite our expanded understanding in the 1990s of Thai cultural and people, we can't forget that Rodgers and Hammerstein were still taking great strides and risking commercial success by creating this amazing musical, the most subtextual love story musical theatre had ever seen. Not a single direct word is ever spoken about the central love story between Anna and the King (perhaps the team were hedging their bets with Tuptim and Lun Tha), and the lead couple didn't even get a love song (unless you count "Shall We Dance"). This is a show about the complexity of real love, not the idealized, simplified love usually found in musical comedies of the 1940s and 1950s. This was an impossible love, an adult, intellectual, and political *Romeo and Juliet.* This was not entirely new territory for Rodgers and Hammerstein, after *Carousel* (which centered on a terribly dysfunctional relationship and a male lead who died in Act I) and *South Pacific* (which complicated love with war, racial prejudice, and death). But Rodgers and Hammerstein generally dealt with American themes, and this was the first time one of their shows was almost entirely about another culture, a theme they had touched on in *South Pacific*.

## The King

It's interesting to note that though Anna is listed first in the title of the book and movie (*Anna and the King of Siam*), the title of the musical puts the King first. It may help to know something about the real King Mongkut, although we have to keep in mind that where there are discrepancies between the character and the real King, the character *as he is written* is whom the actor is playing, not the real man. The real King Mongkut was very educated himself and understood the social, economic, and political value of education. King Mongkut was intelligent, forward thinking, and decidedly visionary in many ways, although he had many obstacles in front of him. His nobles were actively plotting against him, the people of his country were slow to change—and often afraid of change—and the Siamese were deathly afraid of being colonized by England and France, thereby losing their independence. He was tough to get along with but ultimately fair; after all, he did finally agree to give Anna the house he had promised her. And it's at this moment in the show, at the end of Act I, when the King finally agrees to give Anna a house, that she finally sees him as an honorable man, a trait very important to her, and it's at that moment that she falls in love with him.

King Mongkut was not afraid to admit he was wrong, but he had to be careful; he had to do it delicately, without disturbing his people's faith and belief in his leadership; after all, they believed he was divinely inspired. King Mongkut really had to be two people: an old-fashioned feudal lord and religious leader, and also a modern intellectual political leader having to function in a increasingly civilized world. Part of Anna's problem in dealing with the King is that she never knows which of these two personas she's dealing with from moment to moment, and each persona requires an entirely different tack.

The book *Anna and the King of Siam* provides some interesting info on the real King Mongkut. He should've been crowned king as a young man, when his father died, but his older brother usurped the throne until Mongkut was of age. Mongkut left his wife and children to enter the priesthood, in order to escape being murdered. He became a multilingual scholar and rose to become a high priest, studying French, English, and Latin with Western missionaries. He was also a mathematician and an astronomer, and he set up Siam's first printing press, to print in both English and Siamese. While he was a priest he reformed Buddhism by setting up a reform movement within the church and reorganizing the entire church. This was not an ignorant, barbaric king.

The King knew that for his country to survive, his people must be educated, and he would begin with the royal children and the royal wives. In Mongkut's actual letter to Anna, he asked her to teach English, science, and literature, but *not* Christianity, because Siam needed knowledge but not a new religion. He wrote:

> And we hope that in doing your education on us and on our children . . . you will do your best endeavor for knowledge of English language, science, and literature, and not for conversion to Christianity; as the followers of Buddha are mostly aware of the powerfulness of truth and virtue, as well as the followers of Christ, and are desirous to have facility of English language and literature, more than new religion.

## The Conscience of a King

We learn about characters by what they say, what they do, and what others say about them. In *The King and I*, the King rarely says what he feels, and few others are allowed to say what they really think about him, but his behavior speaks volumes. This is a character drawn largely through subtext, which makes it perilously easy to play superficially but also wonderfully full and complex when played intelligently. We see what he thinks of women by the way he treats his wives, by the way he assumes that Anna can be easily dominated merely because she's a woman, and most important, by the way he assumes that Anna will be more like his wives than like him. He soon finds out exactly the opposite is true. Anna and the King are very much alike in many ways, and that forms the basis of their considerable attraction to each other.

The "March of the Siamese Children" scene tells us a great deal about the King's relationship with his children, and his assumptions about Anna. He is stern but he loves them. There are tiny glimpses of his love throughout the scene, and he shows more tolerance with the littler ones. They know that he is a strict disciplinarian but they are not genuinely afraid of him. He cares a great deal about their future, and he wants them to be educated. He also gambles that presenting the children to Anna will wear her down and convince her to stay. He uses the children to dissipate her anger, and it works. This scene shows several sides of the King's personality, and Anna gets her first look at his good traits.

No one knows the King better than Lady Thiang, and her song "Something Wonderful," is an important peek into his personality. Sometimes he's difficult, sometimes he's thoughtless, sometimes he's even mean. But he is a good man, and when his darker side comes out, Lady Thiang knows that he is trying, and she supports him. He is doing great things for Siam (including bringing Anna to the Palace), and has a tough road to navigate ahead of him. She knows that Anna is becoming a confidante to the King and she wants Anna to understand his contradictions. Maybe she feels a bit of resentment toward Anna, that Anna has in some ways taken Lady Thiang's place in the King's life, but she knows that this arrangement is important for Siam, so she will accept it. Lady Thiang says at one point, "I am not equal to his special needs." The King is straddling two worlds, and every day he has to make difficult decisions about what and how much should change. Lady Thiang wants Anna to understand that Siam cannot—and should not—become a fully Western country. There are many things about Siam and its culture that are good and strong, and those things must be preserved. Unfortunately, Anna does not understand that.

## The West

The King sees a great deal of value in Western ways. He wants to learn the West's "scientific ways," but is he forsaking his own culture? Siam must be able to compete in the world and he as King must be respected. He can't allow Western countries to think that the people of Siam are barbarians who can be easily taken over. He must preserve Siam's independence, and that means projecting an image of civilization and progress, *as defined by the Western countries*. But more than that, the King finds the West endlessly fascinating. His mind is hungry to learn about the world around him. He is already an accomplished scholar and he wants to know more. In his mind, Anna represents Westernization, and we see from the beginning that he will fall in love with Anna. In "Something Wonderful," Lady Thiang says that the

King is a man who thinks with his heart, which is not always wise, and she is right on target; and perhaps she knows him well enough to see early on that he will fall for Anna. But Anna is a big challenge—and a dangerous one—just like Westernization, and the King *must win,* for himself and for his country. At its core, this show is about the battle between faith and knowledge, religion and science, as personified by the King and Anna. And neither one wins completely.

Anna proves most difficult when it comes to Siamese culture and beliefs. She refuses to follow the rules about seeing the King, how to speak to him, and other things. The rules are there for a reason, and the King is used to them being followed. The King wants to pay some respect to Anna, because he does genuinely respect her, but she makes it hard. She treats the rules of the Palace with disrespect. She pays no respect to the Kralahome, a high official, a man who has risen to a position of great authority and someone who should be respected. But because she doesn't understand the culture and doesn't understand the Kralahome's position, she dismisses him as unimportant. And what's worse, the King does nothing about that. In her lesson before "Getting to Know You," Anna discards everything the children know and believe, like a bull in a china shop. She replaces their map, and thereby their entire worldview, forcing them suddenly to come to terms with how small their country is, how insignificant it seems. She tells them about snow, and other things, without understanding how profoundly this will shock them. When the Crown Prince objects to her statements (as anybody would), the King arrives and scolds them all for not believing Anna. The Prince and the others are left reeling from this information, so different from what they thought they knew.

And when it comes to the slavery issue, we all agree with Anna that slavery is wrong. Yet it was an important part of Siamese culture, and her awkward, bull moose efforts to change things do not take into account the cultural context. There are better ways to change things. Anna gives Tuptim—already an unhappy slave—Harriet Beecher Stowe's antislavery novel, *Uncle Tom's Cabin,* and starts a firestorm. Tuptim writes a dramatic presentation of the novel for the party for the English, and embarrasses the King in front of some very important guests. Finally, when the King is about to whip Tuptim for trying to escape, Anna intercedes and shames him into not whipping Tuptim. Though slavery is objectively morally wrong, though Tuptim was trying to escape a morally outrageous situation, still Anna has not merely changed the system; she has taken the King's control away from him, has stripped him of his authority and self-respect. If a woman—an outsider, no less—can control the King's actions merely by staring him down, then how can his subjects be expected to follow his commands? If Anna can defy the King, why shouldn't Lady Thiang and his other wives defy him whenever they disagree with him? After the whipping scene, Anna and the Kralahome have the following exchange:

> ANNA: I shall never understand you—you or your King. I shall never understand him.
>
> KRALAHOME: You! You have destroyed him. You have destroyed King. He cannot be anything that he was before. You have taken all this away from him.

At least Anna has finally figured out that she doesn't know everything. But she has no idea what she has done. The Kralahome is right. She has destroyed the King. You might argue that a monarchy is not an ideal form of government anyway, so why not strip the King of his power? But Anna single-handedly destroys Siam's only form of government, and she offers nothing in its place. She feels moral outrage—and perhaps she should—but, like the King, she is thinking with her heart, not her mind, and she is doing great damage she can't undo. The King's attraction to Anna is easy to understand. Not only is she Western, she is a strong, intelligent, independent woman. She is more like him than like his wives, and perhaps a little narcissism is at play here as well. She's a worthy opponent, a strong sparring partner. She questions his ideas, forcing him to articulate them, to alter them, to fix them in their best form. He sees in her so many of his own traits, and therefore finds solace in the fact that so many of his traits are "Western" traits. And yet, he *can't be with her.* She is a foreigner. She is his employee. She is a Christian. And her constant arguing and contradicting him is unseemly and shows disrespect. He has very strong feelings for her that rage against his feelings of loyalty to Lady Thiang, to his country, to his government, to his culture.

"Shall We Dance" is the play's obligatory moment, that moment toward which everything before it leads, and from which everything after it comes. That scene is what the whole play is about. Finally, the physical attraction is satisfied. They can touch. This is a *big deal* in Siamese culture, and they know it. As she teaches him to dance, the dance becomes a metaphor for monogamy. She is metaphorically teaching him how to be monogamous, and as he does with everything else, he learns quickly. This is the last step in converting the King—and in killing him. Just as he finds the joy in romance, in one-to-one pairing with someone who is his equal, he also loses his self—his kwan. When the whipping scene comes, the King realizes that he can no longer live without Anna's respect, so he gives in to her moral pressure. But by gaining her respect, he sacrifices everyone else's. He essentially gives up his throne. He can no longer rule as he once did.

## Anna

Anna begins the story as a terrified twenty-eight-year-old widow (despite the advanced age of many of the actresses who've played her) with a small boy, making a journey halfway around the world, coming to a land where she does not speak the language, a land where she knows from the get-go that weakness will be her downfall. "Whistle a Happy Tune" is more important than it may at first seem. Her behavior throughout the show, her temper tantrums, the way she repeatedly stands up to the King, are all ways of "whistling," of pretending she's brave when she's really scared. But she has been on her own before. Her parents went to India without her when she was six. Her father (an army captain, like her husband, Tom) died when she was seven. She didn't join her now remarried mother in India until she was fifteen. And while she was there, she learned to believe that Western beliefs, or more specifically British beliefs, were superior to all other cultures'. And she saw Britain take over India, further reinforcing her belief that the West was stronger and better than the East. She met Tom (who was named Leon in real life) when she was fifteen, and married him when she was seventeen. They had a daughter, who died within a few months, and Anna mother's died soon after. They returned to London and had another baby, a boy, who died after a few hours. She had two more children in London, who survived. When Anna was twenty-five, Leon/Tom died in India. One year later, King Mongkut of Siam wrote to Anna, asking her to come to Siam. She needed the money or she would have to borrow from her stepfather, so she went. And though she arrived scared of the unknown, her life had prepared her to keep a stiff upper lip and never to show her weakness. This was the Anna who charged into the King's Palace, who confronted him at every turn, who challenged his every belief, and who fell in love with his confidence, his intelligence, and his thirst for knowledge. (And let's not forget that the King went around half-naked all the time, which would have been quite a turn-on for a young woman from Victorian England.)

## Hello Young Lovers

Rodgers and Hammerstein fought convention at every turn, discarded old rules and made up new ones (which would then become the *new* conventions that the next generation, led by Hal Prince and Stephen Sondheim, would discard). But *The King and I* would be the last time Rodgers and Hammerstein wrote a truly groundbreaking show. *Me and Juliet, Pipe Dream, Cinderella, Flower Drum Song,* and *The Sound of Music* would never again draw the complex, fascinating relationships the team had created in their early shows. Never again would they write a score that could compare with the complexity of *Oklahoma!, Carousel, South Pacific,* or *The King and I.*

Still, here in *The King and I* rules were being broken. Tuptim and Lun Tha, the secondary couple, are not funny—in fact, they are horribly tragic—and more startling, they're the only overtly romantic couple in the show. The love between the two main lovers (Anna and the King) had to be entirely subtextual. So the two love songs, "We Kiss in a Shadow" and "I Have Dreamed," both belong to Tuptim and Lun Tha, and yet both songs are love songs with a dark side. "We Kiss in a Shadow" is about how much they love each other even though they can't show their love. And "I Have Dreamed" is about how their love affair has only been consummated in their dreams, and we know that despite Lun Tha's dreams, they will never be able to really be together. Their love is a doomed love. Both couples in *The King and I* have a love that can never be spoken out in the open, that can never be fully expressed. Anna and the King cannot even express their love to each other; at least Tuptim and Lun Tha can tell each other, even though if they're caught they'll probably be killed. Not your average romantic leads. After writing Tuptim and Lun Tha, Anna and the King, Billy Bigelow and Julie, Emile DeBecque and Nellie Forbush, Lt. Cable and Liat, did Rodgers and Hammerstein just run out of ideas?

That Tuptim can read is significant; that Anna gives her *Uncle Tom's Cabin* to read is even more significant. (Did Anna give her that particular book on purpose?) The bravery it takes for Tuptim to present the play *The Small House of Uncle Thomas* is extraordinary. She knows she will likely be punished, but really, how much worse could her situation be? What has she got to lose? She wants to open the King's eyes. She wants the King to see the parallels between the story and real-life events. But the character who parallels the King is the evil, nasty "King Simon of Legree." Surely, she can't think insulting the King will further her cause. Or is she just like Anna and the King, thinking with her heart instead of her mind? Her play is beautifully done (especially with Jerome Robbins' original choreography, fortunately preserved in the film version). It's funny, too, if you know the story of the novel, to see how Tuptim translates uniquely American ideas and idioms into her own culture, how she inserts Buddha into the story, how she explains what snow and ice are, something an American reader wouldn't have to do. But it's also sobering to see this tale of slavery as told through the lens of an actual slave.

Tuptim is also significant in that she is the instrument of destruction between Anna and the King. Tuptim's fate is the issue over which Anna and the King finally find themselves in a confrontation over which neither is prepared to back down. (And it's right after their moment of greatest joy, in "Shall We Dance.") Anna had given Tuptim the book way back at the beginning of the show, Anna helped Tuptim and Lun Tha meet secretly, Anna arranged for Tuptim to perform her play at the party, and now Anna must lose her relationship with the King over Tuptim. This is the only musical in which the love of the secondary couple destroys the love of the primary couple.

Ultimately, Lun Tha is killed, like Lt. Cable in *South Pacific.* Though both romantic couples here are unconventional, Rodgers and Hammerstein keep the secondary couple secondary by killing the man, keeping the love forever impossible. But in *The King and I,* they also kill the man in the primary romantic couple, which of course makes their love even more tragic than before, and as in *West Side Story,* both women have to go on living without their loves. Perhaps Anna's loss is tempered by the fact that she must now stand by the Prince as he becomes the new King, that she still has a purpose in this Palace. And it is some consolation that Prince Chululongkorn agrees with her in many ways. Her battles are finally won, and thanks to the Prince, the government will not fall. The Prince perhaps can see what happened to his father, his confusion, his inability to navigate both worlds at once, and now Chululongkorn sees an opportunity to start fresh, without expectations, to begin anew. Perhaps by watching his father and Anna butt heads, he has learned important lessons, and now he can take the best of both worlds to lead his country toward the future.

## Fake Oriental

Richard Rodgers needed a score for *The King and I* that sounded at once foreign and accessible to the Western ears of his audience. Like many other Western composers before him, he took one aspect of Oriental music and sprinkled it throughout the score—the open fifth chord (or when turned upside down, an open fourth). He used this chord throughout the show, most obviously perhaps in *The Small House of Uncle Thomas* when the chorus sings "Praise to Buddha." He also achieved a "foreign" sound by using chords that don't belong in the key of the song. In "Something Wonderful," the song is in A major, but Rodgers used lots of G-sharp major chords, chords that are just not found in that key. It gives the song an exotic, foreign feel that still isn't too strange to Western ears.

It's interesting, too, that though the songs the Siamese characters sing are "fake Oriental," the songs sung by Anna are more conventional in their harmonies and rhythms. "Hello Young Lovers" alternates between a barcarolle, a staple of operetta, which gives the song not only a Western feel but also a period feel, and a traditional waltz. Anna switches into the waltz whenever she slips back into her memories. "I Whistle a Happy Tune" is a traditional 4/4 show tune. "Getting to Know You" is a soft-shoe. "Shall I Tell You What I Think of You" is the kind of musical scene Rodgers and Hammerstein perfected in *Carousel*. And "Shall We Dance" is a good old-fashioned polka. But the other songs in the score, those sung by the King, by Lady Thiang, by Tuptim and Lun Tha, are full of open fifths, chords outside the key of the song, and other dissonances. None of this is really Oriental music, but real Oriental music is extremely difficult for Western ears to understand, so Rodgers has chosen a sound that is foreign to us. He tells us it's Oriental and we accept that.

The exception to this are Tuptim and Lun Tha's two love songs. They retain some of the open fifths of the other "Oriental" music, but they are far less dissonant. Instead they are very simple musically, almost stagnant, very minimalist. The bridge to "We Kiss in a Shadow" still uses several chords outside the home key, like "Something Wonderful" does. "I Have Dreamed" is a pretty conventional love song, but its bridge uses that minimal accompaniment figure much like the one in "We Kiss in a Shadow," which serves to a small degree to unify the young lovers' music.

The music for *The Small House of Uncle Thomas* ballet, written by dance arranger Trude Rittmann, is the most dissonant of anything in the score. The music is very foreign, full of strange harmonies and rhythms. It's interesting to note, though, the two musical themes from earlier in the show that pop up in the ballet. When the angel comes down and freezes the river, Eva learns to skate to the music of "Hello Young Lovers," and when King Simon of Legree shows up to chase Eva across the river, the music turns to "A Puzzlement," a reference perhaps to the King's inability to see right from wrong?

One of the most dramatic moments is also one of the smallest ones. In the crossover before Act I, scene 3, the priests enter and cross the stage singing their chant, as the children enter from the opposite side of the stage, singing "There's No Place Like Home." First, it demonstrates Anna's—and therefore the West's—influence on the children, and it's funny because it is further advancing Anna's campaign to get her own house by using the King's children against him. But more important, it contrasts the priests and the children, the old Siamese ways with the future of Siam, and of course, the *Westernization* of the future of Siam. The children are singing Anna's song and it subtly suggests that the future will adopt Western ways and, at least to some extent, reject the old Siamese ways.

There are several musical scenes in *The King and I*. The King's "A Puzzlement" and "Song of the King," and Anna's "Shall I Tell You What I Think of You" are all free-form musical scenes, very much like Billy's "Soliloquy" and the Bench Scene in *Carousel,* only shorter. And there's a liberal amount of underscoring in the show, using themes from the songs to identify characters and their emotions. After the King and Anna have their argument in the classroom and Anna storms out, the underscoring is "A Puzzlement" as the King tries to figure out what just happened. This will be his "problem" theme. It's significant that Hammerstein dramatizes the fact that the King is puzzled, confused, even before Anna arrives. He's been thinking about all these things already; Anna just adds to his confusion. When Anna suggests to the King that they have a party for the English and dress the women in European dresses, the music underneath is "Hello Young Lovers," as Anna remembers back to the parties of her youth, the parties she attended with her husband, Tom. But as the King's mind turns to the logistics of how to pull off this party, the music changes to "A Puzzlement" again, the King's "problem" theme. In fact, this time, the music is the bridge from "A Puzzlement," the part in which he wonders if he should form alliances with foreign countries.

When Lady Thiang confronts Tuptim in Act II, we hear "We Kiss in a Shadow," Tuptim's love theme about forbidden love. As it looks like Tuptim and Lun Tha might actually run away together, they say their good-byes to Anna over "Hello Young Lovers," Anna's love theme. Later, when she is caught escaping and Lun Tha is killed, Tuptim says she will join Lun Tha in death, and we hear "My Lord and Master" playing underneath, her theme of disobedience. When Anna reads the letter from the King, expressing his gratitude to her, we hear "Something Wonderful," and as the next transition scene opens, we hear a very slow "Shall We Dance," as Anna remembers how much she loves the King. And as the King dies, we hear "Something Wonderful" again. He was a good King, and Anna has stayed because she loved him and believed in him—perhaps even more than Lady Thiang. It's only when Anna has learned what Lady Thiang knew all along that the story is done, that Anna and the King's relationship is finally in balance. And it reminds us of a lyric from "Getting to Know You," early in the show, about how teachers can also be taught by their pupils. Anna came here to teach the people of Siam, and true to that lyric, she ends up learning a great deal from them, especially from her unofficial pupil, the King.

Once again, Anna has lost a man she loved. But this time, she has a family around her (quite a large one) and a reason to stay.

## Other Resources

The script to *The King and I* is not available commercially, but the vocal selections and the score both are. You can only get the script through the Rodgers and Hammerstein Theatre Library. The movie version, which includes Jerome Robbins' *The Small House of Uncle Thomas* ballet is available on videotape. The original Broadway cast recording is available on CD, as are several revival cast albums. But the best cast album is the 1996 Broadway revival with Donna Murphy and Lou Diamond Phillips, mainly because it's the best acted. An audio recording of *The Small House of Uncle Thomas* is available *only* on the cast album of *Jerome Robbins' Broadway;* it has not been put on any of the *King and I* cast albums because of its length. Margaret Langdon's novel *Anna and the King of Siam* is available, probably at your local library, and the first, nonmusical film based on it is on videotape.

# ▟◤ March of the Falsettos

*Book, music, and lyrics by William Finn*
*Originally directed in New York by James Lapine*
*Licensed by Samuel French, Inc.*

William Finn wrote three one-act musicals about a man named Marvin. In the first part of the trilogy, *In Trousers* (1979), Finn explored Marvin's crushes on teachers and other women, his blossoming neuroses, and his eventual realization that he was really in love with a man named Whizzer Brown (in a wonderfully unsubtle song called "Whizzer Going Down"). In the second installment, *March of the Falsettos* (1981), Marvin tries to force Whizzer, his wife Trina, and his prepubescent son Jason into some kind of hybrid family. When that doesn't work, Marvin leaves Trina for Whizzer, while Marvin's psychiatrist Mendel romances and marries Trina. At the end of *March of the Falsettos,* Marvin has lost Trina and Whizzer both, and in the last song, he tries to reconcile with Jason. In the third chapter, *Falsettoland* (1990), Marvin, Trina, and Mendel plan Jason's bar mitzvah while Whizzer comes back into Marvin's life. But Marvin only gets a temporary Happily Ever After because Whizzer has AIDS and by the end of the show, he has died. The third installment is interesting because when Finn wrote the first two pieces, AIDS didn't even exist yet, so Finn had no idea how Marvin's story would turn out.

After *Falsettoland* was produced in New York, theatres around the country started putting *March of the Falsettos* and *Falsettoland* into one evening as companion pieces. In 1992, Finn and his collaborator, director James Lapine, officially combined *March of the Falsettos* and *Falsettoland* into a full-length musical called *Falsettos.* They did a fair amount of rewriting, adding and cutting things, reassigning lines, altering music, even adding one full song, Trina's hilarious tour de force, "I'm Breaking Down." Once the full-length version was available, the one-acts were rarely produced.

Still, some companies continue to produce the one-acts, and the question is often asked, Why do one of the shorter pieces when you could do the full-length show? The answer is that the two one-acts are very different from the two halves of *Falsettos,* not only in details but also in focus and in the themes explored. In the full-length show, both acts are about Marvin and the development of his relationship with Whizzer. The conflict is about whether or not Marvin and Whizzer can build a life together without killing each other first. But the one-act *March of the Falsettos* is about Marvin and his son Jason. In fact, Jason is the heart of *March of the Falsettos,* a boy who needs his father to guide him toward manhood and yet fears becoming who his father is. The question is not whether Marvin and Whizzer can stay together. Marvin can't sustain relationships with Whizzer, his wife Trina, or his psychiatrist Mendel. Marvin's only salvation is in sustaining his relationship with his son. The one-act isn't about romance; it's about Marvin growing up enough to help Jason grow up. *March of the Falsettos* is a more interesting show, a less conventional musical, a show about deeper, more complicated issues, definitely a show that still deserves to be seen in its original form.

## Time and Place

*March of the Falsettos* was written in 1981 and that's when the story is set. Because of the appearance of AIDS and the subsequent outing of gay celebrities alongside the movement of gay issues into the center of the mainstream press, America was very different in 1981 than it would be just a few short years later, especially for gay men and women. Though there were gay clubs and bars at that time in major cities, though there were gay newspapers and magazines, and even a few movies with gay characters or stories, for most Americans homosexuality was still a foreign, or in some cases utterly unknown, concept.

In 1981, when this story is set, a few gay men in New York, San Francisco, and Los Angeles were popping up with a rare form of cancer called Kaposi sarcoma. No one knew why, but it seemed concentrated almost exclusively in the gay communities of major cities. Soon, it was called gay cancer. Later, it would be called GRID (gay related immune deficiency) and even later, AIDS. But in 1981 most people knew nothing about it. Even those who did know about it weren't sure if it was an epidemic, or if it was sexually transmitted. (And let's not forget that while the AIDS epidemic was beginning, so were massive increases in the incidence of sexually transmitted diseases among heterosexuals—the sexual revolution was not exclusively a gay phenomenon.)

During the sexual revolution of the late '60s and '70s and the simultaneous rise of the gay rights movement, many gay men in large metropolitan centers were finding a kind of sexual freedom and openness they had never known before. After decades of having to hide, of being unable to meet, to date, unable even to recognize who you could ask for a date, gay men celebrated this new freedom with a sexual excess that isn't at all surprising. Whizzer Brown, the character in *Falsettos*, comes from that culture, a culture in which sexual freedom was a hard-won trophy to be enjoyed, in which the gay community had adopted as its ideal a hypermasculine image born in the gyms and gay bars of the 1970s, an image exported to mainstream society in the form of the Village People. The men who were a part of this hypermasculine, hypersexual culture could easily have a dozen or more sexual partners in a single night. The use of drugs and alcohol were pervasive. It's easy from our current vantage point to see this time and place as decadent, but to the people in the midst of it, this was something they had fought for and won, something they were owed.

Also, in 1981, the Kinsey Institute published a new sex study, which concluded that homosexuality was probably biological. Being gay was no longer viewed as a psychological problem, but instead as merely one variation of human sexuality. In 1973, the American Psychiatric Association had removed homosexuality from its list of disorders, and the American Psychological Association had done the same in 1975. Billie Jean King admitted in 1981 that she was gay, and Martina Navratilova's relationship with lesbian author Rita Mae Brown was reported in the mainstream press.

But gay Americans were not being completely accepted into mainstream society. In 1978, openly gay San Francisco city councilman Harvey Milk was assassinated by fellow councilman Dan White. Although White shot Milk and Mayor Moscone at point-blank range, though he confessed to the murders, he was convicted of the lesser charge of manslaughter and would be eligible for parole in five years. In 1979, the Moral Majority had been formed by Jerry Falwell, "to oppose gay rights, pornography, feminism, and communism." In 1980, the film *Cruising* was released and depicted the gay community in a very negative light, focusing on drugs and murders in the leather bars of New York City.

In the America in which Marvin lived, gay bars were regularly raided by police, and gay Americans had virtually no civil rights in most states. When gay characters did appear in movies like *Cruising, The Day of the Jackal, The Eiger Sanction, The Fan,* or *The Road Warrior,* they were usually murdered, or committed suicide because they couldn't live with themselves. It's not hard to see why Marvin married, why he tried to live a heterosexual life, as millions of gay men did (and as many still do today). It's not surprising that he's in psychotherapy, that he's been messed up by a society that has forced him to be something he's not. But it is interesting that despite his serious interpersonal problems, Marvin doesn't seem to have a specific problem with being gay.

And it's not a surprise that Jason is so worried about turning out gay himself. It's not a surprise that Jason thinks his father isn't a real man because he's gay, that he can't bring himself to say "gay" or "homosexual" when he talks to Mendel about Marvin. And it's not a surprise that he can blithely declare that his father is a "homo." Jason is growing up in a world that is less oppressive than the world in which his father grew up, but it's still a world that makes it clear, whether explicitly or implicitly, that being gay is a bad thing, something decadent, something not right.

## All in the Family

Though no one was using the word "dysfunctional" in 1981, it certainly describes Marvin's family. Marvin and Trina have been married at least twelve years, probably exactly that long since there is the implication that they married because Trina was pregnant ("My hands were tied. My father cried, 'You'll marry.'"). During that time, Marvin has been having sex with men, and Trina certainly knew he was fooling around, although we're not sure if she knew it was with men. And now Whizzer shows up and Marvin tries to force his gay relationship into the middle of his existing family, even though he's already divorced Trina.

Like other wives of the time, Trina is thrown into orbit by all this.

She knows next to nothing about homosexuality. All she knows is that after twelve years, her husband has left her for a man. She probably thinks she's partly or entirely to blame. She finds herself without a man protecting her for the first time in her life, so she turns to her ex-husband's psychiatrist, who has a whole bag of his own dysfunctions. As Trina and Mendel try to reestablish a family unit, Marvin tries to force Whizzer into the role of traditional wife. Meanwhile, twelve-year-old Jason has to act as father figure to Trina, asking Mendel about his intentions, trying to protect and look out for Trina, since no one else will. It's a strange, difficult situation, and through it all, Marvin refuses to let go of Trina. He still refers to himself, Trina, and Jason as a family, and he's furious when Trina announces she is remarrying, as if she's the one betraying him.

The reliance of Marvin and Trina on psychotherapy is also a product of their times. Psychotherapy had become not only relatively respectable; it was even trendy. The 1970s had seen the first sitcom with a central character who's a psychologist, *The Bob Newhart Show*. What's funny (and sad) is that these people are still crazy even though they're all going to a psychiatrist, and that Marvin and Trina think Jason's problems can all be fixed by sending him to a psychiatrist. Even the song title, "Everyone Tells Jason to See a Psychiatrist," says a lot. Trina refers to the other boys in Jason's school as "all those guys who have not been analyzed *yet*." She assumes that everyone eventually winds up in therapy. Maybe everyone she knows does. Of course, the question is whether their psychotherapy is ineffectual because they're just too nuts or because Mendel is a rotten psychiatrist.

## March of the Falsettos

At one time, William Finn was going to call this show *The Pettiness of Misogyny*, but instead he settled on the less direct, more ambiguous *March of the Falsettos*, one of those titles that causes arguments in college dining halls. What does the title mean? What is the "march" and who are the "falsettos"?

We have to look at the central action of the show to figure this out. The show isn't about Marvin and Whizzer. If it was, it would end with the song "I Never Wanted to Love You," because that's the end of Marvin and Whizzer's story in this musical. Instead, the show ends with "Father to Son," because this musical is about the fact that Marvin has to grow up in order to be the father Jason needs, in order to be able to help Jason grow up. He can't be a role model until he's made the journey himself. Throughout the show, Jason's unchanged voice sings an octave higher than the other three men in the show. Only in the title song do they all sing in the same register, with the adult men all singing in falsetto. So it's reasonable to assume that a falsetto voice is a symbol of childhood, of not yet being an adult. The march of the falsettos is the journey of those who are still children, who have not yet become adults. In this case, that doesn't just refer to Jason; it also refers to Marvin and Mendel, and to a lesser extent, Whizzer. None of these men have grown up yet; they are all still self-centered, self-involved, and prone to temper tantrums when they don't get what they want. Finn tells us this by having the adults all lose the symbol of manhood—the changed voice—for the title song. The journey—the march—they take is the one from childhood to adulthood.

But there are other journeys going on as well. All four of the adults also take a journey from a world of fantasy and easy, black-and-white answers to the more complex real world in which everything doesn't always make sense, in which life isn't always fair. This is another journey that we all go through when we grow up, when we finally have to confront and live in the real world. Many of us take that step in our late teens or early twenties. Marvin, Trina, and Whizzer get there a lot later. At the end of *March of the Falsettos,* they have only begun that journey. These journeys prove particularly painful and difficult for these people because they're not equipped to handle them, but these are journeys we all must take at some point in our lives. We must all grow up and become adults so that we can nurture the next generation. Even those of us who aren't parents still have a responsibility to the future. The march of the falsettos is a march we all have to go on, one that many of us are still on, in some ways.

At the end of the show, Marvin says to Jason to sing for them all, to speak for them, and to live the life the adults should have lived, as he makes his way in the world. Marvin, Trina, Mendel, and Whizzer have all made messes of their lives, to various extents, but Jason is just starting out and he still has a chance to make the right choices and take the right paths, and as he does, maybe find some redemption for those who've gone before him.

But this song also explores some other issues, most important the idea of what it means to be a man. The concept of marching conjures images of the military, of fighting and war and heroism, of John Wayne and General Patton. One part of the lyric goes:

*Four men marching in one long column,*
*Never touching but always solemn.*
*Four men marching but never mincing,*
*Four men marching is so convincing.*

This passage begins with military images and then reminds us that real men don't touch other men, that physical displays of affection are unmanly, that real men don't show emotion. The reference to "never mincing" brings up the stereotype of the effeminate gay man, a behavior to be avoided at all costs. And in the last line quoted here, the lyric comments on the belief that the appearance of manliness is enough, that gay men are acceptable as long as they act "normal" and traditionally masculine (and stay in the closet), that if you can appear to be a real man on the outside, that if you avoid "mincing," then nobody really cares, or wants to know, what's on the inside. By presenting these accepted social ideas in such a ridiculous context, Finn suggests that they are ridiculous in and of themselves.

Later in this song, Mendel says that Marvin is always wary of things. He sees that Marvin believes in society's restrictions, that he is preoccupied with appearing manly, that he must keep himself in the "masculine" role by forcing Whizzer into what he thinks is the "feminine" role (as cook and housewife). Marvin can't show emotion. He can't allow himself to be vulnerable because that's not manly. It's important that Jason not grow up with this same fear, but with Marvin as his father, it's likely that he will.

Whizzer tells Jason to relax, to stop being scared of whether or not he's going to grow up gay. Whizzer sings, "Asses bared. My delight. Shared with four young men alone in the night." Whizzer likes sex, and he likes sex with men. Whizzer thinks anything between consenting adults should not be judged. In fact, even though Whizzer has come of age in an era of multiple sex partners, unprotected sexual activity, and an overuse of drugs and alcohol, he may have the healthiest attitude about sex of any character in the show. Even though Whizzer is in a pretty unhealthy relationship with Marvin, Whizzer knows that it's okay to be gay. He's telling Jason two things: that Marvin being gay doesn't mean Jason will be gay, and that if Jason turns out to be gay, there's nothing wrong with that. Earlier in the show,

Jason won't listen to his parents, but he will listen to Whizzer. He chooses Whizzer as a role model because perhaps he senses that Whizzer is the least screwed up of the adults in his life.

## Four Jews in a Room Bitching

As mentioned earlier, there is an accepted rule that you can do anything you want in a musical, as long as you do it within the first ten minutes, to make it clear to the audience what the ground rules are for the evening. The opening number of *March of the Falsettos* does that brilliantly. It sets the musical style (frenetic and insistent), establishes the vocabulary (intellectual, absurdist, and sometimes shocking), introduces the characters, and to an extent sets up the relationships. The first line of the song, which is also its title, "Four Jews in a Room Bitching," immediately tells the audience that this show is irreverent and aggressively in-your-face. No punches will be pulled. No feelings will be spared.

The lyric to this song gives us a lot of information. Mendel asks, "Wadda they do for love?" Indeed, *that's* the central question of the show. What *do* they do for love? How far will they go? How much will they give? What will they sacrifice? They admit that they sometimes lie, and that's good to know. It prepares us for the fact that what characters say in this show is not necessarily the truth. They tell us they're "mad" (i.e., insane) and they couldn't be more right. These people are nuts. They don't care about right and wrong; they only care about what they want. Marvin says they are manipulative, also good to know. In the middle of the song, Jason says, "In case of smoke, please call our mothers on the phone and say their sons are all on fire." They are all on the brink of disaster. They are each in a dangerous place in their lives, a place where the choices they make could mean life or death, at least in an emotional sense. This may also be a reference to the old adage, "Where there's smoke, there's fire." It may also be a reference to the term "flaming" as a description of a gay man. Another section in the middle of the song centers on "the bed." This tells us at the outset that these four men are obsessed with sex and sexuality. Jason can't stop thinking about Marvin's homosexuality and his own as yet unknown sexuality. Marvin and Whizzer are both utterly preoccupied with sex. Mendel can't see or talk about Trina without getting all hot and bothered. Sex has an importance to all four of them that borders on the obsessive.

The last lines of the song sum it all up. "Can't lose" tells us that the stakes are very high here, and we will see that they are, for all the characters. (Marvin will later tell us that "winning is everything.") "Loose screws" reminds us that nobody here is really healthy, mentally or emotionally.

## Marvin

Marvin is an unlikely hero for a musical. He's childish, neurotic, almost annoyingly intellectual, self-centered and self-absorbed, overly competitive, and sex-obsessed. But he certainly makes a fascinating character study, and somehow, despite his more despicable characteristics, we do care about him and like him.

In the liner notes for the cast album of the first Marvin musical, *In Trousers,* William Finn wrote, "So Marvin grows up (after a fashion), says good-bye to ladies (more to the point), and learns to live with always getting what he wants." And it's true that Marvin has always gotten what he wants—until now. As *March of the Falsettos* begins, what Marvin *wants* is to make Whizzer his spouse, but also keep Trina. And he finds out that he just can't have that. He can have one or the other, but not both. He's not even sure he's going to get to keep Jason in his life. For the first time in his life, he's not getting what he wants, and he goes ballistic. Trina describes him as a baby who's been denied. Exactly.

We know Marvin's been in therapy with Mendel for a long time. We might wonder if he started seeing Mendel before or after he figured out he's gay, and whether that realization triggered his need for psychotherapy. Surely, even before he knew he was gay, he was still childish, self-centered, and competitive. He says he thinks love is boring. He calls it debris and compares it to a bad biography. This is not a healthy guy. And yet, he's quite the romantic in many ways. He's told Jason that love is the most beautiful thing in the world. He talks about love often, particularly in reference to Whizzer. He wants Whizzer to love him, but apparently thinks Whizzer does not. Still, his relationship with Whizzer is marred by Marvin's incessant competitiveness. Marvin says he's best when he cheats, so he's going to cheat to win, because, he tells us, winning is everything. Even more so than being in love? Possibly. Marvin and Whizzer fight about everything. They even fight about how long they've been together. For Marvin, the longer they've been together the greater the commitment is and the greater the chance that they'll stay together, so Marvin rounds *up,* and says it's been ten months. For Whizzer, the shorter the time they've been together the less permanent it feels and the easier it will be for Whizzer to leave when he wants to, so Whizzer rounds *down,* and says it's been nine months.

Marvin's relationship with Trina is also a complicated one. Even after he's left her for Whizzer, he doesn't want to let go of her. He gets insanely jealous when he finds out that Mendel is courting her. Marvin has been cheating on Trina for quite a while, he gave her syphilis and hepatitis, he admits that she's a good woman, and despite all he's done to her, he still resents the fact that she's found someone else to love her. Maybe this goes back to Marvin's competitiveness. Maybe he can't stand that she's found a new spouse and he hasn't.

His relationship with his son, Jason, is complicated, too. Perhaps we can assume that Jason really does love his father. But Marvin's realization of his gayness has thrown the family into chaos, and Jason is angry at Marvin for disrupting what was a basically happy (though still neurotic) family. Also, in 1981, a twelve-year-old kid isn't going to be real open-minded about homosexuality, particularly when it's his father who's gay. But the blame Jason lays on Marvin isn't entirely fair. True, Marvin has thrown the family into turmoil. But not admitting his gayness would probably be even worse for them all in the long run. One of the most interesting passages in the show is in "Marvin at the Psychiatrist."

MARVIN: We go to ball games.
JASON: The ball is tossed.
MARVIN: The pitcher's handsome.
JASON: And our team lost.
MARVIN: Is that my problem? Should I be blamed for that?

Marvin's right. His attraction to the pitcher did not cause the team to lose, but Jason is only twelve and as far as he's concerned the two things are directly related. Jason invokes some kind of hypermorality that this perceived perversion by his father is so far-reaching that it actually causes the ball team to lose the game. Marvin can't talk to Jason, because Marvin excels only in the realm of words and ideas, while Jason is in an exclusively emotional place. Marvin is at a loss, and he asks Mendel how to reach Jason, what to do about this situation. He knows deep down that Jason is his only salvation. As noted earlier, the relationship between Marvin and Whizzer is not the heart of this show; the relationship between Marvin and Jason is.

## Marvin and Whizzer

Marvin's relationship with Whizzer is one of the most dysfunctional ever depicted in a musical (right up there with *Passion*). One of the most striking characteristics of their relationship is the constant threats and bluffs about leaving or breaking up. They're constantly telling each other the current outrage had better be the end. At the end of "The Chess Game," Marvin goes and gets Whizzer's suitcase and sets it down in front of him. Marvin is probably bluffing again— he's used to being able to push people pretty far and they never seem to break—but this time Whizzer calls his bluff. He actually packs the suitcase and leaves. And Marvin is devastated.

Marvin and Whizzer are actually *proud* of the fact that they refuse to agree on anything. In "The Thrill of First Love," they say that of all the lesser passions, they like fighting the most. To both of them, genuine emotional intimacy is a foreign and frightening concept, so the only way for them to express their passion is through fighting. There is always the danger, though, that one of them will push the other too far.

Yet Marvin is always pushing commitment on Whizzer. In "The Thrill of First Love," Marvin complains that Whizzer doesn't understand the joy of monogamy. But is this love or is this just Marvin's desire for someone to be committed to him, the desire to have someone cook and clean for him? When Mendel asks Marvin if he loves Whizzer, Marvin says, "Sorta kinda." Whizzer is undoubtedly a former boy toy, probably used to being kept by older men, but Whizzer is getting older, enough so that his days as a boy toy are probably over. So Marvin figures Whizzer will be happy to take on Trina's role. Marvin doesn't want to give up having a wife and he clearly intends to put Whizzer in that role.

Yet at times, it's a little unsettling how hard Marvin is working at making Whizzer into Trina. In "The Thrill of First Love," Marvin tells Whizzer to shave his legs. He tells us that Whizzer makes him smile—especially at meal time. He says Whizzer's role is to make dinner. (In an interesting juxtaposition, Trina says elsewhere in the show that *she* was supposed to make dinner.) Even after Marvin has left Trina for Whizzer, Marvin says that he wants a wife who knows what love is, an interesting statement since he clearly *doesn't* want a wife—he wants a man. He acts as if nothing has changed, like the fact that he now wants to be with a man doesn't change the dynamics of the relationship at all. He wants Whizzer to happily slide into Trina's role and he wants nothing to be upset in the transition. Marvin says to Whizzer, "Hate me or need me, just make sure you feed me." It sounds like Marvin doesn't really care that much about love. Or maybe it's just that Marvin doesn't think Whizzer loves him, so he figures he won't even try. Unfortunately for them both, Marvin is wrong; Whizzer does love him, even if he wishes he didn't.

The most frightening (and one of the funniest) moments is in Marvin's therapy session, talking about Whizzer:

MENDEL: When he's naked . . .
MARVIN: Yes?
MENDEL: Does he thrill you?
MARVIN: Yes.
MENDEL: Is he vicious?
MARVIN: Yes.
MENDEL: Would he kill you?
MARVIN: *(Pause)* Yes. I think he's sorta kinda mean.

Certainly this is an overstatement on Marvin's part. It's doubtful Whizzer would kill Marvin, but this is not a relationship built on trust. There is love and there is lust, but there is also suspicion and deceit and lots of mind games.

## Whizzer Going Down

In a lot of ways, Whizzer is probably the least neurotic, least screwed up of all the characters in the show. His past as a boy toy peeks through all throughout the show. Certainly, Marvin is comfortable financially, but he's hardly wealthy, so why is Whizzer with him? Has Whizzer changed his priorities? Whizzer says that what he loves he devours. He uses men and then discards them after he's gotten what he wants from them. But he could have left Marvin long ago. Why is he still here? Does he love Marvin after all? He doesn't *want* to love Marvin. He even goes so far as denying it a number of times, but his actions belie his words. Whizzer is obviously scared of feeling what he's feeling for Marvin. Like Marvin, Whizzer knows that passion eventually dies, but he mistakenly thinks that that means love dies, too, which is not usually the case. Love lives on long after the passion is gone, after the honeymoon, the thrill of first love, is over. Marvin and Whizzer are expecting too much, asking for too much from their hearts and from their relationship. Whizzer has probably never stayed after the passion was gone until now, so he's in uncharted territory, and he's understandably scared. And it doesn't help that the man he loves can be such a jerk.

Whizzer does begin to take on the role of wife, as Marvin wants, but we have to ask if Whizzer is also taking on a role when it comes to intelligence. Is Whizzer really smarter than he seems? Has he figured out that Marvin is threatened by anyone as smart as he is? We know that Whizzer plays games just like the others, and perhaps this is just one more game, one more role-playing opportunity to give Marvin what he wants, the dumb but pretty houseboy who can be put down, to whom Marvin can feel superior, just as he did to Trina. We have to wonder if, for instance, Whizzer already knows how to play chess when Marvin "teaches" him in "The Chess Game."

Whizzer's win over Marvin in the chess game is fascinating. He gets Marvin to take his hand, knowing how horny Marvin is, knowing how that will distract him. Then Whizzer takes his hand away, interrupting Marvin's turn-on to even further distract him. And Whizzer turns the tables—now it's *Whizzer* telling *Marvin* which piece to move, instead of the other way around. He tells Marvin to move the pawn *and Marvin listens to him,* which is a big surprise. There are very specific chess moves in the *March of the Falsettos* script that raise some interesting questions about the characters. Marvin almost makes the move that will prevent Whizzer's win, but Whizzer stops him from moving his knight and gets him to move a pawn instead. Then in very few moves, Whizzer sets up two checkmate opportunities, one with a bishop, one with the queen. The scenario Whizzer creates is called a "Fool's Mate," a comically appropriate label in this case. Marvin cheats to prevent the first checkmate, but Whizzer has a second checkmate waiting, and he wins. So what has happened here? Did Whizzer make all this happen by accident? It doesn't seem likely. Whizzer knew more than Marvin—or any of us—thought he did.

Despite the fact that Whizzer is probably less messed up than Marvin, he still has some unresolved issues in his life. Marvin tells us early on that Whizzer drinks a lot. Is that because he's trying to escape something, his past maybe? Or is it merely because he has lived in the '70s gay club scene for a long time? We can safely assume that Whizzer was a happily successful boy toy once, but now he's getting older, losing his looks, no longer able to be a cute young thing. So what can he do? He probably has no job experience, no marketable skills. Maybe Whizzer needs to be "married" as much as Trina does. Maybe he doesn't see any other option. Maybe that's why he puts up with Marvin, just as Trina did for so many years.

## Trina

Trina is one of those women who was brought up to believe that marriage is the primary goal for any woman. She followed all the rules; she found and married a man. She stayed with him for twelve years. She gave him a son. She put up with all his abuses and neuroses. She might even have known that he was unfaithful but decided it didn't matter. Later in the show, after she's agreed to marry Mendel, she tells us that she won't care if he cheats on her. This is a woman who has no self-respect, no sense of self-worth. While Marvin and Trina are still married, Marvin starts coming home with diseases that he passes on to Trina, diseases he could have only contracted by sleeping with other people (but remember, this is pre-AIDS), and yet she stays with him. Finally, Marvin tells her he's gay and he's leaving her for a man. What does she do? The carpet's been pulled out from under her. The rules no longer apply. She is adrift in a sea that is completely foreign to her, a stranger in a strange land, just as Marvin and Whizzer are, just as Mendel will be when he proposes to her, just as Jason is.

"Trina's Song" is a wonderful glimpse into what makes Trina tick. And often, what is left unsaid, or what is lied about tells us more than what is said honestly. Trina has never been in control of her life. Men have always controlled her, first her father, then Marvin, and now Mendel. She doesn't like it, but it's familiar, it's safe, and though she may complain, she won't take any steps to change things. That would be even scarier. Her life is a mess of contradictions. In the beginning of the song she says that she's happy but not completely at ease, then later in the same song, she says she's *not* exactly happy.

Her relationship with Mendel comes into harsh light in "Trina's Song." She says, "I need those crass, indulgent stares." This says as much about Mendel as it does about her. What about that could she possibly "need"? She says, "He pats my ass and says he cares." Does she think this is the only way she can keep Mendel, to be a sexual object for him, a toy, a child, rather than an articulate adult woman? It's interesting that from her perspective he only *says* he cares. Does she doubt his love just as Marvin doubts Whizzer's love? Has Marvin's betrayal, both real and perceived, made her distrust all men? Still, despite it all, she just continues to pretend that everything's fine, that she's happy and contented. She only requires the appearance of love. She asks only that he make it seem like he finds her attractive. Their whole relationship is based on surface lies, on the appearance of happiness to make up for the lack of real happiness. She says in the reprise of her song that if she has doubts, she'll just ignore them. How sad. She needs to be married. She sees no other options (just like Whizzer). She has an identity, a sense of self, only in relation to the man in her life. She says in the reprise, "I will practice to resemble him in all important ways."

Trina has always wanted to be a Jewish June Cleaver, but she can't seem to get it right, perhaps because June Cleaver was *not a real woman*, because Trina has set a goal for herself that is impossible to reach. She thinks her role is to clip the coupons, check for specials, and show Marvin love. (Isn't it interesting that she equates loving him with her other chores?) She can't handle problems. She wants to be baking cookies for Jason and vacuuming in a dress and pearls. When she calls Mendel in "Please Come to Our House," she says that they'll all act like nothing's wrong—the only way she can get through the day. Even the seemingly innocuous lyric, "Late for Dinner" underscores Trina's inability to get her role as cook and housekeeper right. She can't even have dinner ready on time. June Cleaver would have.

Trina only knows how to be a wife and mother. She even mothers Whizzer from time to time (perhaps she feels a kinship with him because their predicaments are so similar). She comforts Whizzer after his fight with Marvin (just imagine comforting the lover of your ex-spouse, the person for whom you were left). Does she need to be needed that badly? Or does she just know what a son-of-a-bitch Marvin is? Her advice to Whizzer is interesting. She tells him just to forget about it, to pretend it didn't happen. Is this how she dealt with Marvin? She always thought Marvin's abuses didn't matter, but she was wrong. Her life is now in shambles.

The other disturbing detail is the valentine notes Jason leaves for Trina. There's something very weird about that, something a bit too oedipal. Is this the only romance she can get? At that point, it probably is. It's interesting that this adult-child romance is echoed in Marvin and Whizzer's relationship. Is William Finn intentionally setting these two pairs as parallel? Is Whizzer the kid to Marvin's father figure? Trina's comment that "Daddy" (Marvin) is kissing boys takes on new meaning in that context. Marvin's comment that one of Whizzer's jobs is to check for acne seems to indicate that Marvin sees them that way as well.

## The Psychiatrist

What's funniest about Mendel (and there's lots about him that's funny) is that he's far more messed up than any of his patients. Marvin, Trina, and Jason look to Mendel for answers, for guidance, but he's nuts. He asks Trina a question, then stops her before she can answer and says, "Don't—that's a question with no answer." So why did he ask? He says later, "I've never married. Work, work is my passion. Or perhaps that's an alibi. I don't care to discuss it." He hides his fear of intimacy behind being a workaholic, then he calls himself on it, and still manages to avoid addressing the issue altogether. He tells Trina that love is blind, then later agrees with Jason that love is not blind. Does he just agree with whatever his patients say? He tells Trina he's frightened of questions. He's a psychiatrist and he's afraid of questions? When Marvin asks Mendel in "Marvin at the Psychiatrist" what he should do about Jason, what he should do to reach his son, Mendel looks at his watch and ends the session rather than have to answer a question. When Mendel comes to their house to see Jason, he says that they'll talk if they are able to, but probably they won't be able to. He can't communicate with anyone. The whole purpose of the visit is to talk to Jason and yet he admits he probably won't be able to. And he later defends his neurosis by equating himself with geniuses of the past ("Yes I feel guilt. Yes I'm annoyed. So was Jung. So was Freud.").

When the chips are down, Mendel is completely inarticulate and ineffectual. When he proposes to Trina, he babbles hopelessly about her wrist and thigh, about biblical siblings, about horses and zebras. In fact, he rarely escapes being completely crass and inappropriate. He says he thinks Trina is "eager" to fool around. He says to Marvin, "It's queer, Mr. Marvin," and if it isn't enough that he's used that phrase to his gay patient, he then makes it worse by calling attention to it. He speaks to Marvin of Trina's "meager glories," a left-handed compliment if ever there was one. He says about taking Marvin's wife and son, "My acts of theft are incredibly perverse. It's embarrassing but I've got a nice tight family." He acknowledges his amorality, finds it merely embarrassing, and then goes on to gloat about the fruits of his act. He says just a few lines later that he's "bought" a family. He *bought* them??? While Marvin and Mendel discuss Trina during Marvin's session, all it takes is for Marvin to use the word *breast* and Mendel actually has an orgasm in his chair. He asks Marvin if Trina sleeps in the nude when they're supposed to be talking about Marvin and Whizzer, or at least about Jason. When Mendel comes to see Jason, he sees the dinner table as romantic because all he can think about is seducing Trina. He's the worst psychiatrist we've ever met. And unfortunately, his patients are more in need of real guidance than most people we know. It's a combination that can only mean disaster.

## The Kid

Jason is an angry, bitter kid, and can we really blame him? His mother's a neurotic, dependent mess of a woman with chronically low self-esteem. His father is a neurotic, childish man who's just figured out at age forty that he's gay and so tries to force his lover to be assimilated into his (barely) traditional family unit. And his psychiatrist is a lunatic.

Jason declares early on that love is not all that it's cracked up to be. This isn't a surprise since the only love he's ever witnessed is the love between Marvin and Trina, which has gone down in flames, the love between Marvin and Whizzer, which is combative and distrustful, and the love between Trina and Mendel, which is loaded with time bombs. Love hurts everyone around him. He wants no part of it. Beyond that, he also has a genuine fear that he may grow up to be gay like his father, so denouncing love altogether may seem like a safe move for him, taking him out of the action entirely. Instead of love, he invests his energy into games. It's interesting that he chooses that which Marvin loves as well. Marvin's games are mind games, while Jason's are board games, but the connection is still a real one.

He decides he will blame Marvin for all this chaos, but not Trina. He says that Marvin is snide, morbid, and dissatisfied, all of which is true. He sings and dances to "My Father's a Homo," doing anything at all to hurt his parents. Being mean is the only way he knows how to interact with people, and he no doubt learned that from Marvin. This surfaces when Mendel's due to arrive and Jason asks how to behave, whether he should be mean to Mendel. Being mean is all he knows.

The therapy Mendel offers Jason seems silly on the surface, and we're used to Mendel spouting nonsense, but it makes more sense than it might appear. Mendel is telling Jason to *stop thinking* so much, to ignore all the nastiness and mind games going on around him. He's trying to tell Jason to just be a kid. Mendel says, "You can add and subtract at will," in other words, Jason controls how he perceives things and how he reacts to them. Jason keeps starting a sentence with "I hate . . ." and Mendel keeps stopping him and telling him to forget it, to forget the hate, the bitterness, all the energy expended in being angry.

The truth is that Jason is right when he says he's too smart for his own good. No kid should have to deal with all the things he has to deal with. Most kids would be unable to discern all that Jason can understand, and that's how it should be. No kid is equipped to handle this kind of intensity, this kind of emotional complexity, but Jason's intelligence and insight throws him into the middle of the fray. In a very funny and significant moment, Jason turns the tables and throws Mendel's therapy back at him, using Mendel's tactics, even some of his own words. Jason knows more than the adults do. Though the adults all think love is blind, Jason disagrees. He tells Mendel that love isn't blind. Love doesn't have to close its eyes to abuse and disloyalty. Love can be honest. Why can't his parents learn this lesson? And once Marvin is gone, Jason must act as father figure to Trina, screening Mendel, asking him about his intentions. Trina needs someone to watch out for her. If it's not Jason, who will it be? But he's not comfortable in this role. It's not his role. He shouldn't have to do this.

Jason's fear that he might grow up to be gay is an important aspect of his personality. This is a real fear for him, and in 1981 that fear was a lot greater than it might be for a kid today. Jason has no gay role models except Marvin and Whizzer, so if he did turn out gay, who could he go to for guidance? His fear stems from the fact that he really can see himself in Marvin. This is also probably part of why Jason turns against Marvin. He blames Marvin for everything. Interestingly, he doesn't blame Whizzer at all. He chooses Whizzer for advice. In the third chapter of the Marvin Trilogy, *Falsettoland,* Whizzer and Jason become even closer. Jason does love Marvin, but Marvin is a threat to him in many ways. It's only at the end of the show, when Jason finally realizes that he is indeed heterosexual, that Jason allows Marvin to come close, and only then is there finally the possibility of salvaging their relationship.

## Into the Words

The lyrics of *March of the Falsettos* are very unusual in a lot of ways. Finn's voice is unlike that of any other writer working in the theatre. The words he chooses are so often just weird. In the opening number, the men sing that they "stoop" to pray. Generally, a person is said to "stoop" to an amoral or underhanded act, not praying. Mendel says that Trina moves him in "unreported" ways. Marvin, Trina, and Jason sing that photographs can't capture their "magic." Mendel says to Trina in his marriage proposal, "I want you by my side to take my place, if I get sick or detained," as if she's accepting a role as his vice president.

Throughout the show, the characters use overly intellectual vocabulary. They use words and phrases like *a priori, impetus, vis à vis,* and *apoplexy,* not your standard musical comedy vocabulary. Trina makes a reference to Shakespeare when she says to Jason, "Get thee to a psychiatrist." Does she realize she's paraphrasing a line from *Hamlet* that's spoken to Ophelia, who will later go insane? If Trina doesn't know it, Finn sure does. That's no accident. This vocabulary is important since intelligence is such a major issue throughout the show, especially for Marvin, Whizzer, and Jason. And on top of that, Marvin and Whizzer constantly indulge in double entendres. Whizzer says "while I put the steak in," a reference to both cooking and sex. Marvin and Whizzer later say, "We're too busy mounting a display of our affection . . ." The use of the word *mounting* is, again, no accident.

There are also a number of textual themes running throughout the show, including God, music, food, love, and other things. There are dozens of references to games, the show's central metaphor. There's "can't lose" in the opening number; "winning is everything" and "I intend to upset this regrettable game" in "The Thrill of First Love"; Whizzer's song "The Games I Play"; Jason's several song fragments about games; and lots more.

There are references to death and dying throughout the show.

Trina talks about death all the time. She says in "Love Is Blind" that Marvin and Jason acted dead. She tells Mendel she's got a scalpel up her sleeve, and later that she's got rope and that she may be hanging from a chandelier by the time Mendel gets to their house. Her "romantic" dinner table has knives in place but no reference to other utensils, only those that are also instruments of murder. Perhaps they're the only ones she notices. In "Making a Home," Trina and Mendel sing, "Forging ahead, taking our lives, making a home." But Finn uses the music to separate the phrase "taking our lives," by putting a hold on the last note of the phrase and a big break right after it, possibly to give that line added emphasis, possibly to underline its double meaning. After all, Trina has been talking about taking her life through the whole show. Early in the show, Marvin and Whizzer say they would "kill for the thrill of first love." Later in the same song, it's no longer "would kill"; now it's definite: "I'll kill for the thrill of first love." Mendel asks Marvin if Whizzer would kill him. Marvin says yes, he might.

## Reviewing the Situation

*March of the Falsettos* is a complicated, difficult show. And it becomes even more so when it's presented along with *Falsettoland* as a full evening. The music is fast and frenetic. It rarely slows down and almost never stops. The language zooms by, full of Latin phrases, literary references, bizarre phraseology, and hundreds of inside jokes and double entendres. And Finn's music frequently breaks up sentences in places other than where the punctuation breaks them, making things even harder to understand. This is a show that demands an enormous effort from an audience, tremendous concentration, complete focus, and a quick mind. It never condescends. It never underestimates its audience's intelligence. Even after months of studying it, after fifteen years of listening to the cast album, I'm still discovering new jokes, new details, different nuances that I hadn't seen before. And maybe that's why so many people love it. *In Trousers* and *Falsettoland* are both great shows, but they don't have half the complexity or labyrinthine brilliance of *March of the Falsettos*. This show packs more into fifty minutes than most shows can get into two-and-a-half hours. Some people will find that exhausting and unsatisfying. Others will find it exhilarating.

## Other Resources

The full score for *March of the Falsettos* has not been published but vocal selections have. The original cast albums for all three parts of the trilogy are on CD, and the entire trilogy has been published in one volume as *The Marvin Songs*.

# The Music Man

Book, music, and lyrics by Meredith Willson
Based on a story by Meredith Willson and Franklin Lacey
Originally directed on Broadway by Morton Da Costa
Licensed by Music Theatre International

*The Music Man* is one of the greatest of all American musicals, despite the fact that it is not the sweet, slice-of-life, all-American musical we think it is. It is the story of a con man in 1912 Iowa who seduces an innocent young woman merely to keep her from mucking up his plan to swindle the honest, hardworking people of a small Midwestern town, including the young woman's troubled little brother, who's mourning the premature death of his father. Along the way, the show also takes gleefully wicked potshots at most of what Americans hold dear—small town generosity, family values, representative government, education, the Fourth of July, European Americans' view of Native American culture, classical Western culture, and the great hope of so many parents that their child might have the talent to play a musical instrument. Yet somehow, amongst all this darkness and savage satire, we manage to find quite easily a soft, gooey center that winds up as a pseudotraditional musical comedy love story (though just barely). Why is it we consider this show just another sappy, happy, old-fashioned musical? It's really not.

Part of our misperception may be due to the time *The Music Man* came out and the atmosphere on Broadway at the time. When it opened in 1957, its chief competition was *West Side Story*. If *The Music Man* touched on the darker side of human nature in many ways, next to *West Side Story,* it looked like *No, No, Nanette*. *The Music Man* swept the Tony awards that year, though, and ran for 1,375 performances, almost twice as long as *West Side Story*.

The show has an unusually profound sense of unity among its elements, because the book, music, and lyrics were all written by one man, Meredith Willson, who was himself born in Iowa in 1902. He studied at the Juilliard School of Music and played for a while with the John Philip Sousa Band and the New York Philharmonic Orchestra. He was the music director for several radio shows in the 1930s, '40s, and '50s, and wrote the popular hit song, "May the Lord Bless and Keep You." After *The Music Man,* Willson went on to write two other musicals, *The Unsinkable Molly Brown* in 1960, a moderate hit that ran a little over a year, and *Here's Love* in 1963, based on *Miracle on 34th Street,* a critical flop that ran eight months and lost money.

The script and score of *The Music Man* are savagely funny, occasionally touching, filled with wonderfully eccentric characters, and also expertly constructed. The leading man is a genuine scoundrel, yet we like him and we root for him to win the leading lady, even though he only pursues her to ensure that his con is successful. Part of that misplaced loyalty on our part may be due to the uncanny charm and humor of Robert Preston, who originated the role of Harold Hill on Broadway and on film, and whose spirit still hovers about any production. The score is full of memorable songs, not a single one of which is extraneous. Every song adds to the characterization of the people or of the town, or furthers the plot. Music is used in this show not just as a dramatic language (as in most musicals), but also as conscious plot devices—the marching band, the harmonizing board members, Marian's piano lessons, and the rhythm of a great salesman's pitch. Music is an integral part of our country's everyday life; and Harold Hill, the "Music Man," uses that fact to his advantage in executing his con.

The script is peppered with outrageously colorful language, wonderfully odd vocabulary, metaphors, aphorisms, and euphemisms. Harold Hill is called "a bare-faced, double-shuffle thimble-rigger" and a "Saturday night rowdy." Mayor Shinn says things like "You'll hear from me 'til who laid the rails," and "I'll by God horse-whip you 'til hell won't have it again." We hear phrases like "not on your kidney plaster," "the hail stone and sarsaparilla belt," and my personal favorite, "Great Honk." This language serves a few purposes. First of all, it gives us a good laugh, an affectionately comic perspective on these people. Second, it shows us how a small town (and small-town America) at that time had its own lingo, just as certain professions do today, language that keeps outsiders on the outside. It also demon-strates how little the homogenization of the outside world touches River City.

## America in 1912

Two things were going on in America in 1912 that are important for *The Music Man*. In the Midwest at the beginning of this century, there were no department stores, no retail chains. There were just small in-dependently owned stores, most of them specializing in one kind of product—dry goods, hardware, feed, etc. It was about this time that wholesalers, who acted as agents for manufacturers, started popping up. The wholesalers and manufacturers sent travelling salesmen out so that the store owners didn't have to travel to each supplier to see new products and order inventory. Some of these travelling salesmen sold specialty products directly to consumers, which made local re-tailers nervous, fearing that if people started buying from salesmen, they'd stop buying from local stores. So travelling salesmen met with some hostility and the kind of suspicion that small-town folks felt to-ward anything unknown or new. On the other hand, the image of the travelling salesman also embodied the American ideal of the rugged individualist, independently working to build his fortune and realize his own personal American Dream.

Once the cross-country rail system was in place, salesmen were able to get to small towns that were previously not worth the effort or cost of visiting. Around the turn of the century there were literally hundreds of thousands of travelling salesmen in America. And they offered more than just easy access to goods. They were the news car-riers, men who traveled so much that they brought to these small towns news from the big cities, news of social and technological changes. But by the 1920s, chain stores and mail order businesses had pretty much diminished the ranks of the travelling salesmen. Some still existed (and do today), but in much smaller numbers and only in a few industries. The introduction of the automobile also made it much easier for consumers to get to bigger stores, which also killed the travelling salesman's business.

In fact, 1912 was a very significant year in the demise of the travel-ling salesman. That year, F. W. Woolworth was incorporated, which would become one of the biggest retail chains in America. That year,

U.S. automakers were manufacturing 115,000 new cars a month, about a quarter of them Ford Model Ts (the car the salesmen complain about in the opening number in *The Music Man*). Ten years later, 50 percent of the cars in America would be Model Ts. AT&T bought a new device in 1912 that could increase telegraph traffic by 400 percent, thereby making long-distance communication cheaper and more accessible. The A&P grocery store chain, with 500 stores in 1912, opened a new store every three days, across America, for the next three years. Also, in 1912, the first self-serve grocery store opened in California. The way of life depicted in *The Music Man* was changing quickly and drastically, and if Marian hadn't reformed Harold Hill, he might've found himself out of work within a few years anyway.

The other big phenomenon in America at that time was the creation of marching bands, imitating European military bands. In the late 1700s, military bands were being formed in America, and by the mid-1800s, many towns and cities had their own marching bands for parades, Fourth of July celebrations, and other holidays. The bands were comprised of lots of brass instruments—trumpets or cornets, trombones, sousaphones (a travelling version of the tuba), horns— as well as reeds and percussion. Because these bands were based on military bands and because they played primarily for national holidays, they developed a strongly patriotic identity. They were seen as a way to promote physical and moral health in young boys (no girls were allowed), just like sports. The music these bands played ranged from anthems and marches to special arrangements of classical music and opera. Some of these bands still exist today, in many cases playing the same music, but radio and sound movies decreased their popularity.

*The Music Man* couldn't have happened in any other time frame. Harold's profession as a travelling salesman and America's love of marching bands in this time period are vital to the story and to much more—Harold's outsider status; the suspicion with which the townspeople see him; his persona as a sexually experienced sophisticate (Yet is he? Imagine putting Harold Hill into *Chicago* or *Company*.); the townspeople's sheltered lives, which lead them to believe Harold's con; their desire to have a marching band like other towns have; the mayor's status as moral arbiter; the town's lack of influence from outside sources; the relatively bland day-to-day existence, which would make band instruments such a major event; Marian's position as the only source of culture in the town; and the low literacy rate, which kept most adults from being educated enough to see through Harold's lies.

## Professor Harold Hill

What's most remarkable about *The Music Man* is that its hero, Harold Hill, is a lying, cheating con artist. He cares about nothing and no one but himself. He is ruining the livelihoods of other, honest salesmen by making the people he's scammed distrustful of all salesmen. He romances Marian, a lonely, vulnerable young woman, only to make sure she doesn't uncover his scam. He doesn't really care for her until very late in the show. The people of River City may be ignorant, even foolish sometimes, but they are *good* people, hardworking, God-fearing families that deserve better than having their money stolen by Harold Hill. He is also dangerously charming and we see from his "Trouble" speech and "76 Trombones" that Mayor Shinn is right—Hill is a spellbinder. Robert Preston's portrayal of Harold Hill was so successful because he found the most important element of Hill's persona: he never looks like he's working. People are easily conned by him precisely because everything he says and does appears effortless and without guile. He doesn't sound like he's performing, like he's working his magic; he seems utterly genuine. He has the confidence that gives con men their label. If he were to come into town, guns blazing in people's faces, demanding their attention, they'd run him out on the next train out of town. Instead, he is the seducer, and like all great seducers he has learned how to make the object(s) of his seduction come to him. He can never break a sweat until the scene at the end when he has to make good on the promise he never intended to keep. His big songs are not performances; they are seductions.

He knows how to create excitement, by attacking anything that is new, a trick still used by politicians today. Harold knows that some people are afraid of anything new. But that makes the town suspicious of him, too, since he's just arrived, so he has to outweigh that by portraying something else as a more serious, imminent threat. It's not until very late in the show that we see Harold's good side. We learn that he really does dream of being a conductor. We see that despite his intentions, he has actually fallen in love with Marian. But is this too late? Should he be forgiven? Do we not realize how badly he's treating the good people of River City, or do we not care if he steals their money? Perhaps the show's creator, Meredith Willson, has played a trick on the audience. Hill mesmerizes *us* as successfully as the residents of River City.

## Madame Librarian

Just as we think of Harold Hill as a traditional musical comedy hero, even though he's far from it, we also mistakenly see Marian as a typical musical comedy ingenue. On the contrary, she is a strong, smart, fiery young woman, age twenty, working two jobs (the library and piano lessons) as the sole provider for her family. She has some serious psychological issues to deal with, most notably her father's death, her little brother Winthrop, and her social ostracism. She is a bit of a control freak, and a social and emotional coward, but the deck is stacked against her. Even if she wanted to find a nice man and settle down, how could she? She is the only one supporting her mother and little brother. She is an outcast in the town, mostly because she keeps to herself. She could very easily explain away the other ladies' misperceptions, but Marian chooses not to. It's none of their business and she doesn't care if they like her or not.

Her romantic side is so much richer and more complex than that of the usual old-fashioned musical comedy heroines. Mrs. Paroo sums up Marian's personality, motivations, and hang-ups pretty completely in one line in "Piano Lesson": she says Marian's dream man comes from her Irish imagination, Iowa stubbornness, and a library full of books. These three characteristics define Marian. She is a dreamer certainly. Yet she takes no guff from anyone, having created a hard, cold exterior to keep out anyone who might hurt her. And she allows herself to live too fully, too safely in the fantasy of her books, while she escapes from the town—and life—by working long hours in the library.

Marian has no suitors, but we see in "Goodnight My Someone" and "My White Knight" (and the song "Being in Love," added to the film) that she does think about romance, about being in love and getting married, about being rescued from the life she has. But because she has never dated, never allowed herself to be courted, she has never developed emotionally. When she finally allows herself to be wooed by Hill, she has no defenses because she has no experience at this. She has set herself up for quite a fall. She has fantasized her ideal man, a man that does not exist, one that is quiet and contemplative, literate and cultured. How is she going to meet such a man in River City, Iowa, in 1912? We see how far she has fallen for Harold when she rips the page out of the book she gives to Mayor Shinn. For a rule-following straight-arrow librarian, ripping a page out of a book—a reference book, no less—is like splashing paint on the Mona Lisa.

## The Truth

But her complete turnaround is due to Winthrop's conversion. Hill has truly brought happiness to Marian's little brother, a kid no one else could reach. She sees that, whether or not Harold is a real professor (and she already knows pretty much for sure that he's not), he has indeed brought happiness to River City and to her family. She keeps quiet and silently watches her town transform into a magical place. By the end of the show, she has learned that she doesn't need her white knight; she just needs a man who loves life and who can appreciate (even manufacture) the fun and magic of ordinary lives. How many other musical comedy heroines come with this much psychological baggage or this complex a life?

Marian sees a lot of truths that others don't see until the end. And though she's pretty close-minded and guarded at the beginning, it's her clear-eyed pragmatism that allows her to see what even Harold can't see. She sees that he really has delivered what he promised: magic, self-esteem, community pride, and a sense of accomplishment. She sees that Harold isn't selling a boys band; he's selling fantasy, and she realizes that it's okay to sell fantasy if you can really deliver it. Even Harold doesn't understand the power of fantasy the way Marian does, but she's a librarian and has spent her life reading books and escaping her real life through the lives of others (she shares a lot with Fosca in *Passion,* in that regard). Is there a moral to the morally ambiguous story of *The Music Man?* Maybe only that the things Harold promised are things that come from inside, not from others, and certainly not from things you can buy; that the greatest joy comes from having something to believe in, something to come together as a community for. So in the final analysis, has Harold done wrong? Is he a thief? Should the townspeople get their money back or did they get what they paid for? Can Harold really retire from the con man business and settle down with Marian or is River City too quiet for this cosmopolitan seducer? She did say she understands that she can't ask him to stay, that he will probably be moving on. Can she let him go?

## River City-zians

The people of River City, the River City-zians, as Mayor Shinn calls them, are introduced to us in the second song, in one of the richest, funniest expository theatre songs in the canon. In great detail, Willson gives us a character sketch of the townspeople: strong, independent, private, no-nonsense, yet generous when someone is in need. They may be somewhat close-minded, as evidenced by their condemnation of the books in the library by Balzac, Chaucer, Rabelais, and others. They may be illiterate—you'll notice there are no adults in the library during "Marian the Librarian." They may be gossipy, as demonstrated in "Pick-a-Little, Talk-a-Little." (It's fun to notice that both times Maud starts to speak she uses the exact same phrase, "Of course I shouldn't tell you this, but . . ." even though she has every intention of telling.) But these people have created a world where they are safe, where they watch out for one another. Their Fourth of July exercises demonstrate a love of their community and of their country, a fervent patriotism that Hill exploits in "76 Trombones." Everything is in perfect balance until Hill arrives and throws off-balance many of the key relationships in the town: the school board, the mayor and his wife, the Paroo family, Tommy and Zaneeta, and others.

As in most musicals, Harold Hill, the outsider, must either be assimilated into this community or be removed from it. As Jeffrey Sweet discusses in his book *The Dramatist's Toolkit,* many musicals follow the same rule: an outsider is introduced into an established community and by the end of the show he must either become one of them or be removed. In *Carousel, Evita, Pippin, Phantom of the Opera, Sweeney Todd,* and *Cabaret,* the outsider is removed because he or she can't (or won't) fit into the community. In *The Music Man, Company, Girl Crazy, How to Succeed in Business Without Really Trying, Brigadoon,* and *My Fair Lady,* the protagonist successfully becomes part of the community. *South Pacific* manages to do both: Nellie is assimilated into this exotic island community, but Lt. Cable can't overcome his prejudices and he is removed (through death). In *The Music Man,* we even get a little foreshadowing that Harold will eventually become part of the River City community. We find out early on that his old con artist partner Marcellus has already been assimilated into this community; if Harold and Marcellus were once partners in crime, it makes sense that Harold may be similarly assimilated.

## Textual Themes

There are a number of textual themes explored in the show, all of them built around the relationship between Harold and Marian. The first is the theme of fantasy. We see Marian's romantic fantasies in "Goodnight My Someone" and "My White Knight." We see Harold's musical fantasy when we find out he really does dream of being a conductor. We see Amaryllis' romantic fantasy in "Goodnight My Someone," and Tommy and Zaneeta's romantic fantasy in their reading and emulation of *Romeo and Juliet*.

Deception is another big theme, represented most obviously by Harold's great scam on River City, the promise to create a boys band. He deceives Marian into thinking he cares for her. He deceives the school board into thinking he has some credentials. He deceives the whole town in one way or another. He even starts the show by deceiving the other salesmen on the train. He has no scruples. The greatest joke of all is that Harold's biggest con, the boys band, turns out not to be a con after all; he actually delivers what he promises in spite of himself.

Along with deception comes the theme of perception and misperception. Harold creates the misperception that the pool hall is a real danger to the city's children. The ladies have grave misperceptions about Marian, and about her relationship with the late Mr. Madison. Marian and Harold have misperceptions about each other. The townspeople have both their own already established perceptions of what a marching band represents as well as misperceptions about their children's ability to match their preformed perceptions. And most comical is the ladies' misperception of themselves as modern dancers.

## Music

Perhaps the most important textual theme is that of music. The role of music in the lives of Harold, Marian, and River City is key. There's a reason the show is called *The Music Man*. It's not just because Harold's con involved musical instruments. It's because music plays an incredibly important role in American life, and always has, and because Harold brings music (both literal and figurative) to River City even though that was not his intention. Music is portrayed as fiercely American, as wholesome and transforming, as a big part of our national heritage (as evidenced by the singing of "Columbia, the Gem of the Ocean" at the assembly), as patriotic. At that time in our history, music was often the center of small-town life; and yet, the only music in River City before Harold's arrival is the gramophone at the barber shop and the piano lessons Marian gives.

There is an interesting mix in this show of regular book songs (songs that happen within the context of the plot, functioning as heightened dialogue or monologue) and diegetic songs (songs in which the characters are aware they're singing, playing, or dancing). Some of the diegetic music in the score includes Amaryllis playing the piano in "The Piano Lesson," the school board's barbershop harmonizing, the band itself, the dancing at the festival ("Shipoopi"), the school board and the ladies performing "It's You." There are some instances in which it's hard to tell whether the music is diegetic or not. For instance, in "The Piano Lesson," certainly Amaryllis is aware that she's playing piano, but are Marian and Mrs. Paroo aware they're singing, and in counterpoint to the piano? Or is their talking and singing merely the language Meredith Willson chose for them to communicate with the audience? Does Harold know he's singing "The Sadder But Wiser Girl"? We can assume that the school board is aware they're singing "Lida Rose," but it's doubtful that Marian is aware she's singing "Will I Ever Tell You" in counterpoint to them.

## Inside the Score

*The Music Man* employs one of the most interesting and effective but least noticed musical devices in the history of musical theatre. When Meredith Willson wrote the signature tunes for Harold ("76 Trombones") and Marian ("Goodnight My Someone"), he created two songs so rich in music and lyrics, so exactly right for the characters, that he could use them throughout the show to identify the two protagonists. "Goodnight My Someone" is a romantic, old-fashioned waltz, just like the hidden romantic in Marian, while "76 Trombones" is an aggressive, powerhouse march, translating Harold's assertive persona into the language of music. But Willson did something else with these two songs that many people never consciously notice— he built both songs on the same melody. "76 Trombones" and "Goodnight My Someone" use the same main melody and the same bridge melody, with small changes here and there. Because "Goodnight My Someone" is such a gentle waltz and "76 Trombones" is such a hearty

6/8 march, we don't notice they share the same melody. Willson even puts the two songs next to each other in the score, with only a fragment of "Columbia, the Gem of the Ocean" between them. Then when Harold takes Marian back to her house to get a sweater, the two of them even swap songs, Marian taking fragments of "76 Trombones" while Harold takes fragments of "Goodnight My Someone." Not only do they share the same music, which foreshadows the fact that they belong together, they're close enough emotionally to sing *each other's* music. Yet even with all these clues, most of us don't realize what's happening musically. Still, it works on a subliminal level, as we hear unconsciously that these two characters *sound* like they belong together.

And on an even deeper level, maybe Willson is telling us something about Harold that never gets said anywhere explicitly. Marian's "Goodnight My Someone" is a song about her loneliness; but Harold must be a pretty lonely guy as well, in his life as a traveling salesman with his girl-in-every-port, don't-fence-me-in philosophy of love. Maybe the fantasy and seduction of "76 Trombones"—as a representation of his overall con—is a result of his loneliness. He has no real fame or glory in his life, so he makes it up in the song. No one really loves him, so he makes these wild promises of the glories of a River City marching band to win some love from these strangers. If ever there was a man desperate for attention, surely it's Harold Hill. Not only are Harold and Marian more alike than we might think (and surely more than *they* would think), but perhaps their songs are as well, not just musically but also subtextually. Both of them are looking for something to fill their very empty lives.

Another musical device Willson uses is rhythmic talking. We first hear it in the opening scene, "Rock Island." It accomplishes two things here, setting up the salesmen's control and command of the language, and also the sound and rhythm of the train. Like old-time preachers, these salesmen must have complete mastery of their language in order to stir people's emotions and make convincing arguments. But are these men too articulate, too slick, too in control? Mightn't they use that mastery to bamboozle? We see shortly after this scene that yes, they might, as Harold works the townspeople into a frenzy with "Trouble." Interestingly, Marian does it too, during "The Piano Lesson," one more thing she shares with Harold. This rhythmic speech against the piano exercises also sets up the use of a piano exercise for the accompaniment of "Goodnight My Someone."

Willson's use of accompaniment to characterize is masterful. Marian's two introductory songs, "Piano Lesson," showing us her tough side, and "Goodnight My Someone," showing us her tender, hidden side, are both set against piano exercises. Not only does this reinforce her role as piano teacher—strict, authoritarian, no nonsense —but it also says something about how she lives her life. She never jumps into the music of life; she's always just doing her exercises, reading about life instead of living it, creating rationalizations for avoiding romantic contact instead of actually taking a risk. The piano exercises tell us who she is, and connect her to Harold, who's claiming to be a music teacher himself. It's through music that he will win her, through the magic that music brings to River City and to Marian through Winthrop. Similarly, Willson creates an onomatopoetic accompaniment for "Wells Fargo Wagon," a walking bass line that simulates the sound of horses clopping down the street.

Willson uses music as a metaphor for life. When the school board learns to harmonize with each other, they suddenly find themselves in personal harmony with each other as well. Harold uses their new enthusiasm for singing to escape them time after time. By simply starting a song, he can get the board members caught up in music while he slips away. It's ironic that when the school board asks Harold for credentials to prove he's a music professor, he uses music to avoid exposing himself as a fake. Yet his command and manipulation of (and through) music may mean he's more of a musician than even he thought.

## Full Service Score

Unlike most theatre scores, *The Music Man* does not contain an extraneous musical moment. Every song is important and every song has a specific function. Especially in 1957, when the show opened, this was unusual. Though many songs in musicals stop the action to further explore an emotion or a relationship, *The Music Man* rarely does this. Most songs in this show provide us with new information or insights; without the songs, the narrative would be incomplete. Because the same man wrote the book, music, and lyrics, there is a sense of unity and economy that few other musicals have.

It's interesting to note that Willson also broke other rules in writing this score. Most notably, many songs in the show don't rhyme. There is little or no rhyme in "Rock Island," "Trouble," and "Piano Lesson." And half of "My White Knight" doesn't rhyme—these are conversation songs, lyrics that veer closer to real speech than most theatre lyrics would dare to. Willson manages to create lyrics that sound real, colloquial, and genuine, while finding poetry in these characters' words. He said in his book *But He Doesn't Know the Territory*, that he wanted to make the transition between song and dialogue as smooth—even invisible—as possible. And writing lyrics with little or no rhyme certainly accomplishes that. Straying even further from convention, "Rock Island" and the main verses of "Trouble" don't even have melody. Willson was trying to break through to a new language for musical theatre, one that better integrated spoken dialogue with sung lyrics. His solution was to create a hybrid language, one that has the natural vocabulary and structure of spoken dialogue with the rhythm and alliteration of lyrics. This new hybrid form works so well in this show because the characters who use it—mainly Harold and the other salesmen—are men who live by their wits and their command of language. We accept this rhythmic, flowing language from them just as we would accept it from a southern minister, because we already expect these people to make spoken language exciting and musical (the same device is used in *Purlie*). We accept it from Mrs. Paroo in "Piano Lesson" probably because her Irish brogue already makes her language musical to us, and her wonderfully mixed-up language and liberal use of lower-class slang works as a great comic counterpoint to Harold's slick patter. After *The Music Man*, Willson tried to use this device again in *The Unsinkable Molly Brown*, but it failed there because those characters are uneducated and inarticulate mountain folks; for them to have that great a command of language stretches our suspension of disbelief too far. Willson did succeed in creating a new language for musical theatre, but its use is limited.

## Talk, Talk, Talk, Talk, Bicker, Bicker, Bicker

The structure of the score is brilliant. *The Music Man* opens with "Rock Island," the rhythmic patter song that introduces the brotherhood of traveling salesmen, that sets up Harold Hill as an unprincipled con man, and that establishes the time period through the invocation of the rhythms of train travel. The next song, "Iowa Stubborn," establishes the story's setting and characterizes the town of River City, full of no-nonsense, hard-nosed but good people. This song also tells us that these are honest, generous people, no matter how stubborn they may seem on the surface, people who should not be cheated. The central conflict is established between the con man Harold Hill and the intractable residents of River City, and there has been almost no regular dialogue yet.

The action gets under way for the first time with "Trouble," as Harold seizes upon the new pool table in town as a moral threat to the youth of River City. As naturally suspicious folks, the townspeople happily believe that the pool table is dangerous. Following the song, Harold meets Marian and, with the music underscoring him, he tries to impress her and fails. It's significant that their meeting happens to the tune of "My White Knight," the song Marian will sing later about wanting to meet a man and fall in love. The music segues into the Paroo house and the sounds of a piano lesson, establishing Marian's role in the town and the importance of music in her life. To the sound of Amaryllis' piano lesson, Marian and Mrs. Paroo discuss and argue over Marian's refusal to be courted by a man, and Marian complains about the town's illiteracy. After introducing Marian's troubled brother Winthrop, we move on to "Goodnight My Someone," Marian's signature song, establishing her romantic fantasy life, in stark contrast to the cold, independent facade she shows her mother and the rest of the town.

The scene shifts to the high school gym and the Fourth of July exercises begin with a brief rendition of "Columbia, the Gem of the Ocean," establishing the role of music in the town's life, and the connection of music to patriotism, a connection Harold is about to exploit. Within a few minutes, Harold is on stage with another rhythmic speech, just as intoxicating to the townspeople as his "Trouble" speech. This speech segues into "76 Trombones," Harold's signature song, representing both Harold's con and his own fantasy. By using the same melody as "Goodnight My Someone," the two main characters are linked.

The next song sets up one of Harold's great distractions. He teaches the four members of the school board how to harmonize, and they sing "Sincere." For the rest of the show, Harold will set these four men singing whenever he needs to escape them.

Next, Harold sings "The Sadder But Wiser Girl" to Marcellus, explaining why he stays away from innocent, inexperienced girls—the kind of girl Marian is. This will prove important in the next couple scenes. Harold runs into the town ladies who spew forth all their gossip, especially about Marian, in "Pick-a-Little." He is delighted to learn that Marian is "the sadder but wiser girl" he's looking for. The school board shows up, but Harold evades them by getting them singing "Goodnight Ladies." Harold makes his way to the library to look up Marian. He kicks his seduction into full throttle now that he thinks she's the kind of experienced woman he's looking for. Always the control freak, the chaos Harold creates in the library (including a full-scale but "silent" dance break) alternately infuriates, delights, and confuses poor Marian. It's interesting to note that Marian does allow herself at certain moments to get swept away in the excitement of being romanced, because here in the library she is on her own turf; this is the only place where she has allowed romance (albeit imaginary) in her life. To her mind, this is where romanticism and love belong. It's awfully smart of Harold (or of Meredith Willson) to make his move here, where she feels secure.

Back at home, Marian confesses to Mrs. Paroo her romantic fantasies in "My White Knight," the ideal man she dreams of, the life she wants to live. Her dream man is the exact opposite of Harold, yet by now we know they'll end up together. (In early drafts of the show, the first act ended with "My White Knight" sung by Marian in counterpoint to Harold's "The Sadder But Wiser Girl"—the two melodies are written to sit on each other perfectly—another musical device to show us how well Marian and Harold "fit.")

The first act ends up with "The Wells Fargo Wagon" rolling into town, loaded with the band instruments. The lyric is full of great information not only on the personalities of the townsfolk—what excites them, what they value—but also info about their lifestyles, the things they buy, luxury items and higher price items. For the first time since his father's death, Winthrop is happy and talking. No matter what she may think of Harold, Marian knows he's responsible for the transformation in Winthrop. For the first time, we see that Marian likes Harold. Before the curtain falls, she tears an incriminating page out of a book the mayor is borrowing. Marian may actually be in love with Harold now, but he's still just wooing her to keep her from exposing his con. There is a surface happiness here, but underneath, things are not good. Marian will surely get hurt.

And there has not been a single unnecessary song. Every song provides vital information and propels the plot forward. For instance, without "Pick-a-Little," Harold wouldn't have gotten Mrs. Shinn on his side, wouldn't have acquired his misperception about Marian (that ties back to "The Sadder But Wiser Girl") that makes him pursue her more actively, and wouldn't have had an excuse for getting the school board singing again. Without "The Piano Lesson," we wouldn't know Marian's relationship with the other women in town, the illiteracy of the people of River City, or Mrs. Paroo's campaign to get Marian married.

## Act II

Act II begins with another song for the school board members, "It's You," followed by Marcellus and the kids singing (and dancing to) "Shipoopi," both songs about meeting, dating, and being in love. Contrary to the statement above that every song serves a necessary function, these two songs provide another perspective on the evolving relationships in the show, but the story would still work without either one of them. "Shipoopi" works well structurally as a big group number to start off the act with a bang, and also as a comic take on Marian's hard-to-get persona. Still, if these two songs had been cut before the show opened, no one would've known.

We get into the meat of Act II with the reprise of "Pick-a-Little." In its first appearance, this song set up the ladies' resentment of Marian. Now, it underscores the ladies asking Marian to join them, allowing her to fit in for the first time. We also find out in this song that on Harold's advice, the ladies finally read the books they were so dead set against—and they *loved* them. They accept Marian now because they no longer believe she advocates dirty books and is a threat to the children, and because the ladies saw her dancing with Harold Hill and they now perceive her as one of them, a woman who can be courted by a man (could they have worried unconsciously that she was a lesbian?). Though Harold Hill is really the central character, the outsider who is at odds with the community and who must be either assimilated or removed, Marian is actually in that position as well. Although she lives in River City, she is very much an outsider socially. She, too, must be assimilated, although for different reasons and in different ways. This reprise signals the beginning of her assimilation; what's significant is that the assimilation only happens because of Harold. He brings about Marian's assimilation, and later, she'll return the favor.

The next number is a double song, the school board singing "Lida Rose" in counterpoint to Marian singing "Will I Ever Tell You." "Lida

Rose" is not particularly essential to the plot line (although it does set up a nice moment later), but "Will I Ever Tell You" is a wonderful glimpse into Marian's psyche. She's finally accepted the fact that she loves Harold, but this being her first time in this situation, she's not brave enough to do anything about it. He's going to have to make the first move, and this information is very important.

The next song is "Gary Indiana," a song Harold has taught Winthrop about Harold's home town. Though this is a very lighthearted moment, there is a dark subtext. Winthrop is excited because Harold has taught him a song with "hardly any Ss in it," presumably so that Winthrop can be less conscious of his lisp. But when Winthrop starts singing, we realize the song is absolutely loaded with Ss. In fact, Harold has conned Winthrop just like he's conning everyone else in town. He's promised the kid a song without Ss, and doesn't deliver. In context, it seems very innocent, but the bottom line is that Harold will lie to anyone for any reason.

The scene in which Charlie the anvil salesman arrives to expose Harold is accompanied by the offstage voices of the school board singing "Lida Rose." Marian offers to pass on Charlie's message to the mayor, even seduces him briefly to keep him from delivering the message himself, and she keeps him occupied until his train is leaving and he has to run to catch it. So "Lida Rose," a song about a man returning to claim the girl he loves and marry her, underscores a scene in which Marian vamps Charlie to protect Harold, the man she knows is scamming her and the ones she loves, a man she knows will be leaving town soon. Very ironic, but very dramatic.

The musical climax of the show happens on the foot bridge, the place where lovesick young couples go to be alone, a place Marian has never been with a man. Marian tells Harold she knows everything about his false identity, which naturally surprises the hell out of Harold. He's thought all along that he was keeping her off balance, when in reality, she's been far more in touch with reality than he was. Even though he's been trying to con her, she realizes that he has brought great joy and excitement into her life and the lives of her family and friends. Harold really has made life better in many ways. She sings "Till There Was You," to explain to him how he has transformed her very ordinary life into a life full of color and happiness. This is the one song that is not written in period style. Instead it's in the style of traditional 1940s and 1950s Broadway love songs, and we have to forgive Willson for this. This is the most potent emotional moment of the show and instead of putting it in a period style that could be emotionally distancing to the audience, he has set it in the musical language his 1957 audience expects for a musical comedy love song. He made it more familiar for them and allowed them easier access into this moment, and there's nothing wrong with that. It's beautiful, complex music that captures perfectly the emotion of the moment.

Harold and Marian go back to the Paroo house so Marian can get a sweater, and it's here with Marian in the house and Harold waiting on the sidewalk that they swap their signature songs. They begin singing their own songs, alternating phrases to give us another chance to recognize the fact that their signature songs share the same melody. Halfway though the song, Harold realizes he's in love. He picks up Marian's song instead of his own, and she picks up his. We see—we hear, actually—that they really do fit together.

Back at the ice cream sociable, the ladies do their hilariously bad interpretive dance, when Charlie returns to announce that Harold is a fake and that he's cheated the whole town out of their hard-earned money. A massive chase ensues, with the whole town after Harold, to music that includes a badly fractured "76 Trombones"—Harold's magic spell, as represented by that song, has been broken. Back at the Paroo house, Winthrop runs into Marian and Harold. Winthrop is devastated and Marian tries to explain to him that everything Harold promised really did happen. This all happens over underscoring to the tune of "Till There Was You." Harold picks up the melody and finally expresses his love for Marian. But he's stayed too long and the crowd catches him. The underscoring continues with "Till There Was You," and as the scene changes, the music also changes to a very solemn, hymnlike version of "Iowa Stubborn." These townspeople are funny but they're also hard-nosed, and if they are the way they described themselves in their opening number, Harold hasn't got a prayer.

Harold's "trial" is held in the gymnasium where he first wowed these people with his hypnotizing "76 Trombones." Despite the mayor's desire to tar and feather him, Marian gets up and speaks for him, possibly jeopardizing her newfound acceptance in the town. But the crowd knows she's right. River City has been a wonderful place to live since Harold arrived. He is given one last chance to prove himself. The band has been assembled, now wearing their newly arrived uniforms, and he has to conduct them. They begin to play the worst "Minuet in G" we've ever heard, and one by one parents start popping up yelling with pride that their sons are playing in that band. It turns out that it doesn't matter if the band is any good. The joy of music isn't about being good; it's about expressing yourself, about sharing yourself, a lesson that Harold only now really understands. As the show ends, Harold and Marian are together, the town is happy, and Harold (we presume) is going straight. He and Marian have both been assimilated into this community and the play can end. Though it's not written in the script, most productions use the curtain call music, an instrumental "76 Trombones," as a chance to bring a real marching band (or sometimes, several marching bands) on stage to finish the show, somewhat the way the movie does. We finally see the band as the parents see it—marching in perfect unison, playing strong and clear, making great music.

Willson's great accomplishment is that by the time the show's over, we forget what a snake Harold was to begin with (until his conversion only about twenty minutes before the end of the show). He hurt people, he stole their money, he used their children to make a fast buck. Suddenly because he's fallen in love with Marian who's never let a man touch her, Harold is a good guy. In fact, as the townspeople chase after Harold, we feel sorry for him. We see the townspeople as an angry mob instead of as justifiably angry people who've been cheated out of their hard-earned money. One of the greatest scumbags ever on the musical stage becomes a shining, all-American hero and we don't even realize it's happened. We've been mesmerized just like the people of River City.

## Historical References

There are a lot of obscure references that it might be helpful to define. In "Rock Island," the salesmen make references to several products and items common to general stores of the period. A *hogshead,* a *cask,* and a *demijohn* are all containers for wine and other spirits. A hogshead is a large container holding sixty-three gallons of wine. A cask is a bottle of any size, but usually one holding liquor. And a demijohn is a large wine bottle with a narrow neck and usually a wicker enclosure around the bottom. A *firkin* is a small wooden tub for butter or lard. A *noggin* is a small cup or mug of wine, usually a quarter-pint. A *piggin* is a small bowl with a ladle for serving cream. A *tierce* is a wine cask holding forty-two gallons. Uneeda Biscuits are soda crackers, introduced in 1889 by National Biscuit Company (now better known as Nabisco), the first crackers to be sold packaged with a brand name instead of just out of a cracker barrel. This marketing experiment paid off and by 1900, Uneeda Biscuits were selling more than ten million packages a month, while all other brands of packaged crackers *combined* totaled only 40,000 packages a month. This was a huge change for marketing food in America. This is an important reference because it's one more sign for the salesmen that things are changing (and not necessarily to their advantage), that the old rules for selling things to people no longer apply.

The various authors referred to in *The Music Man* include Honoré de Balzac, a French novelist (1799–1850), Geoffery Chaucer, an English poet (1340–1400), who wrote the very racy *Canterbury Tales,* and François Rabelais, a French satirist and humorist (1490–1553). Obviously Mrs. Paroo is mistaken when she says "Balzac and Shakespeare and all them other high-falutin' Greeks." (Maybe this is a quirky variation on the old saying, "It's all Greek to me.") In the first library scene in the film version, when Marian and Mrs. Shinn discuss "dirty books," Mrs. Shinn mispronounces *The Rubáiyát of Omar Kayyám,* a book of erotic twelfth-century Persian poetry translated in 1859 by English poet Edward Fitzgerald. Marian also refers to Elinor Glyn, a "naughty" Hollywood novelist of the early part of the twentieth century (who Mrs. Shinn mistakenly thinks is another girl in town).

Dan Patch, mentioned in "Ya Got Trouble," was a champion harness-racing horse at the turn of the century. As another example of arbitrary rules of morality, it's funny that riding *behind* a horse in a race is considered wholesome, but riding *on* the horse is not. *Captain Billy's Whiz Bang* was a monthly humor magazine first published in 1919, which reached a circulation of 425,000 in 1923. Technically, this reference is a mistake, since the show is set in 1912. Dime novels were cheap, paperback adventure novels, in vogue from the 1850s through the 1920s. A cistern was a tank for storing water that had to be kept full (by pouring water into it manually) for the family to use, before people had indoor plumbing. Bevos, cubebs, and tailor-mades were various kinds of hand-rolled cigarettes, and Harold knows when he mentions them that cigarettes were illegal (and considered immoral) in Iowa at that time. Sen-sen is a popular breath freshener, very small but very strong.

Harold's comment in the intro to "76 Trombones" about all the famous musicians coming to town on the same day is presumably a joke, although an obscure one. The joke is that it would have been highly unlikely for all these extremely famous men of widely varying ages to actually come to one small town, especially all on one day. Hill is just throwing out names that sound impressive, names that the River City townspeople might know. John Philip Sousa (1854–1932), a world-famous bandleader and composer, was known as "the March King" for writing many of the famous marches that marching bands play today. Patrick S. Gilmore (1829–1892) was a famous Irish American bandleader who also wrote "When Johnny Comes Marching Home Again" (under a pseudonym). W. C. Handy (1873–1958) was a famous American blues composer and bandleader, who wrote "St. Louis Blues." Alessandro Liberati (1847–1927) was an Italian-born cornet player, bandleader, and composer, who came to the United States in 1872 and played with many bands, including Gilmore's. He had his own touring band from 1889 to 1909, and was active in music (opera, other bands, teaching) until his death. Pat Conway (1867–1929) was a conductor, bandleader, and teacher, who directed several bands from the 1890s until his death and was the founder of the Air Force Band in World War I. Conway and Sousa were friends, and their bands often performed together. Giuseppe Creatore (1871–1952), also known as The Great Creatore, was an Italian conductor and composer who brought a band to the United States in 1902 to tour. He was active as a conductor through the 1930s.

Mayor Shinn mentions peck horns, a nickname for the alto horn, which looks like a small tuba and has the same range as a cornet. It was once a very common instrument in marching and military bands, especially in Europe. The song "Seventy-Six Trombones" also mentions some less well-known band instruments. A cornet is just a different version of a trumpet, shorter in length (the same amount of tubing, just wrapped around more), with a longer bell and a somewhat darker sound. A euphonium is like a baritone, which is itself like a small version of the tuba, but the euphonium has a larger opening in the bell and produces a mellower sound and better low notes than the baritone. Harold also mentions a flugelhorn at one point, which is like a cornet, but with a larger opening in the bell.

One of Harold's comments to Mrs. Shinn during "Pick-a-Little" includes a reference to François Delsarte, a French musician and dance teacher (1811–1871) who taught a dance method based on the mastery of certain bodily attitudes and gestures. In "The Sadder But Wiser Girl" Harold makes references to the Roman goddess Diana and to Hester Prynne, the heroine of Nathaniel Hawthorne's novel *The*

*Scarlet Letter,* who had to wear a red *A* in punishment for her adultery. In "Being in Love," a song written for the film but sometimes performed in stage versions, Marian refers to a teacher who sang, "In the Gloaming," a popular song written in 1877. In "The Wells Fargo Wagon," one man mentions getting a gray mackinaw, which was a thick, blanketlike coat, usually plaid, named for a kind of blanket that northern and western Native Americans made.

## Other Resources

The vocal selections and piano vocal score have both been published. Recordings of both the Broadway cast and the film soundtrack are available on CD. The film versions stars original Broadway cast members Robert Preston (Harold), Pert Kelton (Mrs. Paroo), and the Buffalo Bills (the school board), and it's available commercially on videotape. Music Theatre International has published a very thorough study guide for the show.

Meredith Willson wrote a hilarious and charming account of the creation and production of the show called *But He Doesn't Know the Territory* (Putnam's Sons, New York, 1959), which may be hard to find, but it's worth the effort. Not only is it extremely entertaining, it also offers invaluable insights into the intentions of Willson and the original creative staff. It's a must-read for anyone working on the show.

# 6   Passion

*Book by James Lapine*
*Music and lyrics by Stephen Sondheim*
*Based on the film* Passione d'Amore, *based on the*
  *novel* Fosca *by Iginio Ugo Tarchetti*
*Originally directed on Broadway by James Lapine*
*Licensed by Music Theatre International*

A handsome military officer who is having an affair with a married woman is also being stalked by an obsessive divorcée whose ex-husband was a fake count and who is dying of a mysterious disease. Is this some over-the-top story line from a soap opera? No, strangely enough it's a Stephen Sondheim musical, based on a 1981 Italian-French film based on an 1869 Italian novel, based heavily on the author's real life. It contains many of the elements Sondheim seems to look for in a project and everything his fans expect from his musicals: deeply complicated, profoundly intense, real-life emotions, a central character who is an outsider, a love that seems impossible. Sondheim is not a writer who tolerates easily tied up resolutions to difficult situations. The endings of his shows often leave loose ends, questions unanswered, moral ambiguities — just like real life. *Passion* is no different.

On the other hand, *Passion* was different from most other musicals — it was clearly an alternative work, playing with notions of time and space, using letters as a narrative device, and portraying emotions more extreme than anyone had ever seen in a musical before. And the show's central themes, that beauty is power, that emotional longing is dangerous, are as true today as they were in 1863 Italy, yet it's hardly the message with which a musical theatre audience expects to leave the theatre, even today. *Passion* does not suggest that love is the answer to all our woes, as many musicals do; it suggests instead that love can destroy your life.

The novel in which the obsessive dying Fosca first appeared was at least somewhat autobiographical. Like the handsome soldier Giorgio Bachetti, the novel's author, Iginio Ugo Tarchetti, also ended an affair and was then granted sick leave in Milan where he met a married woman named Clara, whose name is Italian for *light* (these events are not in the stage musical but are in the novel). Like Giorgio, Tarchetti was transferred to Parma soon after he began an affair with Clara, where he met Angiolina (renamed Fosca in the novel, which is Italian for *dark*), the dying cousin of his commanding officer. Tarchetti and Angiolina developed an obsessive relationship and conducted a scandalous affair. He was eventually discharged due to illness, and died at the age of twenty-nine, before finishing the novel. Interestingly enough, Angiolina survived him, unlike her literary counterpart.

Some of the theatregoers who saw the original Broadway production of *Passion* were confused. It was a love story, of course, but a very different kind of love story, one about unwanted love in a world consumed by physical beauty, one that began with a Happily Ever After and then deconstructed it. People didn't know what Sondheim and director/bookwriter James Lapine wanted them to think about this obsessive, demanding, selfish woman. Should they feel sorry for her, laugh at her, root for her? In all their shows, Sondheim and Lapine refuse to tell an audience what to think; they present people and situations that aren't black and white, and leave audiences to draw their own conclusions. Though audiences may accept that from straight plays, it still confuses them when a musical is presented that way.

## A Passion for Passion

This was one of only two projects Sondheim himself had ever initiated—the other was *Sweeney Todd*—and it's not hard to see similarities in these two very dark, very tragic stories. In both *Sweeney* and *Passion,* the central character has loved and lost before the show even begins. In both shows, the central character's existence centers on an obsessive love: Sweeney for Lucy, Fosca for Giorgio. Both central characters are sociopaths, abandoning the constraints of "polite society" and deciding instead to operate according to their own rules. Both musicals are European period pieces focusing on madness (or at least perceived madness) in a repressive and oppressive society. And both shows end with the death of the main character. In *Sweeney,* the few characters who survive are mad (with one exception), and in *Passion*, Giorgio survives but in an asylum.

This was Sondheim's first musical that told a nonironic love story. So often, Sondheim and other writers use irony to stand back from their characters—and to let us as an audience do the same—and comment on their follies. But here, Sondheim and Lapine charge headfirst into the depths of real love and real death. There is no irony to keep us back at a safe distance. When we watch *Crazy for You* or *Oklahoma!* we can stand back, and although we're happy for the young lovers, we know we're not as sappy as they are. We can still feel superior to them in some sense. They're silly, so we can dismiss them as just characters in a musical comedy. But the emotions in *Passion* are so real, run so deep, that we can't dismiss them. We're forced to deal with them on a serious level and that can be very scary for audiences.

This is a work of inordinately profound emotion, even for Sondheim. Robert Brustein called it "Sondheim's deepest, most powerful work." Brustein believed the reason audiences were confused was that *Passion* is not really a musical and doesn't really belong on Broadway; he thought it is an opera. Sondheim himself has said that Fosca is not really a musical theatre character; she's an operatic character living in a musical, a character of supernatural emotion and extreme tragedy. After all, how often does someone really die of love in a musical? Or in real life?

## What's Love Got to Do with It?

Sondheim has said that *Passion* is about how the force of somebody's feeling for you can crack you open. This is a kind of love we're not used to seeing in musicals, violent and extreme, obsessive and upsetting. The show explores many aspects of being in love, including questioning the very definition of love. The show isn't really about Fosca, as it appears on the surface; it's about Giorgio's search for the meaning of love. That is the action that propels the plot and the story doesn't end until that search is over. The show asks several questions about the nature of love. Is true love selfless or selfish? Fosca's love for Giorgio is both. She will do anything to get him, but she would also sacrifice anything for him. She would literally give her life, something Clara probably would not do.

Giorgio says several times in the opening song that he had thought he knew what love was (perhaps in the affair from the novel which precedes the action?). He thinks he finally understands love now that he's with Clara, but he will find out later that he does not. He will continue to search without success until the end of the show. None of the three central characters in *Passion* has ever had a healthy, loving relationship. Fosca was married to a con man bigamist who stole her money and ran off. Giorgio is in love with a married woman who can't make any real commitment to him. Clara is stuck in a loveless marriage and is fooling around on the side, yet she won't leave her husband because she would lose her son. In addition, there is an argument to be made—supported more by the novel than by the text of the musical—that Giorgio is every bit as obsessive as Fosca is. No wonder these three don't know what real love is. At first, Giorgio and Clara think love is just about being happy. Of course, it's not that simple. The Rousseau novel Giorgio lends to Fosca, *La Nouvelle Heloise,* says, "Tortured love provides a disturbing pleasure that replaces happiness."

*Passion* can be seen as a study of what drives love. Clara and Giorgio's love grew out of pity, and that is certainly the basis for Giorgio and Fosca's relationship as well. In an early version of the script, Clara had said that pity can sometimes be stronger than love. Fosca tells Giorgio that pity is only passive love, pointing up the fact that both of Giorgio's relationships are built on pity and he is, as a result, the most passive character in the show. He makes very few decisions for himself; life happens to him, rather than because of him (much like Bobby in *Company* and George in *Sunday in the Park*), at least until his breakup with Clara. Fosca has learned over her life to use pity and guilt to manipulate those around her. Her parents were motivated by pity and guilt. Her cousin, Colonel Ricci, is motivated by the guilt he feels for having introduced her to the adulterous, thieving Count, and by pity for her physical condition and lonely life. Giorgio succumbs just as easily as the others. When the Colonel says in the flashback that the enemy was love, he immediately corrects himself; it was selfishness more than it was love. He knows that his happiness for Fosca's marriage was partly relief in being rid of her, and he assumes her parents felt the same way. Yet Fosca's willingness to ignore the danger signals was motivated by selfishness as well, so should the Colonel really feel guilty?

Another driver of love in *Passion* is beauty. The lyric, "beauty is power," verbalizes one of the central themes of the show, though

Fosca has learned that her lack of beauty can also be turned into a kind of power. Clara's beauty clearly plays a part in Giorgio's love for her; Giorgio repeatedly tells Clara she's beautiful throughout the show. How differently Giorgio would feel about Fosca if she were beautiful, and she knows it. Meanwhile, Clara is worried that when she gets old and is no longer beautiful, Giorgio will no longer love her. The Count says to Fosca in the flashback that he gave Fosca his looks, the privilege of being married to a handsome man, in exchange for Fosca's (or more exactly, her parents') money. He knows the value of physical beauty and he knows how to use it to his advantage, just as Fosca later learns to use her ugliness to her advantage. On the other hand, using that beauty has its consequences; as the doctor says, being beautiful is something we must pay for.

Flowers are a metaphor for beauty and femininity throughout the show, and eventually, for Fosca as well. Clara speaks repeatedly of having flowers in bloom in the room where she and Giorgio meet. In the flashback, Fosca says that a woman is like a flower. Flowers are connected with death when Giorgio sees the hearse pulling up to the greenhouse and Fosca faints. Fosca's bitterness over her ugliness is expressed in the story she tells Giorgio about the poison flower in "I Read," thereby establishing flowers as a symbol for Fosca and also as a dangerous thing. The characters who get what they want with their looks—Clara, the Count, even Giorgio—either end up unhappy or directly cause great unhappiness. Beauty and the worship of beauty is dangerous, Fosca is saying. But does she ignore her own warning by desiring Giorgio's beauty? Is her attraction to him only intellectual? Later in the show, Fosca asks Giorgio why the violets and daisies are blossoming in the fall. Giorgio answers that the flowers, already established as a symbol for Fosca, mistake the autumn warmth (i.e., Giorgio's artificial politeness) for April (genuine warmth and affection).

## All This Happiness

Happiness is also a recurring theme in the show. All three central characters find happiness only through other people; none of them can find happiness within. Even at the end, when Fosca does develop a sense of self-worth, it's only because Giorgio finally says he loves her. Without Giorgio's love, Fosca would not have found that sense of self-worth.

For the first half of the show, Giorgio and Clara keep singing about how happy they are, but over time they both realize their happiness is not as solid as they thought. They both find that being in love with someone isn't always easy and can sometimes be extremely painful. Love is an extreme emotion, and can make people both extremely happy *and* extremely unhappy. But as Clara says, unhappiness can be very seductive. It was Giorgio's unhappiness that first attracted Clara, and perhaps Giorgio is seduced by Fosca's melancholy as well. They all want happiness, but they are drawn to unhappiness.

## Permanent as Death

Like many of literature's great love stories, *Passion* intertwines love with death. The first two lines of the show both mention death ("I'm so happy I'm afraid I'll die here in your arms."). Fosca's story of the poison flower in "I Read" presents death as the result of an attraction to beauty and acts as both a warning to Giorgio and the foreshadowing of Fosca's own death. It also links sex (represented by flowers, pollen, etc.) and death. The offstage hearse at the end of scene 3 even connects death back to flowers and beauty.

One of the most important details of Fosca's character is that she's dying and there is no hope of a cure. She is in many ways the embodiment of death, and she brings death to Giorgio's relationship with Clara, to Giorgio's military career, and almost to her cousin's life. In contrast to Clara's association with flowers in bloom, Fosca's environment is bleak and colorless, without life. She says she thinks the ruined (i.e., dead) castle is beautiful *because* it's ruined, because there is no life there. When Fosca is compared to flowers, they are poison (as in "I Read") or the comparison only illustrates how Fosca is a failure (as in the flashback). At the end of the show, Fosca is the reason behind Giorgio and Colonel Ricci's duel, from which one of them should be killed. In one of Fosca's most chilling speeches, she says she's not afraid of death, that in fact she looks forward to it. Instead it's the image of being locked in a coffin and buried under the earth that terrifies her. It's strange enough that death doesn't scare her, that she has a kind of relationship, even a romance with the concept of death. But her fear of what will happen to her after death is even stranger. Why does she care if she's locked in a coffin and buried? She won't be alive to know it. Perhaps she sees herself as already dead. Perhaps she sees the end of her marriage to the Count as a death, and the idea of being shut up in a coffin reminds her of her present life, shut up in her dark room with no love, no friends, nothing at all to live for.

Life and death, beauty and ugliness, happiness and despair, health and sickness. *Passion* uses opposites to tell its story. Could Fosca and Clara be more opposite? Or Giorgio and the Count? Yet these pairs are also each alike in many ways. Certainly, Fosca is one of the most extreme characters ever written, definitely the most extreme ever on the musical stage (with the possible exception of Sweeney Todd). Throughout the show, the lyrics reflect this juxtaposition of opposites—like "so much" and "nothing," as Giorgio's reunion with Clara is set against his rejection letter to Fosca. All the symbols surrounding Fosca and Clara are also opposites. For instance, Giorgio can only visit Fosca at night and can only see Clara in the daylight hours.

Passion and spontaneity, in the person of Fosca, is juxtaposed against rigid control, in the person of Giorgio. But there are different kinds of control. Fosca controls Giorgio through her passive-aggressive behavior (another set of opposites). The military controls Giorgio's life as well. Clara's husband has control over her, just as the dictates of "polite society" exert control over Giorgio and Clara's relationship, forcing them to keep it secret and making it impossible for Clara to run away without losing her child. And those same dictates keep Giorgio from being rude to Fosca even though she utterly ignores the rules of society.

## A Damned Exasperating Woman

A friend once suggested to me that we are all Fosca. Or would like to be. After all, she says and does exactly as she pleases. We're often afraid to say or do outrageous things because of their possible consequences. But Fosca has nothing to lose; she's dying anyway. On top of that, everyone has to be polite to her because she is the colonel's cousin. Though she is dying, she well may have the strongest life force in the show because she has no rules, no constraints, and just one all-consuming purpose to her life.

Fosca is sick, and this is perhaps her most important characteristic. Almost everything else stems from this single fact. The real woman Fosca is based on suffered from epilepsy. This explains Fosca's seizures, but this is certainly not all that is wrong with her. She is sick because of her lack of love (in the flashback, she says longing is a disease). Her sickness didn't begin until the Count left her. But losing her husband may not have been all that affected her. In the London production, the colonel had an additional line after the Count leaves: "There was to be a child . . . but . . ." We can only imagine the rest. It certainly deepens Fosca's tremendous loss and humiliation, and the reason why it all left her physically debilitated. To add insult to injury, Fosca's sickness makes her ugliness even more profound. She wields her sickness like a weapon, to manipulate those around her, to prevent anyone from acting badly toward her (at least to her face), to punish those who do. In a sense, being sick is what she's all about, what she's best at. It is all she has and she does it well.

She is always exhausted, but also peaceful in that she knows and accepts the fact that she's nearing death (which unnerves Giorgio), even though she's only in her late twenties. She has a kind of resignation, a melancholy, a sense of preparing for death, knowing there's no more to be done or accomplished. In the novel, Giorgio (as narrator) says that Fosca's ugliness is less physical deformity than the feeling when looking at her that you're staring death in the face. This implies not only a sense of her sickness but also of danger, of dark power.

But Fosca doesn't fit the usual tragic romantic mold. There is no beautiful soul inside this ugly exterior. She is demanding, selfish, manipulative, and deceitful. We understand why she is this way, but it is no excuse. Giorgio comes into her life not because he is noble and sees beyond the ugliness. He comes to her out of pity, out of an overdeveloped sense of propriety (that is curiously lacking when he's sleeping with Clara, a married woman), and out of guilt. The doctor is so sure that Giorgio couldn't love a woman so ugly, that he has no hesitation in letting them be alone together in Fosca's bedroom. Had Fosca been beautiful, the doctor probably would not have even considered allowing such a thing. In fact, Fosca is a predator, not a damsel in distress. Despite her weak physical condition, she is stronger than Giorgio. She is a vampire, sucking the life and the will out of Giorgio. (In the film *Passione d'Amore,* Fosca even looks a lot like Max Schrek in *Nosferatu*—ghostly pale, painfully thin, with a receding hairline, bug eyes, buck teeth, a long hooked nose, and long spindly fingers.) This role of vampire is reinforced by the fact that Giorgio visits Fosca only by night. Count Ludovic quite accurately tells Fosca that he knows she's not the victim she appears to be. The truth is that Giorgio (and perhaps Clara) is the victim.

Yet we must consider that perhaps the reason Fosca acts so horribly toward Giorgio is that she knows he'll reject her anyway, so if she treats him badly enough she can blame his rejection on her outrageous behavior rather than on her own (perceived) intrinsic lack of value. We have to remember that Fosca never got the chance to learn the courting ritual. She never had the chance to be an adolescent, which also explains why so much of her behavior is childish and awkward. She is going through her adolescence now, along with its excesses, inconsistencies, mistakes, and heartbreak. She has only ever had one suitor before, only one chance ever to be courted, and he didn't really want her. Part of the reason she behaves so inappropriately toward Giorgio is that she was never taught how to behave around a man she found attractive. She doesn't know what a woman is *supposed* to say or do. Though she is in her late twenties, she has the emotional and social development of a child.

Yet all of this is not to say we can't understand why Fosca is the way she is. She lives in a very Catholic country in 1863. In that time and place, a woman had only two choices, to be either a wife or a daughter. There was nothing else. And Fosca was neither. Her parents are dead, and her one attempt to be a wife failed miserably. None of the prevailing philosophies of the time—as embodied by characters in the story—could explain Fosca. The doctor's science could neither explain nor cure her. Giorgio's literary romanticism could not understand or predict her. The colonel's nineteenth-century Catholic morality could not define or excuse her.

Fosca was a feminist before there even was such a thing in Europe. She believed that intellect was the true measure of a person, not beauty, even though she knew no one around her agreed. Giorgio's eventual feelings of love for her prove in a way that Fosca was right; he ultimately chooses heart and mind (Fosca) over beauty (Clara). It's significant to note that the American Women's Suffrage Association was founded only a year before Tarchetti wrote his novel, and five years *after* the musical is set. For him to write a novel about a woman without any of the traditional feminine characteristics (the doctor says she's too weak even to have sex) and what would have been considered masculine habits (like intellectual literary discussion) was remarkable. Tarchetti was not only toying with the notions of morality and propriety, but also with the traditional roles of men and women —Giorgio crying, Clara as the adulterer, Fosca as the manipulator, the Count as the one using his looks to get ahead.

Can we wonder that she's as sociopathic as she is? Her parents spent her childhood telling her how beautiful she was. Yet their fawning over the Count and their relief when he proposed perhaps demonstrates that they knew she was unattractive. She was passed from parents who deceived her to a husband who fooled around on her, lied to her, and stole from her. All he left her was the skill for manipulation. Fosca learned from the Count how to get what she wanted. No matter how much he hurt her, Fosca knew she could learn from him and had a grudging respect for his talents at manipulation. She says that when she confronted him about his lies, that "*to his credit,* he made no attempt to deny it" [emphasis added]. In comparing Fosca's first conversation with the Count and her first conversation with Giorgio, we can see that she has appropriated the Count's con game, using his words, even using the same music.

Along with her skill at manipulation, she has learned, during all her years of watching the world go by without her, from years of reading about life instead of living it, how to read people. Her success at manipulating Giorgio is due in large part to how well she figures him out. She knows his politeness will allow her to get away with some pretty outrageous things. She knows his pity for her will allow her to push him further than anyone else could. As she repeatedly tests the limits to which she can push him, she learns more and more about how his mind works. When she dictates the letter from him to her, she is speaking in his voice. Everything she says is true, every feeling she describes accurate. She can articulate for him the things he feels but would never say out loud. We know in that scene that Fosca will ultimately win. She knows Giorgio, his weaknesses, his feelings, his needs. In much of the show, characters sing each other's words as they read letters, but here, for the only time, one character articulates another's feelings that even he doesn't yet understand.

It's also interesting to note the amount of rhyme in this song, "I Wish I Could Forget You." Sondheim has said that in his shows, rhyme connotes intelligence and presence of mind. The more intelligent or lucid a character is, the more rhyme we'll hear in his songs. Characters who are less intelligent or more flustered will rhyme less. Intellectual statements rhyme more than purely emotional ones. So, in much of *Passion* there is less rhyme than we're accustomed to from Sondheim, less of those triple-decker internal rhymes that dazzle the ear and mind. But "I Wish I Could Forget You" is much more heavily rhymed than the rest of the score, full of multiple rhymes and internal rhymes, because Fosca is playing out an intellectual conceit. She is choosing her words carefully to achieve her goals, and her rhyming illustrates this.

## Reading Is Fundamental

One of the continuing textual themes underneath the action of the show is the juxtaposition of reader and writer, observer and participant. This is underlined in the many letters read during the show. Characters often interact throughout the show without being in the same physical place at the same time, by reading letters. Sometimes characters read their own letters, sometimes they read letters written by others to them. (One of the joys of a good production of *Passion* is to watch the acting of the character whose words are being read by someone else—seeing Giorgio actually experiencing the sensations he's written about as Clara reads them, in the castle garden scene, for instance.) Sometimes they interact through letters with one character while interacting directly with another. At the ruined castle, Giorgio interacts with Clara by letter while he interacts with Fosca directly. On his first leave, he interacts with Fosca by letter while being reunited in the flesh with Clara. As mentioned above, Fosca turns this convention upside down by dictating to Giorgio a letter from him to her, another instance of Fosca not following the rules, in this case the rules of the musical in which she is a character. In a sense, Fosca "reads" Giorgio better than she reads her books. She understands him better than he would like her to. At the end, Fosca even speaks to Giorgio (and to us) from the grave by way of a letter. When Fosca writes to Giorgio that her love will live on in him, it's true; and her voice lives on in her letter.

We find out early on that both Giorgio and Fosca are avid readers. When Fosca first meets Giorgio, she says that Rousseau's character Julie is a great mystery; in reality, Fosca herself is the character who is a great mystery. The line between fiction and reality, writer and reader, past and present is hopelessly tangled. Has she gotten the notion that dying for love is somehow romantic from the novel Giorgio has lent her, Rousseau's *La Nouvelle Heloise?* In fact, reading is what unites Fosca and Giorgio, and it is the reason they first meet; she came to see him (or at least so she says) to thank him for lending her his books. We find out they even have the same taste in books. The colonel says reading is Fosca's only passion, but that won't be true for long. Fosca's first big song, "I Read" sums up her life and philosophy brilliantly. For her, books are her way to escape a world in which she doesn't fit:

> *I do not read to think.*
> *I do not read to learn.*
> *I do not read to search for truth,*
> *I know the truth,*
> *The truth is hardly what I need.*
> *I read to dream.*

Not only does this lyric tell us a great deal about Fosca; it is also her first step in creating pity for her in Giorgio. With that step, she becomes active, perhaps for the first time in her life. She is no longer on the outside looking in, no longer just an observer. She is actively pursuing something she wants, finally putting the Count's lessons to good use. All her years of observing, of reading, of studying the world instead of living in it will pay off. She is smart and has learned well. She moves from the ranks of passive female characters like Snow White and Sleeping Beauty to the ranks of strong, willful women like Mother Courage and Dolly Levi.

When the Colonel discovers Giorgio's letter to Fosca (the one *she* dictated), Giorgio says something that's very important to him, that Fosca is not a child and should not be treated as one, that though she may be sick, she is still an adult and still responsible for her actions. But Giorgio learns this too late. Perhaps his greatest blunder was in underestimating her.

## Every Good Boy Does Fine

Sondheim said that when he first saw the movie on which *Passion* is based, he realized right away that it wasn't a story about Fosca. It was a story about how Giorgio falls in love with Fosca, not about her falling in love with him. It was about how Giorgio changed and what he learned. Midway through the show he tells Fosca what love is supposed to be about, and what it isn't about:

*Is this what you call love?*
*This endless and insatiable,*
*Smothering*
*Pursuit of me,*
*You think that this is love?*

He tells her that love isn't sudden and obsessive and extreme. He believes that it's slow and tender and gentle. Yet by the end of the show, he's changed his mind. He realizes that he's never felt pure, unconditional, all-or-nothing love before. He realizes that the love Fosca offers is so much freer and truer than the love Clara offers. He has changed his tune—well, actually, it's the same tune with new lyrics. He says to Clara:

*Is this what you call love?*
*This logical and sensible*
*Practical arrangement,*
*This foregone conclusion,*
*You think that this is love?*

He now has a different understanding of love. He tells Clara that love isn't convenient or safe or easy. It's risky. It's scary and often difficult. This is somewhat the same lesson Bobby learns in Sondheim's *Company,* that love requires hard work and sacrifice. Clara is not willing to make tremendous sacrifices for Giorgio (like giving up her child); Fosca is. Interestingly, in the novel, Giorgio does not come to recognize the compensations of Fosca's kind of love, if in fact they can be called compensations. In fact, in the novel Giorgio doesn't really learn anything at all. His break-up with Clara isn't his decision; Clara breaks it off because her husband is having some sort of trouble and needs her. This may be a result of the fact that Tarchetti died before finishing the novel.

But there is an argument to be made that Giorgio does not treat Clara fairly. Giorgio comes to the conclusion that Clara's love is not as profound as Fosca's because Fosca will sacrifice everything and Clara will not. But the sacrifices the two women would have to make are not at all comparable. Clara has a happy, comfortable life; Fosca has nothing. Clara has a child which she would lose; Fosca does not. Fosca asks Giorgio if Clara would die for him, because Fosca would. But

Fosca's going to be dead very soon anyway; Clara has a long healthy life ahead of her. Fosca has nothing to risk; Clara has everything to risk, most notably, her son. Can Giorgio's love really be that deep if he wants Clara to give up her child to run away with him? Isn't that far more selfish than anything either Clara or Fosca does? The deck is stacked in Fosca's favor here. She can claim the ultimate sacrifice as proof of the depth of her love, but that sacrifice is an easy one. It sounds very dramatic and selfless, but in reality it is not. Giorgio's conclusions about Clara's and Fosca's love are shallow and adolescent.

To add to his woes, Giorgio does not fit in with the other officers at his post. In a letter to Clara, he calls the other officers pompous little men. Judging by their gossip, the other, less literate, less intellectual officers don't much like Giorgio either. Giorgio doesn't gamble or gossip. He doesn't talk about women or horses. He is a solitary man who reads in his spare time and keeps a journal. He likes gardens. He is frighteningly like Fosca. When Fosca says, "They hear drums, we hear music," she's absolutely correct. In the early part of the novel, we're told that Giorgio had just ended a relationship and it was so heartbreaking for him that he became sick—just like Fosca. He was transferred to Milan, where he met Clara. The description of their early relationship is curiously like Fosca and Giorgio's relationship. He is nearly as obsessive about Clara as Fosca is about him later.

The novel also gives us some insights into Giorgio's emotional health. He says that Clara resembles his mother, which certainly puts a whole new slant on their relationship. According to the novel, Clara also loves reading and playing music—just like Fosca. In the opening scene of the musical (and periodically throughout the show), Giorgio can't stop talking about how beautiful Clara is. When he lists her attributes in the first scene, he lists only physical characteristics—her feet, her skin, her smell, her breath, her hair, her breasts and lips—and never mentions anything about her personality. She is only a body to him. Their relationship is much more superficial than either of them can acknowledge.

Giorgio's two women, Fosca and Clara, are set up as opposites from which he must choose. As mentioned earlier, Clara's name means *light* while Fosca's name means *dark*. Appropriately, Giorgio only sees Clara in the daytime and usually sees Fosca at night (or on cloudy days). Also appropriately, Clara's hair is blonde and Fosca's is dark; and Clara's voice is a light soprano while Fosca's is a dark alto.

## Mister Manners

Much of what happens with Fosca and Giorgio stems from the fact that Giorgio is too polite. He has been taught never to be rude to a woman, but he's never encountered a woman like Fosca before. She knows he's too polite to fight back and uses that to her advantage. Giorgio is playing by rules that Fosca won't play by, and that's how she wins. Had he made his anger and disgust clear at the beginning, perhaps none of the trouble would have happened.

In some ways, Giorgio *is* Fosca and becomes even more like her as the show progresses. The closer he gets to her, the sicker and the more like her he gets. After the duel, he lets out a wail of despair just like the ones we've been hearing from her throughout the show. That's why she can read him so well and manipulate him so successfully. When Fosca tells Giorgio that the two of them are the same, she couldn't be more right. Perhaps that's part of what scares Giorgio so much about her. Many people tend to abhor the things in others that are most like themselves. At the end, he even approaches death—in the duel—just like Fosca. At the end of the show, Giorgio's song of realization, "No One Has Ever Loved Me," has basically the same melody as Fosca's piano motif. He has finally learned to see things her way, to feel her love, to hear her music.

The big question is whether or not what Giorgio learns about love is true. Is obsessive, unconditional love, love that isn't "pretty or safe or easy," *really* truer and deeper? Is Giorgio's love based only on pity and guilt? In an early version of the show, Fosca says to Giorgio on the train, "After I've died for you, you'll be compelled to love me." Some would argue—many people who saw the show on Broadway *did* argue—that Fosca's love is not healthy in any sense, that Fosca and Giorgio's relationship was without any redeeming value. Certainly, nothing good comes of it. Clara is left abandoned and unhappy, Fosca dies, and Giorgio winds up in an asylum.

And one has to wonder what it is about Giorgio that makes these woman want him so desperately. He's not overly intelligent. His understanding of love is shallow and incomplete. He's uptight and neurotic. Is it only his looks? Some people who saw the show wondered how Sondheim and Lapine could believe that this kind of love was good. But we learned with Sondheim's *Assassins* that the opinions expressed in a Sondheim show aren't necessarily those of its authors.

Sondheim and his collaborators tell stories they find interesting and leave it to their audiences to form opinions.

## You Are So Beautiful

Clara is a difficult character to understand. Because of the nature of the story, she gets less stage time, less dialogue, and less music. Yet what she does say and the way she has led her life is often very illuminating. What kind of a marriage must she have? She's sleeping with Giorgio for an extended period of time, and her opinions of love are strange indeed. She says she has always thought love was what kindness becomes. She remarks on how quickly pity can become love. She says that she has always associated love with shame. Her understanding of love may be, in its own way, as backward as Giorgio's and Fosca's.

And as much as Clara says she's utterly happy with Giorgio, we have to wonder about that. They both readily admit that their love is based on pity. How healthy is that? Clara tells Giorgio he's the one who makes her happy; she can't find happiness in herself, only in Giorgio. Clara and Giorgio can only spend afternoons together; they've never seen a sunrise together. She won't risk her child, but she will risk her marriage. She is too careful, too self-involved to give herself over completely to unconditional love. Yet despite all of this, she doesn't see what's wrong with their relationship. She is surprised when Giorgio suggests that their love is not as complete as they believed.

Yet Clara deals with everything as most of us would. She wants to be with Giorgio, but she won't give up her child. How many women would? Her marriage is bad, but she finds some happiness in her affair with Giorgio—it's not the life she might have envisioned for herself, but it's the best she can do. She is the practical one among the three. She tells Giorgio they must figure out a way to create a life around the obligations they already have. Only Clara deals with the realities of life. Fosca says she does, but she doesn't really. Perhaps Clara is not a paradigm of virtue or self-knowledge, but who is?

## War Is a Science

Fosca's campaign to win Giorgio's heart by metaphorically beating him into submission is not just a random string of events. She knows what she's doing and is careful to evaluate each move and its results.

She tests his limits and makes adjustments to her battle plan. She is as savvy and shrewd as any general (the colonel tells us early in the show that Fosca's been reading military handbooks), which is why the drums and bugle call motif pervade even her music, why even the melody of "Loving You" is based on the bugle call. To our modern eyes, Fosca appears to be nothing more than a stalker. But she is much more—she's a brilliant strategist.

Her attacks are designed to keep Giorgio off guard, to test his defenses. Both "I Read" and the scolding in the garden of the castle are groundwork for her later actions. She shows him that practically anything can set her off, can upset her, and that he must be extremely careful in what he says. This lesson to Giorgio will serve Fosca later when she makes ever increasingly outrageous demands of him. She both produces guilt in him for provoking her anger and also fires up his emotion, creating passion in him about her, even if it is a negative passion. One of the weaknesses of the original production was that Giorgio almost never showed his anger; he did not become passionate about Fosca until he announced that he loved her, and at that point, it was too sudden for the audience to accept it. Giorgio must demonstrate his anger, his extreme emotion for Fosca, and we must see it build over the course of the show so that we can believe his passion at the end. In an early version of the script, Giorgio happily agrees to the duel with the colonel, saying "Fine. I feel the need to kill a man." It is easier to go from extreme anger to extreme love than to go from absolute apathy to extreme love. By losing his temper from time to time Giorgio illustrates that, like Fosca, he is not always in control of his emotions, an important piece of information that will help the audience accept his conversion at the end.

We see then that the title of the show refers to many kinds of passion, not just romantic love, but also Fosca's passion for reading and music, Giorgio's passionate anger at Fosca, the colonel's anger at Giorgio at the end, Fosca's fear of losing Giorgio and her fear of death, as well as the characters' sexual and spiritual passions. Also, it's important to remember that *passion* can mean the *object* of someone's passionate feelings; in other words, Giorgio is Fosca's passion, and as he finds himself talking and thinking about her more and more, Fosca becomes Giorgio's passion. In fact, each of the three central characters is the passion of someone else. Perhaps the title also refers to the Passion of the Bible, the story of Christ's persecution and crucifixion, drawing an analogy to the suffering and martyrdom of Giorgio. Then again, maybe it's Fosca who is the true martyr, since she actually gives up her life. It's interesting that the Latin word that *passion* comes from means suffering or submitting, meanings that are definitely a major part of the fabric of this story.

## The Campaign

Fosca's first important move is to force Giorgio to deal with her unattractiveness. In her first song, "I Read," she demands that he look at her and acknowledge what is being left unsaid—that she is ugly. She confronts the issue head-on, so that it can no longer be a source of unspoken embarrassment. She not only demands that he look at her, but also discusses how her view of life is affected by her ugliness. She immediately then wedges her way into Giorgio's life, deciding (not offering, not asking) that she will show him gardens around the area. She simply assumes that he will not decline her invitation, and Giorgio is too polite to hurt her feelings. Moments later she brings him flowers, just as the Count did to her. Fosca has decided that since Giorgio will not court her, she will have to court him. Of course, this makes him even more uncomfortable than before, but he's too polite to say so.

Despite several unpleasant conversations between Fosca and Giorgio, she keeps asking for his friendship each time she has pushed him too far. Like an overly polite idiot, he keeps agreeing. Fosca builds a relationship between them, even without Giorgio's conscious help, even if it isn't the kind of relationship she wants. She figures that once the relationship is established, it can be converted into the kind she wants. To secure his friendship, she writes him a letter scolding him for promising to be her friend but then avoiding her. She calls into question his integrity and honor, and he sees no alternative but to be her friend as he so rashly promised.

Fosca confronts Giorgio before he leaves to see Clara the first time. She drops to the ground and locks her arms around his legs. She kisses him, hugs him, and declares her undying love. He is made clearly uncomfortable by all this, but Fosca has accomplished something. She has told him in no uncertain terms that her love for him is passionate and unconditional. Even though he rejects her as he leaves to be with another woman, Fosca still loves him. She makes him promise to write her while he's gone.

Now she involves the doctor. Fosca allows her physical condition to worsen and convinces the doctor she is letting herself die because of Giorgio's rejection. The doctor (on questionable judgment) enlists Giorgio's aid. He asks Giorgio to go to Fosca and *pretend* to love her, in order to save her life. Giorgio thinks he has no choice. If he refuses, he will essentially be killing Fosca. She has forced him into a situation from which he can see no escape. His decision to go to her locks him once and for all into a path that will lead to tragedy. Once he goes to her and declares his false love, there is no turning back. Giorgio is so polite, so afraid of offending, so easily manipulated that Fosca actually convinces him to lie on her bed beside her. Meanwhile, back in Milan (across the stage), Clara talks of waking up beside Giorgio. Fosca has physically replaced Clara—at least for the moment—as Giorgio's partner in bed. When Fosca wakes, she even echoes Clara's words, saying that she thought having Giorgio there was just a dream.

## Checkmate

Now Fosca makes the most brilliant move of all. She asks Giorgio if he will write a letter for her, which she dictates from her bed. Of course, he complies. But when she starts dictating, he is embarrassed to find that Fosca is dictating a letter *to* herself *from* Giorgio. He starts to object, but again his politeness and his pity stop him. She has won her most important victory; she knows Giorgio's mind completely, and with this letter, she shows him the feelings he has that he's been afraid to acknowledge. The letter doesn't say what Fosca wants to hear so much as what she wants Giorgio to hear.

When Fosca finally pushes him past the point of even his amazing tolerance, and he explodes, the battle is essentially over. She has made him feel real passion for her. No matter that it's anger; the fact remains that he has felt more for her than he does for Clara. The next time Giorgio prepares to leave to see Clara, Fosca follows him. Giorgio must not be allowed to be with Clara, to think about Clara, without also thinking about Fosca. In sharp contrast to the rest of her campaign, she now expresses a very tender, very quiet declaration of love, in the song "Loving You." She knows she has won the battle and has only to secure her victory. With no artifice, no manipulation, no subtext, she sings a simple, short love song. This is unconditional, pure love, a kind of love no one has ever expressed to Giorgio before. There's only one more thing Fosca must prove to Giorgio—that his happiness matters to her more than her own. Fosca says she'd die for him. She knows Clara would not.

Later, when Giorgio goes to see Fosca for what will probably be the last time before he leaves, she surprises him one last time. He tells her that he and Clara have ended their relationship, and Fosca shows genuine sadness. Giorgio sees that Fosca's love really is selfless in many ways, that his happiness really does matter to her more than her own. Finally, he lets his emotions out. He sings in a final revelation that no one has ever loved him as deeply as Fosca does. Fosca has shown him what love can be:

> *Not pretty or safe or easy,*
> *But more than I ever knew.*
> *Love within reason—that isn't love.*
> *And I've learned that from you . . .*

What we thought at the beginning could never happen has, in fact, happened. Giorgio has fallen in love with Fosca. This resolution is bittersweet, in that not only will Fosca be dead soon, but even if she were to live their relationship would not be a healthy or particularly happy one. They are both neurotic and ill-prepared for the complications of a real relationship. Still, they have both now felt a kind of love that few people ever feel, a level of passion that few people ever know.

## Corpus Delicti

Fosca's campaign to win Giorgio's heart (or is it a campaign to shatter his mind?) can also be traced through the progressive amount of physical contact between the two of them. At first, their physical contact is limited to Giorgio taking Fosca's hand to help her up, as any gentleman would do in polite society. It then progresses to full-fledged hand-holding at dinner when Fosca won't let go of his hand. This is the first time contact goes beyond the realm of normal politeness, and it's the first time that Giorgio can be sure this contact is intentional and calculated. Before he takes his first leave, Fosca embraces him, wraps her arms around his legs, and finally throws herself at him and kisses him squarely on the mouth. This is a test to see how far he'll let her go. His response is shock and anger. This is more than he'll accept.

After that, things begin to progress more quickly, their physical relationship growing more intense just as their emotional and psychological relationship does. As Fosca worms her way into Giorgio's consciousness, she also manages more and more touching between them. When Giorgio visits her bedroom for the first time, at the doctor's insistence, Fosca is the absolute picture of infirmity; she knows how pitiful she looks and knows that physical contact now will seem far less "dangerous" to Giorgio. Fosca starts with holding his hand again, this time kissing it as well. She convinces him to sit on her bed beside her, then to put his feet up as well. We know where she's heading, and Giorgio does too. He doesn't lean back (although how that would help if someone were to walk in I can't imagine). In her most brazen move yet, she takes his hand and presses it against her breast, holding it there. This makes Giorgio clearly uncomfortable, but his belief that she is dying (because of him, to some extent) keeps him from reacting as he otherwise might. He makes the huge mistake of allowing this potent and very sexual move without objection. She convinces him to lie back and sleep beside her. Before he leaves her room, she asks for a kiss. Not content with the peck he gives her, she pulls him down and gives him a big wet kiss. Finally, at the end of the show, in their last scene together, Fosca kisses Giorgio again, but significantly, the kiss is instigated by Giorgio this time. Just as his heart gives in to her, so does his flesh. He picks her up, carries her to the bed, and they collapse on each other, kissing passionately, caressing and groping. Though the lights fade, we know they are about to make love.

In a sense, the show is criticizing Giorgio and Clara's love for being merely physical. Yet here, Fosca and Giorgio's love seems to be inextricably tied to the physical as well. Apparently, their love cannot be fully expressed without sex. Has Giorgio learned to see Fosca's love as the superior kind of love he spoke of in the castle garden, or is all love connected to sex for him? Or is sex merely an expression of a much deeper love he now feels for Fosca? If that is so, then do we need to know they'll have sex? Aren't their musical declarations of love ("Loving You" and "No One Has Ever Loved Me") enough for us to understand the depth of their passion? On the other hand, the dictionary definition of *passion* includes both love and sexual desire.

## Connect

*Passion* uses textual, visual, and musical motifs throughout the show to connect characters and situations, and to show subtle, unexpected relationships between characters. One of the visual motifs we see throughout the show is physical touching between two people—not just ordinary human contact, but an obsessive need for tactile contact that the three central characters seem to crave so desperately. In the original production of *Passion,* Donna Murphy, as Fosca, was touching her face, her neck, her chest, almost every minute she was on stage, as if Fosca needed human contact but could only get it from herself. Fosca is so repellant to those around her that only she can bear to touch herself. Meanwhile, when Giorgio and Clara are together, they also are touching almost every moment they are together. Even when they're not directly sexual, they are touching, caressing. This tactile obsessiveness is echoed in several lyrics. In "Happiness," both Giorgio and Clara talk about touch. In Giorgio's letter about the castle, he talks about how Fosca's touch—or the touch of any woman, really—makes him think of Clara. These are people obsessed with the physical, Fosca because she never experiences physical human contact, Giorgio and Clara because their relationship is such a sexual one.

This obsession with the physical is also reflected in the musical and textual phrase, "God, you are so beautiful" (which we'll call the "beauty" motif or theme), beginning as a phrase used repeatedly between Clara and Giorgio. But it becomes Fosca's phrase when she sings those same words to Giorgio in her bedroom. Not only has she reversed the roles in this courting process, but she has also appropriated Giorgio and Clara's music (and their love?) from them and will soon take over Clara's physical relationship with Giorgio.

Sondheim deftly shows us that Fosca learned to manipulate people by watching the Count manipulate her. We find out that many of the things Fosca says to Giorgio during their first meeting are actually things the Count once said to Fosca. She has learned his tricks and even stolen actual lines from him. Is this revenge against the world or men in general? Or was this an education in survival the Count unwittingly gave her? Is this what she got for her parents' money? Fosca is imitating the Count's seduction very closely. Since she has ascertained that she and Giorgio are very much alike, she figures he will fall for the same lines she did. But Fosca has moved up in the world. In the flashback, she is the victim; she is passive. But she goes from being the object in the flashback to being the viewer in the present, from being acted upon in the past to be the one acting upon others in the present. She is in control now.

Sondheim has frequently used the image of a social outcast observing life from a window, as in "Finishing the Hat" in *Sunday in the*

*Park with George,* and the image of seeing someone else framed or imprisoned in a window, as Anthony sees Johanna in *Sweeney Todd.* The window also represents passivity. Fosca is first observed by the Count as he passes by, as she sits in her window. Later, Fosca observes Giorgio while he's walking and talking, as she sits in her window. She is passive, watching as the world goes by without her. She is not a participant, only an observer, yet she does learn from her observations, as we see in her adoption of the Count's methods. When she pursues Giorgio, it is the first time she has been genuinely active in her entire life. Until now, she has always been taken care of, by her parents, (ostensibly) by the Count, and then by her cousin. Giorgio is something she wants badly enough to finally become active. Like he does is so many other ways, Giorgio follows in Fosca's footsteps, completely passive until Clara and the doctor stand in the way of his being with Fosca; only then does he become active, first by breaking up with Clara, then by demanding that the doctor arrange one last meeting between himself and Fosca.

## Rhapsody in Black

Sondheim has called *Passion* "one long rhapsody, one long song of rapture." A rhapsody is a free-flowing, loosely structured musical fantasy about an epic or heroic character, sometimes very improvisatory or even completely lacking in conventional structure and form, sometimes involving improvisatory treatments of an existing theme or song. *Passion* does not follow the traditional musical theatre structure of alternating dialogue scenes and songs (Sondheim has abandoned traditional structure in several of his shows, including *Company, Follies, Assassins,* and others). There are no real stopping points in this show, no intermission, no place where the music stops and allows the audience to applaud. It's a constantly moving, extended one-act musical. This lack of a strict, traditional structure is especially appropriate for a story contrasting Fosca's no-rules behavior against Giorgio's rules-obsessed behavior and Clara's rules-breaking behavior.

The songs do not follow the traditional verse-chorus-verse-chorus structure we're so used to. For instance, in "Loving You," there are only two short verses, no intro, no choruses, no bridge. And Sondheim doesn't follow normal harmonic rules, either. The key signature of the song is B major, but it actually starts in E major. Halfway through the first verse it finally moves into B major. Then when it modulates into a new key for the second verse, it doesn't move up a step as traditional theatre songs do. It actually moves down a step and a half, from B major to A-flat major. Underneath the last two lines, it moves into yet another key, finishing the song in D-flat major. Yet it's all so smooth, so subtle, that you don't notice while listening to it that you've gone through four different keys in a short, thirty-two-bar song. All this lack of traditional structure in the hands of a lesser playwright and composer could make it hard to follow the story, hard to focus on the music. But Sondheim grounds the score with a number of leitmotifs (short musical phrases associated with a particular character or idea) that he uses throughout the evening to lend unity and coherence to the score. Lapine grounds the book by focusing on a few very specific textual themes and eliminating the use of any subplots, which are usually a staple in musical theatre.

One thing that unifies the show textually is the use of triangles. Throughout the show, *Passion* focuses not on couples like most musicals, but instead on a number of interrelated triangles. The central triangle is Giorgio, Fosca, and Clara, two women in love with the same man. But that central triangle shares one side with a triangle consisting of Clara, Giorgio, and Clara's husband, and also shares one side with a triangle including Fosca, Giorgio, and Colonel Ricci. This last triangle is not a romantic one, but it is significant. In a sense, there is also a triangle of Fosca, Giorgio, and the Count—Fosca and her two suitors. Just as significant is the triangle of Fosca, Giorgio, and Doctor Tambourri. In some ways, this is one of the most interesting and significant triangles in *Passion*. Sondheim's *A Little Night Music* also deals with a number of interlocking triangles, but they are all happily resolved by the final curtain, whereas the triangles in *Passion* are not.

## Putting It Together

*Passion* is an exceedingly difficult show to do. While I was directing a production of *Sweeney Todd*, I talked to the artistic director of another theatre company about their *Sweeney Todd*. I remarked how hard we were all working on *Sweeney*, and he said, "If you think *Sweeney* is tough, don't ever do *Passion*." I laughed since we'd already announced *Passion* to open the next season.

*Passion* is a hard show to do because it rarely lines up with a musical theatre audience's expectations. Maybe Broadway was not the best place for this show to be presented. It had only a short run, with extremely mixed reactions from audiences and critics. Many people thought that James Lapine was not up to the directing demands of the book he wrote for the show. Putting such an intimate, personal show in a big Broadway theatre on a big Broadway stage (with very minimal sets, which made the stage only look bigger and more cavernous) did not allow the audience to be as close to the characters, physically or psychologically, as they need to be. Instead of being overwhelming, it looked small and far away. The Broadway production was very slow, dark, and quiet, very brooding and deliberate. Many of the transitions were staged as intricate, choreographed marching exercises that seemed terribly out of place in a show in which most of the scenes take place with the central characters sitting or lying down. Lapine may have hoped these transitions would add visual excitement to a mostly psychological drama, but instead they just robbed the show of a stylistic unity. Subsequent productions have addressed many of the problems the original production had, and have solved most of them.

A production I directed in St. Louis was presented in a small experimental basement theatre. The actors were three or four feet from the first row. We staged the transitions more as static tableaus, which more easily fit into the fabric of the rest of the show. We moved the action along at a brisker pace, never stopping to let the audience process intellectually what they were seeing. This story is about momentum, about an unstoppable force, about not having time to stop and step back; the production should be the same. We made the audience feel as overwhelmed as Giorgio; we forced them to react viscerally, without the benefit of rational thought, just as Giorgio does. Though many productions of *Passion* have inserted an intermission, we decided for the reasons just stated that an intermission would be a mistake. The audience can't be given fifteen or twenty minutes to discuss, process, or analyze what's happening halfway through the evening. We wanted to keep them off-balance, overwhelmed. An intermission would destroy the snowball effect of Fosca's outrageous actions, the mounting insanity of this unlikely story, the confusion of Giorgio's dilemma. (Other directors told me audiences wouldn't sit still for two hours without an intermission, but people see movies that long or longer without an intermission, so why not?) Most of our audiences were literally on the edges of their seats, actually physically leaning forward through most of the show, and a good number were sobbing at the end. They believed in Giorgio's love much more completely than we had anticipated, and I think our new approaches to the show's problems helped enormously.

Perhaps *Passion* demands things of an audience that the average Broadway theatregoers were not intellectually prepared to give. Sondheim's *Assassins* had the same problem and never even made it to Broadway, yet both shows can be utterly riveting. *Passion* moves continually, like a river, never pausing, never slowing down, almost never even giving the audience an opportunity to applaud. Audiences want release, breathing room, and *Passion* doesn't give them that. Perhaps *Passion* belongs in alternative theatre spaces, in front of audiences who are used to less mainstream work, used to performance art, to plays and musicals that break rules. Maybe if audiences could bring fewer rigid expectations with them, they'd have a better time watching this show. On top of all this, *Passion* requires absolute concentration from the audience (as do all the other Sondheim shows); you have to listen to every word, think about all that is happening, and ultimately, come to you own conclusions about what has transpired. People used to seeing *Nunsense* and *Cats* find such demands excessive. People who are used to alternative work find these demands exhilarating.

## Lessons Learned

It's also tough to do this show because it's hard to figure out what the show means to say. Unlike the novel, in the stage version of *Passion*, Giorgio and Fosca each learn something. Giorgio learns that there are layers of love. He has never before felt unconditional love, love worth dying for. This may not be the kind of love that can last a lifetime, but it is something Giorgio needed to understand. Certainly, it has changed him; his next relationship will be very different from his past relationships. Maybe he saw in Fosca how obsessive he had been with Clara, and maybe he will be more mature in his next relationship (if in fact this episode hasn't caused him to swear off women forever). Giorgio has confused love with passion. He tells Clara that love can't wait, but he's wrong. Love can wait; passion can't. Does he really expect Clara to give up her child for him? If she won't, does that mean she doesn't love him? Couldn't she love both Giorgio *and* her child? Why must it be one or the other? If Giorgio really loves Clara, would he ask this of her?

Fosca learns that you can't demand love. *Or does she?* Really, her outrageous demands end up paying off pretty much as she had hoped; perhaps she has learned that her sociopathic behavior is precisely the means to this particular end. She also learns that she is worthy of being loved, even though she is ugly. Giorgio's love does not really blossom until Fosca offers a quiet, nonmanipulative declaration of love in "Loving You." It is what's inside her that Giorgio falls in love with. On the other hand, he has been practically beaten into submission. Is the love he feels genuine? Or has he come to embrace his nightmare, as torture victims often defend their tormentors after they're released? Certainly Sondheim loves exploring insanity and nervous break-downs (*Gypsy, Anyone Can Whistle, Follies, Sweeney Todd, Assassins,* etc.); is this one more example? Fosca presents her love to Giorgio as so profoundly noble, but what kind of a sacrifice is it to offer your life when it's already over?

So what are we as an audience to take with us as we leave the theatre? Sondheim has said that art is meant to create order out of the chaos of our lives. What order does *Passion* create? What about life is easier to understand after seeing this show? And who in the show has really found love? Is that kind of love something any of us would really want? Does Giorgio really see things more clearly at the end, or has he been dragged down into Fosca's madness with her? He is, after all, in an asylum at the end. Perhaps it is, more than anything else, the asking of all these questions that is the gift *Passion* gives us.

Ultimately, the primary dramatic challenge of *Passion* is to make an audience believe that Giorgio could fall in love with Fosca. Whether or not that happens will depend on each audience member's personal experiences, insecurities, and current romantic state. In this society obsessed with physical beauty, is it possible to get an audience to believe a handsome army captain could fall in love with an ugly, demanding, obsessive, sickly woman? The trick isn't to get them to believe Fosca's behavior—we all know obsessive people and many of us have acted like Fosca at one time or another—it's to get them to believe *Giorgio's* behavior. And that requires going deep below the surface of the dialogue to figure out what makes Giorgio tick, and then communicating that to an audience.

This show presents extreme emotions that will make audiences uncomfortable. The only way to succeed is to play those emotions honestly and fully. Don't be afraid to go too far. Let Giorgio and Clara's joy be extreme, even giddy. Let Fosca's obsession, her rage, her attraction, her neediness be full and reckless. Let Giorgio and Fosca's anger be full-throttle. Don't be afraid of how an audience will react. Play everything as honestly and bravely as possible, and your audience will trust you. If you get scared, if you pull back or soften the emotions, the audience will sense your anxiety and they will turn on you. They won't believe the characters.

## Doctor, Doctor

One of the most difficult things to deal with in *Passion* is the character of Dr. Tambourri. He is a dramatic enigma, constantly contradicting himself in his words and deeds, yet he is the one that sets all the important events in motion so we must both understand him and believe him. Early in the show he tells Giorgio that Fosca's body is so weak it can't produce a mortal disease, yet a few scenes later, he says she'll die if Giorgio doesn't go to see her. He forces Giorgio to visit Fosca in her bedroom, then at the end absolutely forbids Giorgio to go to her. In early previews of *Passion,* we got a much clearer picture of Dr. Tambourri's motivation in two lines that were later cut:

GIORGIO: Why did you bring this woman into my life?
TAMBOURRI: Perhaps to get her out of mine, even if just for a short while.

These lines give the doctor a motivation for thrusting Giorgio into such an awful position that is absent in the version we all know and that better explains the doctor's often contradictory words and actions throughout the show. They create an entire backstory for the relationship between the doctor and Fosca. They tell us that Fosca had forced herself upon the doctor, perhaps just as obsessively, although perhaps in a different manner, but extremely enough that the doctor needed to escape her. With this in mind, we can see the doctor's plans as early as the second scene, when the doctor and Giorgio first discuss Fosca in detail. The doctor is the one who first brings her up— and even encourages Giorgio's curiosity about her. Even at this early moment in the action, the doctor is planning to shift Fosca's neediness onto Giorgio. Later, the doctor arranges the first meeting in Fosca's bedroom, telling Giorgio that Fosca will die, that in fact Giorgio will be killing her, if he doesn't go to her.

In the film on which the musical is based, *Passione d'Amore,* the doctor has an interesting line that helps that first conversation make more sense. Instead of saying that Fosca's body is too weak to produce a mortal disease, the doctor tells Giorgio that "every victory, even death, is the result of a struggle. In Fosca, all these diseases compensate each other. She's not in danger unless something upsets the balance." This is so much clearer and sets up beautifully the reason why Giorgio's rejection should prove so dangerous to Fosca's health.

But things go awry. Instead of Giorgio lessening Fosca's illness, she is actually creating illness in Giorgio. He is in fact taking on her characteristics (just as a vampire's victim does), growing dangerously ill. The doctor's plan doesn't go as he expected, and suddenly, he finds himself having to save Giorgio from a situation he put Giorgio in. He tries to rescue him but it's too late; Fosca's spell is too powerful and Giorgio refuses the doctor's rescue attempts. The doctor realizes he is the cause of Giorgio's illness just as he earlier said that Giorgio was the cause of Fosca's illness—or at least its greater severity. By the end of the show, the doctor is genuinely scared that he may be killing Giorgio. And perhaps he is.

To create a consistent character through all this is not an easy assignment. When I directed the show, we took a cue from the film, in which the doctor describes himself as "a mediocre doctor, fast forgetting what little he knew." Historically speaking, if this doctor was any good, he'd be in private practice. Being an army doctor probably meant he wasn't that great. Our doctor was an incompetent, and as a logical outgrowth of his incompetency—and his painful knowledge of his incompetency—he drinks. As Giorgio's health grows worse and worse, the doctor's drinking gets heavier, as he tries his best to grapple with the consequences of his interference. Dr. Tambourri is such a major player in the events that unfold in *Passion* that great care must be taken with his character. If the audience gets confused about his actions and spends time trying to understand why he acts as he does, it pulls their focus away from the central conflict of the show.

## Can They Bare It?

The original Broadway production of *Passion* used nudity in the first scene. The decision whether or not to do so in other productions is not an easy one. Many subsequent productions of the show have not used nudity. Originally it was meant to communicate two things to the audience. First, it's important for the audience to understand how physical Giorgio and Clara's relationship is, that sex is central to the relationship, in stark contrast to Fosca's relationships. Second, Giorgio and Clara are physically nude at the beginning, but Fosca is much more exposed—psychologically and emotionally—as the show progresses. Ultimately, Giorgio finds himself more exposed, more naked at the end of the show, with his clothes on, than he was when he was nude in the opening scene.

Apparently, in the earliest previews of the Broadway production, both Giorgio and Clara got out of bed, completely nude, during the song "Happiness," even chasing each other around the bed. As previews continued, the use of nudity lessened. At first, Giorgio stayed in bed, but Clara still got out of bed nude. Later, they both stayed in bed, but Clara's breasts were seen above the sheets. She got out of bed but slipped into a robe, so she was barely exposed below the waist. Once the show opened, Giorgio stayed in bed throughout the scene and was never exposed below the waist. Some later productions stuck with this scenario; others changed the opening scene. In some cases, the opening was moved to a garden and sex was not a part of the scene at all, though this changed one of the central points of the scene. In other cases, they were still in the rented room, but had already begun to dress after sex when the scene starts. In this way, the actors could be partly undressed and themes of physical love and sex were retained but without the shock of frontal nudity.

The question a director of *Passion* must answer is how will the audience react to nudity? In many cities, nudity is still so rare in theatre, especially in musical theatre, that its use is very distracting. The audience thinks about the nudity, about the actors, about whether or not they're cold, about the relative merits of their bodies, about what rehearsals were like, about the actors' spouses, rather than paying attention to the music and lyrics. The song "Happiness" contains important information and sets up some important textual and musical themes that will be developed throughout the show. It would be a shame for an audience to miss all that because they're preoccupied with the nudity onstage. A director has to decide what the authors meant to say, and if it can still be said without nudity. On the other hand, there's nothing that draws publicity like controversy, and there are few things more controversial than nudity. Some might argue that the titillation factor is a valid concept to explore in and of itself.

## Other Resources

The script, vocal selections, and the full piano-vocal score have all been published and are commercially available. The original cast album is available on CD (though it does not include the entire score). It should be noted that actors should not try to learn their songs from the cast album; the leads on Broadway took enormous liberties with the rhythms and tempos of the song, and trying to learn the songs from this recording causes much more confusion than understanding of this complex music. A live CD of the London cast (who reunited for a concert performance after the show had closed) is also available commercially and has much to recommend it.

The original Broadway production was filmed for PBS in the fall of 1996, and has been released commercially on video. The film on which the show is based, *Passion d'Amore*, is available on videotape, and it's fascinating to watch when you're working on the musical. The novel on which the film is based, *Fosca*, has been translated into English. The translation, by Lawrence Venuti, has been retitled *Passion*, published by Mercury House in San Francisco. This translation has a fascinating foreword by the translator that discusses Tarchetti's life and work, and the autobiographical aspects of the novel. Be warned, though, that the novel differs greatly from the stage play in several significant ways; it's interesting to read if you're working on the show, but it's not a sound reference work since it's so different.

# ▛▟ Ragtime

Book by Terrence McNally
Music by Stephen Flaherty
Lyrics by Lynn Ahrens
Based on the novel by E. L. Doctorow
Directed by Frank Galati
Choreographed by Daniele Graciela
Licensed by Music Theatre International

R agtime is the next Great American Musical, comfortably taking its place among other masterpieces like *Show Boat, Carousel, West Side Story*, and *Assassins*, those rare musicals that are enduring and timeless, that address important themes that continue to spark societal debate, that are uniquely "American" at their core, created by Americans with American settings and with something to say about the American consciousness, the American way of life, and the American Dream. *Ragtime* is muscular, expansive, emotional, and could only have been written by Americans. It embodies everything that the American musical has come to represent while it addresses the great social issues of the twentieth century, issues that we have been struggling with for over a hundred years—racism, immigration, social violence, political activism, poverty, and women's rights.

Written within the luxury of a three-year development process, including several workshops, a concept album, and two major, lengthy, pre-Broadway engagements in Toronto and Los Angeles, *Ragtime* is a musical in which every word, every note counts, in which music is not just a medium but also a serious dramatic device, in which not only does content dictate form, but form actually *becomes* content. It is inspiring, heart-wrenching, and overwhelming in the best ways. And it is a textbook example of how to structure a serious musical score. Each act is constructed of one long dramatic arc instead of several smaller arcs, like most musicals. The scenes flow seamlessly into each other, the book, music, and lyrics so perfectly in synch, so perfectly in the same voice, that it almost seems as if one writer wrote book, music, and lyrics. The proof of its greatness is that even after a year on Broadway, with many of its leads gone, the show still delivered, still held the power it had on opening night. No one will ever inhabit those characters like the show's original cast—Brian Stokes Mitchell, Audra McDonald, Marin Mazzie, Peter Friedman, Mark Jacoby, Steven Sutcliffe, and the rest—but even without them, the show is still dazzling, still thrilling. It is a masterpiece.

## Size

*Ragtime* is epic, telling not just one big story but *three*, full of big, soul-stirring anthems, and that's what its detractors criticize most and its supporters love most. It tells a big story, a story of big ideas, big themes, and big emotions. It needs anthems to tell its story. Its language is formal, full of symbolism, and grand in its intent and ambition. It's about big journeys, interior and exterior, both of the characters and of our country. Like Stephen Sondheim's *Follies*, it is about enormous changes in our individual and collective lives. Lyricist Lynn Ahrens and composer Steve Flaherty said that when lighting designer Jules Fisher came to see the second reading of the show, he told them he wasn't sure what they wanted him for, that he thought the show was already so powerful just as a reading. And yet it's interesting that so many of the "big" moments in the show are played on an empty stage (the lengthy opening sequence, "Your Daddy's Son," "Back to Before," etc.). Even when the show uses sets, they are mostly small set pieces. There are only two realistic sets in the show—Mother and Father's house, where Sarah and Coalhouse finally get together, and the Morgan Library, where Coalhouse makes his final stand. The show could work in a small theatre on a small stage. *Ragtime* isn't a show that *has* to be big, like *Phantom of the Opera* or *Miss Saigon*, a show in which spectacle hides deficits in the material. *Ragtime* is a show in which the material itself has size and power even with no set at all.

## The People Call It Ragtime

The only really surprising thing about *Ragtime* the musical is that someone hadn't already done it, that it took more than twenty years for the novel to be made into a musical. With a name like *Ragtime,* you'd think someone else would have thought of it. It's a novel whose central character is a musician and composer, a story in which music is a metaphor for so much. The title, *Ragtime,* has multiple meanings, some obvious, some subtle. Most obviously, it refers to the musical form that was first appearing at that time. Though ragtime had been around for a while, it wasn't called ragtime until 1896, when it suddenly caught on with middle-class white America. Before records were popular, sheet music was the only way songs became well-known across the country. In 1897, the first sheet music was published with the label "rag-time." By 1902, when the story of *Ragtime* begins, ragtime was the most popular musical form in America. The label referred to the syncopation that characterized ragtime, a "ragged" kind of rhythm that had shown up in jigs, "coon" songs, cakewalks, and other forms for a while but really caught fire with ragtime.

It was the beginning of a tradition that would continue until the end of this century and beyond, the phenomenon of a black music form becoming popular and being absorbed into white mainstream music. Ragtime, jazz, blues, rock and roll, rhythm and blues, and now rap, all began as uniquely black musical forms that moved into the mainstream. The history of American music would be practically nonexistent if not for the contributions of African American musicians and composers. And that phenomenon is reflected in *Ragtime* as the black family—Coalhouse, Sarah, and their baby—move into and forever change the white family that takes Sarah in. Just as black music in America transformed white music over and over, so too do Coalhouse's passions transform Mother's Younger Brother into a political activist, Sarah's crisis transform Mother into a woman of action, and Coalhouse's actions force Father to confront the social changes that are transforming America.

Ragtime music is syncopated, the beat always off, notes played ahead of or behind the beat. Again, this mirrors the events in the story of *Ragtime,* never what we expect, never what "should" happen, always a surprise, always different than the characters planned. In addition, the majority of ragtime composers were black men. As we see in *Ragtime,* this was the first time in American history that black men were becoming famous. We see Booker T. Washington, a greatly respected black man of national fame. Coalhouse was seeing men like him becoming famous for the first time, and this fed his ambitions. If Scott Joplin could be famous, so could he. He saw that with fame, with notoriety, came power as well. When his pleas for justice go unanswered, he decides to become famous, or more accurately, infamous.

The title of the show also suggests that this is a "time" of "rags," a time of a tremendous influx of poor immigrants (transported to America on "rag ships"), literally clothed in rags and housed in crumbling, disease-ridden tenements. This was a "ragged time" in American history, a time of great social upheaval that included the creation of labor unions. With so many immigrants coming to America, with so many former slaves looking to build lives, the resulting tumult was inevitable.

## America

The period in which *Ragtime* is set was a fascinating one. In 1902, the United Mine Workers began a five-month strike that President Roosevelt ended by giving in to their demands. Other strikes followed across the country. That same year, Roosevelt instituted antitrust proceedings against many giants of American industry, and immigration to the United States reached record levels. In 1903, J. P. Morgan made $40 million in a single stock deal. The Ford Motor Company incorporated and their new Model A cost $750. And the first World Series was played. In 1905, U.S. auto production reached 25,000, ten times what it was only six years earlier. In 1906, Emma Goldman founded *Mother Earth,* an anarchist journal. It is 1906 when the main action of *Ragtime* begins.

America itself is a character in both Doctorow's novel and the musical, and much that happens in the stories and relationships of the characters acts as a metaphor for America's own struggles and growth. Just as we meet and get to know the fictional characters and actual historical figures over the course of the show, we also get to know America at the turn of century, its triumphs, its problems, and its shames.

Each real person depicted in *Ragtime* represents an idea of living and succeeding in America. Harry Houdini, the famous magician, represents the millions of immigrants who came to America and reinvented themselves, in many cases giving themselves new names and new identities, often trying to erase or hide their ethnicity and their past, believing that success could only come through assimilation. They couldn't see that being American didn't have to mean no longer being Jewish or Italian. At that time, success in business usually meant denying who they were. America's image as the Great Melting Pot is usually seen as a positive thing, but it's not entirely. The idea is not that America accepts all nationalities; the idea is that we all become the same, that we lose the things that make us individuals, that we homogenize.

Booker T. Washington was a new kind of American—a famous black man. He represents the fight for political power, the fight to change the system, to find equality and fairness by working *through* the existing system. Emma Goldman represents the fight for political power and equality by working to abolish the existing system and replace it with a fairer system. She represents the power of the ordinary people to effect change. Anarchism and other radical politics were new to America, the idea that the people might take back the government, which was supposed to be theirs to begin with, and that they could seize the power that theoretically came from them anyway, that righteous anger from good people can create change. And these ideas find their voice in Emma Goldman, Mother's Younger Brother, and Coalhouse.

Evelyn Nesbitt represents fame and celebrity in America. Nesbitt was the first sexual celebrity in America, the first American to be famous for nothing more than her sexual life, the precursor to contemporary celebrities like Monica Lewinsky.

Henry Ford represents American capitalism at work, financial success, the now-familiar rags to riches American Dream. Ford is the iconic American, who used brains, creativity, courage, and hard work to achieve success and wealth. J. P. Morgan is another icon, but he represents even greater wealth and greater power. Together, they are the boys club that excluded women, blacks, and immigrants for decades and even still today. They also represent the industrial revolution that had taken hold of America, with its inhuman working conditions, impossibly long hours for workers, and the countless other abuses that demanded action and unwittingly inspired the labor unions that sprang up across the country to oppose this oppression.

Early in the show, Mother's taking control of the household and making difficult decisions represents how women were just beginning to take control of their public and private lives, becoming political, demanding the vote, going to work, and finding their strength and their collective power. Mother and Father's growing marital problems echo the growing tension in American culture between long-held traditions (including unpleasant traditions like racism) and the new ideas that were gaining exposure and popularity in some places. *Ragtime* presents a microcosm of the entire country in a single family. In addition, the racial integration in Mother and Tateh's new family at the end of the show represents America's slow movement toward complete racial and ethnic integration. Not only is Mother a WASP and Tateh a Jew, but they have three children, one white, one Jewish, and one black. These three children also represent the promise of the future, the idea that with each new generation, less and less of our past prejudices and racism are passed on. It's the perfect final image for this musical, an image of profound optimism after the horrors and despair that have peppered this story.

The three families in *Ragtime* become inextricably linked, just as the various ethnic groups in America were becoming connected—in both cases completely unexpectedly and yet somehow inevitably. These three families and the events in the story are also a microcosm of America, not just at the turn of the century but throughout the twentieth century. In fact, the complete blending of races at the end with the kids is only now beginning to really happen in America.

It's interesting that the members of the white family have no names—Mother, Father, Mother's Younger Brother, Grandfather—not even a surname. They've given up their identity to the Great American Melting Pot. Only those white people who are famous, who get into the papers, who make a name through personal achievement (or infamy) get names in *Ragtime*. And yet, the little boy has a name—Edgar (named for the author of the novel, E(dgar) L. Doctorow)—perhaps because he is the promise of the future of America, in which everyone won't have to give up their identity to be proud of being an American. At the end of the show Younger Brother and Father even switch roles as Coalhouse's hostage, perhaps saying that these Americans who have given up their individuality are interchangeable in some way. Likewise, Tateh has no name ("tateh" is Yiddish for father) and his daughter has no name either, because they hope to become a part of the melting pot themselves. Only later, when Tateh finds success and wealth, does he get a real name.

## Coalhouse Walker Jr.

Coalhouse Walker Jr. *is* the show. He *is* ragtime—the music, the era, and the musical. He is the moral center of the show, a tragic clash of pride and prejudice. He is also a fascinating, unusual character. He acts and talks like a white man of that era, embodying the idea that blacks and whites are the same at their core, that the only difference is in how they are treated. He is like his music—a blending of white culture and black culture. Ragtime music combined European classicism with the rhythms and blues notes of black music to create a uniquely American musical form. Mother is at first wary of Coalhouse—she has probably never interacted with a black man who wasn't a servant before, and has certainly never encountered one so well spoken, well dressed, and well mannered. In the song "What Kind of Woman," she admits that she never thought about the lives of servants before now. Mother is experiencing an awakening of her social conscience, and she soon sees that Coalhouse is more like her and the men around her than he is different, so she invites him into her home.

Coalhouse has anarchy in him when we first meet him. He doesn't follow social norms. His ambitions and dreams far exceed his appointed station in life, yet that doesn't seem to bother or intimidate him. He does not acknowledge prejudice, assuming that he will be treated with the respect he believes he deserves. This repudiation of social rules and expected behavior immediately connects him to Younger Brother, who feels that he doesn't belong, doesn't conform himself; and through Younger Brother, Coalhouse is connected to Emma Goldman and the idea of social and political activism. While Booker T. Washington tries to persuade the white majority to treat black Americans equally, Coalhouse Walker Jr. *demands* it. But Coalhouse's assumption that he should be treated like any white man makes the destruction of his car at the hands of racists even more jarring, even more gut-wrenching.

Coalhouse thinks that by *acting* like the white men around him, he will attain their social position, but reality is uglier than that. It is a horrific shock to him to discover that he is judged entirely on his skin color. The racist firemen who destroy Coalhouse's Model T describe him as "a nigger who don't know he's a nigger," and the insult is more accurate than we would like to believe. Coalhouse will not be what the world expects him to be. He won't fit neatly into a narrow social category. He blurs the lines of class and color. Interestingly, in Act II Coalhouse's men call Mother's Younger Brother "a cracker who don't know he's a cracker." It's not just the white people who want everyone to fit into nice, neat categories—*everyone* wants that. It makes things easier. It also confines and imprisons, making it harder to escape those categories. And when someone transgresses, crossing those social boundaries, they must be punished. White America literally shits on Coalhouse's car, his prized possession, the wheels of his dream, the ultimate symbol of the American Dream both then and now. In a way, these white men have desecrated the American Dream itself.

In his last scene, Coalhouse becomes a mythic character, almost Christlike. He also becomes like King Arthur in the finale to *Camelot*. In the song "Make Them Hear You," he tells his men to go out and tell their story, to make people understand all that has happened and understand what they were fighting for. By keeping the story alive, by keeping the idea and ideals alive, the fight lives. Like Arthur, Coalhouse may not survive, but his ideas and dreams will, and through them he will too. Like Arthur, what he tried to do won't be forgotten.

## Themes

Many major themes run through *Ragtime*. Most obvious, perhaps, is the theme of storytelling. Unlike most musicals, *Ragtime* is very Brechtian. The actors directly address the audience and tell us much of the story in narrative form. They break the imaginary fourth wall by narrating and commenting on the action. And unlike any other musical ever written, the characters also talk about themselves in the third person and the past tense, stepping out of character to tell us about the people they portray. It's an unusual storytelling device, but it's the thing that preserves the atmosphere and unique voice of the novel. The ensemble comments on the action in the opening number, in "Crime of the Century," "Henry Ford," "New Music," and other songs. In Act I, Mother's Younger Brother talks about Emma Goldman in "The Night That Goldman Spoke," and Goldman then comments on Mother's Younger Brother in "He Wanted to Say" in Act II.

Less obvious and more subtextual is the theme of responsibility of the main characters to their families and respective communities, but that gets more complicated than the characters expect. There is also a battle *between* the conflicting responsibilities of family and community. There is Mother's responsibility to Father (as the dutiful wife) versus her responsibility to do the right thing (taking in Sarah and the baby). There is Coalhouse Walker Jr.'s responsibility to his family versus his responsibility to his people and to what he believes is just and fair. There is Younger Brother's responsibility to the family and the family business versus his responsibility to important social causes. It's interesting that in each case where such a choice exists, the character chooses community over family.

Another major theme in the show is that of change, the changing and growth of characters of course, but also changes in America, in relationships, in styles, and in other ways. The narrative framing device of the show points this up beautifully and simply. As the show opens, the boy Edgar comes downstage and picks up an old-fashioned stereopticon (kind of an old-fashioned viewmaster). The slide that he views becomes the scene onstage as the opening number begins. At the end of the show, the boy returns, on an empty stage again, this time coming down to an old-fashioned movie projector. Technology has changed. Time has passed. And this connects back to the theme of storytelling—the movie projector is evidence that technology has transformed entertainment in America. It has changed the way we tell stories. The idea of change in America still has resonance for us today. A hundred years ago, America was changing from an agricultural nation into an industrial one, and today, a century later, America is changing again, moving from the industrial age into the information age, a change just as monumental and far-reaching.

The changes we see in the main characters are fascinating. Mother goes from contented, sheltered housewife to strong liberated woman. In Father's absence, Mother must run both the household and the family business, and she finds she's good at it. She likes it. But as she discovers those things, Father loses his mystique in her eyes. She didn't need his protection as much as she thought. She isn't as dependent on him as she thought. Coalhouse goes from an irresponsible playboy to a respectable citizen and responsible father to an angry political activist. Mother's Younger Brother goes from an aimless young man with silly crushes to a serious political activist, a man fighting for what he believes in. Tateh goes from poor immigrant to successful movie director. Sarah goes from lost soul at the end of her rope to political martyr. Though she sings a great deal, Sarah hardly speaks in the show, perhaps symbolizing the fact that black women at the turn of the century had no voice, no control over their lives. And when she does speak out, when she asks to be heard, she is beaten to death. She is pure innocence thrust into the middle of explosive social issues, completely ill-equipped.

Father is the one character who really does not change, and that is his great tragedy and the reason that his marriage falls apart. He is a proper Victorian gentlemen caught in the wrong time. Mother grows beyond him, leaving him right where he was. When Father leaves for the North Pole, he tells Mother nothing will change while he's gone—and he believes it. But he couldn't be more wrong. Everyone around him will change, as will the country he so loves.

The changes wrought on America during the relatively short period of *Ragtime* are just as profound as the changes wrought on the characters. It is, after all, the turn of the century (and it's interesting that *Ragtime* would be written and produced so close to the turning of another century—and a millennium) and the industrial revolution is bringing America great wealth, more leisure time, a larger upper-middle class, the creation of labor unions, strikes, violence, and the rising up of oppressed groups. There is a great change in popular music that goes along with the other changes, and there is a change in other forms of popular entertainment. At the beginning of the show vaudeville is king, but as the show ends, movies are becoming the greatest force in American entertainment ever created.

Entertainment is another theme in the show, symbolized by the stereopticon at the beginning of the show and the movie projector at the end. There are Tateh's movie books and, later, his silent movies, Evelyn Nesbitt's vaudeville, Harry Houdini's magic act, the ball game Father and Edgar attend, and the entertainment on the boardwalk in Atlantic City. There's also the subtextual fact that *Ragtime* itself is an entertainment even while it is a social document. In fact musical theatre is an art form that existed in *Ragtime's* time in much the same form at is exists now. And of course, ragtime music is the entertainment form at the heart of this show. It represents change, popular entertainment, Coalhouse himself, an important era in American history, and functions as a form of storytelling.

There's also the theme of traveling, of journeys, and of transportation that lies beneath the surface throughout the show. There's Father and Tateh's ships crossing in the night, representing not only their literal journeys but also internal journeys. There's Coalhouse's Model T car, representing America's industrial age, the oppression of workers, and the realization of Coalhouse's American Dream—a lot of symbolism for one Model T. There are the trains that Mother and Edgar take, and that Tateh and his daughter escape on after the riot in Lawrence, Massachusetts. There's the elevated train under which Coalhouse dances with Sarah in his memory. And in the original production, the entire set is based on Penn Station in New York, with its giant clock above the playing area, symbolizing journeys, the progression of time, and the change that brings with it.

## A Perfect Score

The *Ragtime* score is one of the most beautifully, artfully, and carefully constructed scores ever written for the stage, blending ragtime, early jazz, early gospel, Sousa marches, work songs, and other turn-of-the-century musical forms. It is made of great music and great lyrics, but more than that, it is great theatre. There is a rule in musical theatre that an audience will accept any content, any form, any breaking of the rules, as long as it's done in the first ten minutes. *Ragtime* is a textbook example that proves the rule. The show begins with a solo piano, the signature sound of ragtime music. This musical theme will reappear throughout the show, providing a kind of unity that few theatre scores possess. In fact the first few measures of music contain a melody that will belong to Coalhouse and will set to the words, "My life has changed," words that verbalize the most important textual theme in the show. The Little Boy (Edgar) walks out onto an empty stage and talks directly to the audience. In the first minute, the creators of *Ragtime* have introduced the musical sound of the show and its storytelling style. The people of New Rochelle appear and sing the title song, a song that not only establishes many ideas in *Ragtime* but also subtly tells us about America at that time. Things were calm and ordered in America, but there was distant music, the music of change on the horizon. Something is coming, transforming America in hundreds of ways, literally "giving the nation a new syncopation," a new rhythm, a new beat, a new way of living and perceiving the world. Life would soon speed up as people bought automobiles, and the rules would change as blacks and immigrants wove themselves into the fabric of the American mainstream.

Notice the amazing command of language Lynn Ahrens displays in this lyric. Not only are there acrobatic rhymes everywhere, alliteration also abounds. Notice the *S*s in the phrase, "Simple and somehow sublime, giving the nation a new syncopation." Notice the *L*s in "lavender pink, lemon and lime." And there's a rhyme that goes unnoticed but it's beautiful, the only theatre lyric that's ever rhymed the schwa sound (the *uh* sound in unstressed syllables). You don't notice it when you read the lyric because the line breaks are different in the printed lyric than they are in the music. But when it's sung, it goes like this:

> Giving the nation a
> New syncopation—the
> People called it ragtime!

Ahrens rhymes *a* with *the,* both falling on the same beat. You might not even notice it, but it adds to the flow and smoothness of the line. Of course, it's really a double rhyme, since she's also rhyming *nation* and *syncopation.*

As Mother's Younger Brother introduces himself, the music changes to "Crime of the Century," foreshadowing both his crush on Evelyn Nesbitt as well as the violence that would become a part of his life. The people of New Rochelle continue the song, noting the symbols of the lives of leisure and comfort they led. The verse ends with the statement that there were no Negroes. Of course, there *were* African Americans in America, but most of the white people didn't have to deal with them, and certainly not in the wealthy, isolated community of New Rochelle (which is where E. L. Doctorow lived when he wrote the novel). But as black people became more and more visible in America, so too the blacks take the stage in *Ragtime,* much to the discomfort of the whites. But they still don't interact. Coalhouse introduces himself and notes that ragtime was a music that belonged to the blacks—a music that would later move out of the black community and become a part of mainstream entertainment. As Booker T. Washington introduces himself, the music changes to "Till We Reach That Day," the song of social and racial inequality and social protest.

The residents of New Rochelle take back the song and sing another verse, this time adding the fact that there were also no immigrants. But no sooner do they say it than the immigrants take the stage as well, again to the discomfort of the whites. We meet Tateh and as he introduces himself, we hear the music of the song "Success," the song about the American Dream, a dream so far from the immigrants at this point but a dream Tateh will someday achieve. Houdini appears to the strains of "Harry Houdini, Master Escapist," as he performs one of his daring escapes while dangling over the stage. The people of New Rochelle return to the song, now with some awareness of the changes to come, singing, "And there was distant music, changing the tune, changing the time." Nothing will ever be the same.

J. P. Morgan and Henry Ford introduce themselves, followed by Emma Goldman, who responds to their elitist philosophy with contempt. Goldman then introduces Evelyn Nesbitt and her two lovers, as the music turns to "Crime of the Century." Goldman notes that "although the newspapers called the shooting the crime of the century, Goldman knew it was only 1906 . . ." What was shocking then would be out-shocked over and over as the century continued. The main song continues with this lyric:

> And there was music playing,
> Catching a nation in its prime . . .
> Beggar and millionaire,
> Everyone everywhere,
> Moving to that Ragtime!

This moment in American history is a special one. The changing of the century before this would include the writing of the Constitution, and the changing of the century after would be the beginning of the information age, but at this time America had never seen such change and in many ways had never been more ready. No one would escape the fallout from those changes, not the immigrants living in the tenements, and not J. P. Morgan.

The number moves into an instrumental section in which we see the three groups—the whites, the blacks, and the immigrants—circle each other warily, with Mother, Coalhouse, and Tateh at the center of the storm. The script says, they "find themselves in moments of contact or confrontation; there is the potential for violence." It is the foreshadowing of everything to come in this story. The main song returns, now singing of "A strange insistent music, putting out heat, picking up steam," a music that can't be ignored or turned back, a music that will generate tremendous amounts of energy, violence, creation, and destruction. The lyric describes "distant thunder," the sound of the violence and profound change on its way, only barely sensed by the people in its path.

The final stanza of the song describes not only the time of the events in *Ragtime*, but also a time a century before, and a time right now in American history:

*It was the music*
*Of something beginning,*
*An era exploding,*
*A century spinning,*
*In riches and rags*
*And in rhythm and rhyme,*
*The people called it ragtime.*

Notice the technical brilliance of the lyric. It's chock full not only of evocative, muscular language, but also of an abundance of alliteration. There's the pairing of *era* and *exploding,* then the *S* sounds of *century* and *spinning,* then five Rs—*riches, rags, rhythm, rhyme,* and *ragtime.* It explores all these thematic ideas in one number, introducing almost every character, establishing numerous musical themes that will be used throughout the show, and connecting it all back to the title of the show, the central metaphor for all that's coming. It also establishes the style of music for the evening—a mixture of period styles and contemporary theatre music—and the texture of the show—a seamless blend of book, music, and lyric, in which it's often impossible to tell where the book leaves off and the score begins. And all in under ten minutes.

## Journey On

As Father departs for the North Pole, Mother sings "Goodbye My Love," which segues directly into "Journey On." In "Goodbye My Love," she's not just saying good-bye to her husband who's leaving on a long trip; she's also saying goodbye to their relationship as they've known it, and to the safety of her life. She doesn't know it yet, but things will never be the same. Mother and Father will both take journeys, but even though Father will go to the North Pole and Mother will stay in New Rochelle, she will travel further. It's interesting to look at Mother's language. She describes certain people as "planted like flowers, with roots underfoot." Gardening and raising children are all she knows so when she reaches for a metaphor, that's where she'll go. Later, in Act II, we'll see this again in the song "Back to Before," where she'll say her feet were "solidly planted," and where she'll describe herself as "a princess asleep and enchanted," reaching to the fairy stories she reads her son for a metaphor.

In "Journey On," Father comes up against his prejudices for the first of many times. Admiral Peary's first officer is a black man, which startles Father, and the man on the other ship out in the distance— Tateh—is an immigrant. We see how similar Father and Tateh are ("For a moment in the darkness we're the same.") as they sing their duet. Father is physically leaving America here, but though he'll be back, he's also leaving forever the old America he knew. He'll be coming back to a new America, one that includes black men and immigrants like Tateh. Father thinks Tateh has no chance for success or happiness in America, but he's wrong. That may have been true in the old America, but no more. In fact, Tateh will find great success here in America. When Tateh speaks, he says that Father is "a fool on a fool's journey" and in a way he's right. If Father hadn't left, Mother might not have changed, and he might have kept the life he loves. When Tateh wonders what Father's lost, neither of them knows the enormity of the loss. Once again, Lynn Ahrens' language dazzles, as the song ends with the phrase "In the darkness of the dawn." It evokes so many feelings and meanings (and includes yet more alliteration). On the one hand, it's surprising because we think of dawn as a time of light. On the other hand, it's incredibly accurate metaphorically, as all three—Father, Tateh, and Mother—embark on the beginnings (the "dawn") of new lives, having no idea (being "in the dark") about what will come their way.

## What Kind of Women

The next number is "The Crime of the Century," a raucous comedy number about Evelyn Nesbitt and her husband's murder trial for killing her lover. On the surface, it's very funny, very silly, but underneath (like the musical *Chicago*) it's very serious. Like every other comedy song in *Ragtime,* this one has serious purposes and foreshadows dark things, in this case, the violence and death to come. It also dramatizes the awakening of Younger Brother's passions, directed now toward Evelyn but soon to be redirected toward social justice and, interestingly, connected already here to violence, foreshadowing the rest of his story as well.

Throughout the show, every scene is linked to the scene following it, sometimes by music, often by an idea of textual theme. In this case, the scene shifts to Mother's garden and we hear her humming a reprise of "Crime of the Century," just before she is about to discover another crime, one that will change her life. As she digs, Mother finds Sarah's baby buried in the garden, still alive. Mother sings "What Kind of Women," wondering who could have buried a child and left him, but within moments, she's telling the police she will take responsibility for both Sarah and the child, and her lyric changes, now wondering what kind of woman would do what she's now done, thus connecting her to Sarah. Women in New Rochelle just don't do this, don't take in single black women with babies, but Mother is beginning to realize she's not an ordinary woman. She realizes for the first time that if Father had been there, he would have not taken Sarah in, he would have let the police take her away, "protecting" his family from the outside world. She has done what's right, but she is no longer protected from the world. She has invited it into her home. Again, as the police mention attempted murder charges, the theme of death returns. It is everywhere in *Ragtime*.

## Amerike

We now meet the immigrants fully, as they come to America singing in their native language—a different language and different music—but they will assimilate. As the song "Success" begins, we hear the assimilation in the music. As they come through each successive gate, closer and closer to living in America, the music finally turns to the title theme. They are finally here and they hear the music of America. But as they sing of success, J. P. Morgan appears and describes his own success, which has resulted in oppression for immigrants just like them. There is a dark side to success and a dark side to America. Houdini appears, and the idea of escaping the chains of oppression, the prison of the tenements, returns. There is oppression in America, but here is also hope.

The scene shifts to Harlem, and Coalhouse appears—a black man who has made his success in America, which connects him thematically to the dreams of the immigrants in the previous scene. Before "The Gettin' Ready Rag" begins, "His Name Was Coalhouse Walker" moves through a variation on the title song, and then into Coalhouse's love theme, as he talks of Sarah. It's the music of the song "New Music," which will be the reunion music for Coalhouse and Sarah later on. As "The Gettin' Ready Rag" ends, Coalhouse is bragging about getting a Model T Ford, the symbol for him of success in America, and once again, a segue is provided to the next scene, as Henry Ford appears to sing about his wondrous car.

But to Henry Ford, success means exploitation of workers and depersonalization. He describes his assembly line as "every worker a cog in motion." His workers are part of his machine; they have become more machine than human in his eyes. They have no individual identity. And yet they praise Ford almost as a god. There's a funny line midway through the song, as the workers sing "Hallelujah! Praise the maker . . ." We think they're talking about God, but after a beat they finish their sentence, "of the Model T." And we see how powerful Henry Ford really is. Later in the song, Ford's demands to speed up the assembly line act as a kind of metaphor for America itself, as it becomes more mechanized and less personalized. As the song ends, Coalhouse drives off proudly in his new Model T, the symbol that he can live as white men live, but it will become the symbol of how easily it all can be taken away from him.

## Family

"Nothing Like the City" gives us a glimpse into the future, as Mother, Edgar, Tateh, and his daughter meet coincidentally on a train platform in New Rochelle. Aside from Coalhouse's son, this is the family that will end the show, but none of them know that yet. And even Coalhouse's son is present in a way, when Edgar tells the girl that they have a "Negro baby" in their attic.

We move from these parents and children to another scene of mother and child, as we find Sarah singing to her baby, trying to explain why she left him in the garden. "Your Daddy's Son" is the best argument ever for writing musical versions of great novels or plays. No printed or spoken word could ever convey the sorrow, desperation, and profound emotion Sarah feels like this song does. Music and the poetry of lyrics elevate this moment to greater heights of emotion than spoken word could ever achieve. We must understand how she could bury her child and leave him to die. If we don't, we can't care about her and we can't understand Coalhouse's deep love for her. She describes the terror of the childbirth, the pain and the blood, and her desperate fear of being a single mother, of raising a child without a father. It is a powerful moment, and Ahrens and Flaherty make one of their most brilliant choices by setting this song as a lullaby, lending the song more emotion, more gentleness than it could ever have otherwise. Despite her act of desperation, Sarah loves this child.

## The Courtship

Again, the connection between scenes is perfect. The music of "Your Daddy's Son" continues into the next scene as Coalhouse—the daddy of Sarah's son—comes to the house in New Rochelle to see Sarah. It's interesting to see that Mother holds some racial prejudices but forces herself to get over them, and Edgar isn't old enough to have formed those prejudices. When Coalhouse finally sees his son for the first time, the melody he hums to his son is "Your Daddy's Son." As the ensemble sings about Coalhouse coming to the house every Sunday, the music returns to the main title theme, the theme that represents change. This is probably the first time a black man has been welcomed into a New Rochelle home as a guest. We see here that Mother has brought great changes to her life and the lives around her. When Coalhouse sits down to play the piano, he plays ragtime, his music, his language and the language of his love, and one of his greatest charms in Sarah's heart.

Father returns to find the life of his family turned upside down, Mother now a strong, independent women running the family business, a black woman and her baby staying in his house, and a black man sitting at his piano. Father does indeed hear "new music." Perhaps he senses that these changes cannot be reversed, that this is where the world is heading, and that he cannot participate. He readily admits he can't "sing" this "new music." He can't accept all this, and he can't love with the passion that Coalhouse and Sarah display. He can only play by the old rules. We see right here that Mother and Father have already been irreparably torn apart, even though they will remain man and wife for a long time. Meanwhile, Sarah comes down and reconciles with Coalhouse. She hears his music, and through his music, his passion and love for her and their child. He really is a different man now, changed and successful. The last line of the song, "Hear it forevermore!" tells us that the changes in this family (and by extension in the country) are permanent. The characters can never un-hear all they've now heard. The themes of family, of change, and the future ring throughout the scene.

The next scene finds Coalhouse and Sarah having a picnic, the

Model T sitting behind them. Again, the themes of family and change connect the last scene to this one, and the image of the car picks back up the theme of success. Coalhouse and Sarah sing "Wheels of a Dream," singing of the great future ahead for their child and of the greatness of America and its great social mobility. Unfortunately, Coalhouse's dream isn't entirely real. He sings:

> Any man can get where he wants to
> If he's got some fire in his soul.
> We'll see justice, Sarah,
> And plenty of men
> Who will stand up and give us our due.

But it's not true. They will not see justice. Even though America had made progress at that point—Coalhouse could buy a car, could be invited into a respectable home in New Rochelle—America was still a racist country (and still is today in many ways). For a black man at the turn of the century, the moment he stands up for himself and demands equal treatment, he becomes a threat to the white establishment. The racist firemen who later destroy Coalhouse's car can't stand to see a black man who's more successful than they are. Coalhouse's car is a symbol of his success and with "Wheels of a Dream" it becomes a symbol of a great future for his child, the realization of the American Dream. But soon the car will become Coalhouse's greatest nightmare and will set events in motion that will take Sarah's life and, eventually, Coalhouse's life as well. It will leave his son an orphan.

## The Beginning of Violence

In "The Night That Goldman Spoke at Union Square" Mother's Younger Brother finally finds the spark, the fire that he's been looking for, a direction for his passions. He accidentally steps into a political rally and finds a profound connection to the activist Emma Goldman. Emma describes Younger Brother's heart as fiery (we've already been told he's a genius with explosives), making a connection to Coalhouse ("fire in his soul") and also to the events to come: the explosions and fires that Coalhouse will cause and that Younger Brother will help with. It is Goldman that will eventually bring Younger Brother to Coalhouse, but it's also the fire the two men share, and the fire with which Younger Brother has expertise. This scene describes the violence already under way and foreshadows the violence to come.

With another strong connection, the scene shifts to Lawrence, Massachusetts, where a strike is under way that becomes violent, and Tateh and his daughter are in the middle of it. They escape from the violence, barely getting themselves onto the back of a train. The violence fades into the background as Tateh soothes his daughter with one of his flip books and a song. We see again the fragile innocence that Tateh's daughter shares with Edgar, the innocence that let Edgar talk to Coalhouse without fear. He sings a simple waltz, "Gliding," to calm the girl, invoking the memory of his lost wife, connecting to the idea of family. (Unlike most of the other leads, Tateh will never be forced to choose between family and community.) The accompaniment to "Gliding" will show up again in Act II in the song "Our Children." When the train stops, the conductor buys Tateh's flip book and Tateh realizes he can make money by selling these books. The first blush of success has come to Tateh. We won't see him again until he has become the Baron Ashkenazy.

As the scene shifts again, Booker T. Washington delivers a monologue on the strength that struggle and persecution bring to an oppressed people, over the music to "Till We Reach That Day." Coalhouse and Sarah drive home and encounter Willie Conklin and his firemen, who trash his beautiful Model T, as Booker T. Washington continues to talk about patience, self-control, and forebearance. The music of "Wheels of a Dream" returns as the dream is destroyed, as the dream turns into a nightmare. Coalhouse's confidence that there is justice for black men is gone, and the lyric returns, this time in bitterness and anger. But it's important to note that Coalhouse *tries* to claim his justice through peaceful means, but is thwarted at every turn by white bureaucrats. Another dark image of America is invoked, the dark side of the American Dream. Coalhouse declares that he will not marry until he receives the justice he's due. He chooses justice and community over his family.

When Sarah tells Mother and the family about what has happened, she tries to call back the dream, singing snippets of "Wheels of a Dream," but the dream won't come back now. It's dead. For the first time Mother and Younger Brother see the real injustice in America, something they've never seen before, and it shakes them to their roots. Sarah goes to see the vice president, who is in town for a rally, but when she tries to get to him, the police mistake her actions for a threat, even though she's only an unarmed black woman. Due to the recent assassination of President McKinley, the police are paranoid, perhaps understandably. Sarah is beaten and killed.

The scene shifts to Sarah's funeral. The mourners sing the anthem "Till We Reach That Day," calling for change, for genuine justice for all Americans, for the dawning of a new day (an image we encounter throughout the show) for America. The song tells us "We'll never get to heaven till we reach that day," in other words, America will never truly be a great nation until all Americans are free and equal—something that has still not come to pass. The first act comes to a close on a note of tragedy, but also of strength, and most important, of resolve. Coalhouse's passion has been twisted, perverted by Sarah's death (murder?) at the hands of white America. Like Sweeney Todd, his grief overwhelms him and chokes out his reason. He can see only revenge now.

## Act II

Act II opens with the little boy Edgar having a nightmare about his hero, Harry Houdini. In the nightmare, Houdini is locked in a box with a bomb and suspended high above the stage. The bomb explodes but Houdini has escaped. It has been established in the show that Edgar is prescient. He knows when he sees Tateh and his daughter at the New Rochelle train station in Act I that Mother and Edgar will know them at some point in the future. Edgar keeps telling Houdini to warn the Duke, even though no one (including Edgar) knows that he's talking about the upcoming assassination of Austrian Archduke Franz Ferdinand, which will trigger World War I. Here in this dream, Edgar sees the explosions that Coalhouse will cause throughout New York.

"Coalhouse's Soliloquy" is set to the same music as "Your Daddy's Son," a song of regret. Whereas "Your Daddy's Son" was Sarah's lament over abandoning and almost killing her son, this soliloquy is Coalhouse's lament over Sarah's death, which was caused indirectly by Coalhouse's own actions. The music segues into "Wheels of a Dream" as Coalhouse describes his *new* dream, not one of promise and possibilities now, but one of anger and revenge instead. The music segues into the title song as he decides to take action. The lyric from the opening number, "something beginning, an era exploding, a century spinning" takes on a new, more sinister color here. Things will literally explode, signaling the beginning of a reign of terror, the beginning of a new battle for equal rights in America, with new rules and new battlegrounds. Ragtime is Coalhouse's music and his music has changed. "Coalhouse Demands" uses musical material from "Till We Reach That Day," connecting the justice that both songs describe. But this is an angrier, more aggressive song. The music contains elements of ragtime—Coalhouse's music—but it's more muscular, more restless. Coalhouse has moved beyond the hope for justice; he has decided that justice won't come—and Sarah's death will be for nothing—unless he makes it happen. This has become Coalhouse's "new music," the music and emotions that drive him.

## America's Past Time

Mother asks Father to explain to Edgar all that is happening, but instead Father decides to take Edgar to a baseball game. He thinks he can escape everything. He remembers ball games at Harvard. But the world is different now. It has passed Father by. As he will soon find out, nowhere in America can he escape social discord, racial unrest, and the other things that now define America. The quiet, sheltered days of only a few years before, as described in the opening number, exist no more. When they get to the game, Father finds that it is no longer a game for rich college boys; it is now a populist sport, the fans vulgar and aggressive, the players a racial potpourri that mirrors the new America. Father has never lived in the real world, only in the sheltered worlds of his father's house, Harvard, and New Rochelle, but Mother's decision to take in Sarah and her baby has thrust the family into the middle of the real world and all its issues. Baseball also mirrors the America that Emma Goldman, Booker T. Washington, and Coalhouse are working for, a place where the players of various ethnicities are all equal on the field (although it will be some time before African American players are welcome).

## Atlantic City

Again, the theme of escape figures prominently as Father and Mother decide to escape the press and the furor over Coalhouse by going to Atlantic City. Before he goes, Father reprises a short section of "New Music." When he returned from the North Pole, the strange new music was Mother's new independence and strength. Now, the strange new music is a world in which Father's morals and values are under constant attack, in which all he believed in no longer makes sense. The scene shifts to Atlantic City, where we meet Houdini and Evelyn Nesbitt, who are both disillusioned. They got their Happily Ever After, and now we see what happens *after* the Happily Ever After (a theme explored in Stephen Sondheim's *Into the Woods*). Earlier drafts of *Ragtime* included several different songs for Houdini and Nesbitt for this spot in the show. (One version, "The Show Biz," made it onto the original concept album but was almost immediately dropped after that.) Eventually, it was decided to give them brief reprises of their signature songs within the framework of a bigger song that is more connected to the main plot. In fact, Houdini and Evelyn Nesbitt represent Father and Mother here, as Father searches for escape from the chaos that has enveloped his life and his family and Mother faces the difficulties of leaving the traditional mold for women by choosing to be an independent woman in an age in which that is simply not done. Both Evelyn and Mother lost their husbands, Evelyn to jail, Mother to the North Pole, and both had to learn to make their own way in the world. Evelyn says, "Justice is never fair." She's talking about her own problems, but it connects her (and the song) to the greater unfairness of Coalhouse's story.

## The Baron

It turns out the elaborate Atlantic City sequence we've been watching is actually part of a movie being filmed by the Baron Ashkenazy. Father and Mother meet the Baron and he tells the story of his success. The Baron is really Tateh; his success with the flip books led to his job directing silent movies. He is the embodiment of the American Dream, literally going from rags to riches through hard work and a few lucky events. His talent is in seeing and seizing opportunities.

The next morning, Tateh and Mother stand on the boardwalk and watch their children playing together, another image of racial integration. The accompaniment of their song, "Our Children," echoes the accompaniment of "Gliding," Tateh's Act I song to comfort his daughter, and reminds us that Tateh's fervor to find success was always about giving his daughter a good life. We are also reminded of that day they all met in New Rochelle (in Act I). Mother and Tateh sing, "Children run so fast, toward the future, from the past," another metaphor for the quickly changing times in America and for the promise of future generations. The children hear "music of their own," another example of the characters' emotions and values being described as music. This new music the children hear is free of racism or prejudice. There's an interesting reference to the children being silhouetted against the sky, connecting back to Tateh's early days selling silhouettes on street corners. We see a connection here between Mother and Tateh. Mother no longer sings duets with Father; now she sings with Tateh. And remember that "tateh" means "father"—he is taking Father's place in several ways.

## Coalhouse and Sarah

The scene shifts to Harlem and we hear ragtime music coming out of a club, music that quotes from the title song. But Coalhouse isn't playing his music; he's standing outside listening, watching others dance to the music. He is no longer a part of the world of ragtime. He has lost his music. Coalhouse remembers back to the night he met Sarah, as "Sarah Brown Eyes" begins. The intro quotes a line from "New Music," the music that accompanied the line "Sarah, my life has changed." His life has changed more than he could ever know. Instead of changing to win back Sarah, he has changed to avenge her death. This song was written because Sarah died in Act I and the original Sarah, Audra McDonald, was such an amazing singer the writers thought she should have another song. But it serves an important practical purpose as well. It reminds us of *why* Coalhouse is doing all this. It's not about him; it's about Sarah. She is always on his mind. Reminding the audience of that helps keeps Coalhouse from becoming monstrous.

Coalhouse and Sarah sing this duet and we see the joy and love that they once shared, the joy they should have been allowed to enjoy for the rest of their lives. It shows us the tragedy of Coalhouse's life and also makes his resolve even stronger. Midway through the song, they dance to the music of "New Music," and we realize that when Coalhouse won back Sarah's heart in Mother's house (in Act I), he was playing her the music of the night they met.

In the next scene, Mother's Younger Brother comes to see Coalhouse, as Emma Goldman and Coalhouse's men act as a Greek chorus, commenting in "He Wanted to Say." At the beginning of the scene, one of his men is whistling and Coalhouse says, "I said, no music." He has banished music from his life. Evelyn ignited Younger

Brother's passion, Emma Goldman directed it, and now Coalhouse will give him an outlet for that passion, a cause that's worth fighting for. The song quotes sections of "Journey On," underlining the interior journeys both men are taking, and also connecting them to Mother's interior journey and to Father and Tateh's physical journeys, both heading for the unknown at the beginning of the show.

## Journey On

Back in Atlantic City, Father has been called back to New York to help the police with Coalhouse. Before he leaves, he tells her that everything will be like it was. He's wrong, of course. Nothing will ever be the same. It can't be and Mother doesn't want it to be. Connecting back to the previous scene, Mother sings a song of where her journey has taken her. In "Back to Before," she realizes that once Father left, once she was forced to confront the real world, she would never be the same again. She can't be the passive wife anymore. But Father has not changed and she knows he won't. They no longer belong together. They can never go back to their happy marriage because their happiness and peacefulness depended on not seeing the injustice all around them. Now that Mother's eyes have been opened, she can't look away anymore. It's interesting to note her vocabulary. She still speaks of what she knows—gardening and raising children. She says her feet were "solidly planted," that she was "a princess asleep and enchanted," an image right out of a children's fairy tale. In a way, she was like a child, living in a fairy-tale world, but she has grown up and now lives in the real world. At the beginning of the show, Father is taking a journey while Mother stays at home, but now Mother is taking a journey while Father stays where he is. He's stuck in the past while she moves toward the future. Again, Mother's journey is a metaphor for the changes happening in America. Things were changing and society could never go back to the way things were before. She travels the furthest of all the characters in *Ragtime*.

## The End

Coalhouse has taken over the Morgan Library and is threatening to blow it up. Outside, the women of Harlem stand vigil, singing "Till We Reach That Day," a song about justice and death. The scene shifts back and forth between singing and spoken dialogue, and the underscoring is important. Under Booker T. Washington's sermon, we hear the music from "Coalhouse Demands." Under Washington and Coalhouse's debate over his tactics, as Coalhouse insists that they must demand respect, we hear the music from "Till We Reach That Day." As Washington appeals to Coalhouse to leave a legacy of dignity and decency for his son, we hear "Your Daddy's Son."

Coalhouse's final anthem, "Make Them Hear You," is a plea to his men to keep his ideas alive. Coalhouse knows he will probably not survive, but if the story of his struggle, the story of the injustice can be preserved, someone else will pick up the fight where he left off. If his ideas can survive, he has won the fight, even if he dies.

In the final number, echoing the style of the opening, each character steps forward to tell us of his fate. Edgar comes forward to a small movie projector, just like he came forward to a stereopticon at the opening, showing us much has changed since the beginning of the story. Father dies and Mother marries Tateh and adopts Coalhouse's son, forming a multiracial family, again echoing the racial progress of America, and echoing the structure of *Ragtime* itself, incorporating the stories of a white family, a black family, and a Jewish family in one show, and here, in one family.

Coalhouse and Sarah appear and sing a brief reprise of "Wheels of a Dream." Even though they're not here, their dream for their son really has come true. Mother, Tateh, and their children have moved to California, the destination Coalhouse and Sarah dreamed of in "Wheels of a Dream." Coalhouse is not here to show his son America as he promised, but Mother and Tateh have taken his place. They will show Coalhouse Walker III America, a new America, a better one, perhaps better in some small part because of Coalhouse and his dream. Likewise, Ahrens, Flaherty, and Terrence McNally have shown us America in this epic musical masterpiece—America's past, America's struggles, and the possibilities for America's future.

At the end of the show, the company sings:

*Beyond that road,*
*Beyond this lifetime,*
*That car full of hope*
*Will always gleam*
*With the promise of happiness*
*And the freedom we'll live to know.*
*We'll travel with heads held high*

*Just as far as our hearts can go*
*And we will ride—*
*Each child will ride—*
*On the wheels of a dream.*

To the characters who populate *Ragtime,* we are the future. But *Ragtime* is as much about our future as it is about theirs, about where we should go from here. E. L. Doctorow said in one *Ragtime* interview, "We are a society in suspense . . . We don't know how things are going to come out."

## Other Resources

There are two recordings available. The 1996 concept album ("Songs from *Ragtime*") includes "The Show Biz," which was later cut, plus earlier versions of "He Wanted to Say," "The Night That Goldman Spoke," and others, plus shorter versions of songs that were later expanded. The full two-CD cast album includes *all* the music in the show on opening night on Broadway. Vocal selections have been published, but at press time the script had not been. Many collectors have videotapes of several TV specials, including a two-hour special that was broadcast locally in Los Angeles at the time of the pre-Broadway, L.A. opening, and a PBS special broadcast before the Broadway opening. Both include a lot of performance footage.

# 8 Sunday in the Park with George

Book by James Lapine
Music and lyrics by Stephen Sondheim
Originally directed on Broadway by James Lapine
Licensed by Music Theatre International

*S*unday in the Park with George sits precariously on the line between traditional plot-driven musicals and the concept musicals developed mostly by Stephen Sondheim and director Hal Prince. Like concept musicals, *Sunday* explores an idea more than it tells a story, and yet it does still tell a story. The difference is that the exposition and conflicts are established in the 1880s but the resolution comes a hundred years later to a protagonist who is a different man and yet the same.

The central action of the story focuses on George Seurat (in French, it's "Georges" but in the play it's just "George"), a real painter about whom we know very little. The story that bookwriter James Lapine has fashioned is almost entirely fictional even though it's based on a real person. *Sunday* explores the eternal battle between Seurat's work and his life with his mistress Dot. Dot loves him for his talent, and yet it's his painting that keeps them apart. At the end of the first act, Dot leaves for America with another man, leaving George to finish his famous painting, *Un dimanche après-midi à l'Ile de la grande jatte* (which translates as "a Sunday afternoon on the island of La Grande Jatte," which is literally "Big Bowl Island"). In Act II, Seurat's great-grandson, also named George, is in the midst of a personal and artistic crisis of his own, facing the same issues as his ancestor. By the end of the show Dot returns, and she and George (the twentieth-century

George) reunite. Their musical argument from Act I (in 1886), "We Do Not Belong Together," returns at the end of Act II (in 1984) as the inspiring "Move On." There are two Georges and yet they are the same George. As an illustration of this, Dot sings in Act I (in another context):

> *And there are Louis's*
> *And there are Georges—*
> *Well, Louis's*
> *And George.*

Though most of us are not one of a kind, George is; so much so, that even when there are two of them, separated by a hundred years, they are really the same man.

James Lapine and Stephen Sondheim discussed at great length the idea of turning Georges Seurat's famous painting into a musical. But they couldn't figure out how to approach this musical they wanted to write. Lapine wondered why no one in the painting is looking at anyone else. He also noticed that the central character is missing: the painter. Those two observations were enough to start the two men writing a musical about the (completely fictional) events leading up to the creation of this painting. But it's about more than just why the people in the painting aren't looking at each other; it's more specifically about why the woman in front is placed so prominently. Sondheim and Lapine's answer was that she was Seurat's mistress, Dot, and the show became about George's struggle (and the struggle of all serious artists) to reconcile his obsessive passion for his art with his often ignored personal life, represented by Dot. (Some people have complained that Dot's name is a heavy-handed, too-obvious joke on George's pointillistic painting style, but Sondheim counters that Dot was a common woman's name at that time in Paris. And besides, Seurat's pointillist paintings were done mostly with small brush strokes, not dots of paint as commonly believed.)

This is a musical with great relevance to our modern world. Though on its surface it is about an artist trying to find his voice and reconcile his life with his art, it's about much more. As with any great work of theatre, the more particular it gets, the more universal it becomes. It's the shows that *try* to be universal that fail. This is a show about our epidemic inability to sustain relationships, as evidenced by a 50 percent divorce rate and skyrocketing domestic violence. This is a show about juggling a career with a relationship, an issue that speaks strongly to women at the end of the twentieth century. It's about the struggle between art and commerce, an issue that has become a political firestorm as Congress works to eliminate funding for the arts, as corporate arts funding dwindles, and as computers make it cheaper to replace musicians and other artists with software.

## Que Seurat Seurat

*Sunday in the Park with George* does on stage what Seurat's painting does on canvas—it catches people in the midst of living their lives, but in a formal, unnaturalistic style. The musical just sits back and watches people come and go, being lazy or combative, happy or otherwise, and because we only get snippets of most of these characters' lives, we don't get resolution to their many problems. Like the hundreds of people we each encounter every day without really *knowing* them, most of the characters in the show just pass through this park, but in this case they are frozen there for all time, caught not all at one moment but at many moments at once.

Some critics of the show complain that all the characters other than George and Dot are treated as two-dimensional objects, stereotypes with no real inner life. What these critics fail to understand is that this is done intentionally and, in fact, is one of the points of the show. We see all the other people as two-dimensional because that's how George sees them. He can't understand the people and world around him; he can't connect with anyone because he doesn't take the time to know them. Dot is the one person he does actually expend some effort in trying to understand (although it takes one hundred years and four generations for him to do it). These critics see only the surface of the show, the passion and pain of being an artist, but that's not what the show is about. That's been done, to the point of being nothing more than a cliché, and Sondheim and James Lapine deserve more credit. *Sunday* is about something much more complex, much deeper, about how isolated the artist feels, how difficult it is to be faithful to his work *and* live fully in the real world, interacting with those around him. It's about the conflict between being an observer (which the artist must be) and an active participant, about the conflict between paying attention to those around you who need attention, and paying attention to the work which literally defines your life. In some ways, George's conflict is similar to Robert's conflict in

*Company* (though for different underlying reasons). It's important to remember that George is the only character in Act I who is not in the painting; everyone else is just a figure to be drawn. George gets to know them only enough to create the tension and drama he needs. And Lapine has done the same.

One of the interesting things about the show is the fact that the two acts are set a hundred years apart, yet are intimately related. One of the devices to help connect the two acts is the use of the same group of actors in both acts, all playing different though sometimes parallel roles. The actor playing Seurat also plays the modern George. The actor playing Dot also plays her daughter Marie, who is the modern George's grandmother. The actor playing Seurat's mother later plays an art critic and friend of the modern George (anyone looking for a connection between being a mother and being a critic hasn't had a mother). Jules, the more conventional, commercially successful painter and colleague of Seurat, later becomes the director of the modern-day museum, in both cases walking the tightrope between making art and making a living (as evidenced by the museum director's comic monologue about selling the air rights over the museum for condominiums). The actor playing the sweet but bland Louis the baker in Act I becomes the bland boyfriend of a rich arts patron in Act II. The crass, uncultured American couple in Act I become a crass but rich arts patron and a museum publicist in Act II. Interestingly, some of the connections were different in the first workshop production of the show. For instance, George's mother later became a rich arts patron and Jules' wife (who didn't really understand very much about art) became the critic. It's also interesting to note that the character pairing from the Broadway production was not re-created exactly in London.

## Act II Trouble

When *Sunday* opened in New York (and still today as it's done around the world), critics complained that Act I is complete in and of itself, and that Act II is unnecessary. Clearly this is not true; there is no resolution of the central conflict in the first act—the inability of George to grow as a person and to connect to other people. The Act I George has a clear vision of his art, but not his life; the Act II George has lost the vision for his art, and only by returning to the art of his ancestor (the painting and then the site of the painting) does he find the answers. A protagonist in a narrative has to learn something, and the Act II George learns both how to connect to others and how to move forward in his art. He learns to recapture his artistic vision from his great-grandfather through Dot; and he learns for both himself and for his great-grandfather how to connect to others in his personal life. He finally connects to the Act I George's lover, Dot.

As with many Sondheim protagonists (Robert in *Company*, Frank in *Merrily We Roll Along*, Fosca in *Passion*), George's great lesson is to connect. He has to learn to find as much in other people as he does in his art. Dot has to learn to connect to George by loving what's good in him and not trying to change him to match her idea of what he should be. But George tries to change Dot, too; he wants her to be the perfect model and a literate and educated mistress. Though she tries desperately to be these things for him, he doesn't notice her efforts, only the fact that she falls short. By the end of the show, George finally sees that Dot has something to teach him as well. And Dot has finally come to an understanding of George's passion and she sees how she can help and guide him. The lyric from Act I, "We do not belong together," becomes "We have always belonged together" in Act II, as it should be. The love song is finally resolved, after a hundred years and four generations.

The critics who claim that the first act is a complete play in and of itself and that Act II is superfluous have missed the point of the show. George has a long journey to make and it can't happen in only one lifetime; it has to be finished by his great-grandson. Act II is absolutely necessary to resolve those conflicts and get George (although a different George) and Dot back together again. No other musical (or play, to my knowledge) has ever reunited lovers in quite this strange a fashion, yet it is somehow satisfying for us. If this show is viewed as just an excuse for making a pretty tableau, then Act I is a complete work; if, however, the show is about the centuries-old battle between life and art, then Act I is only half the picture.

One of the problems facing the show's creators was how to create a late twentieth-century equivalent to Seurat's groundbreaking pointillism. (Seurat also called it "divisionism" because it was a deconstruction of the shapes and colors of traditional painting, just as Sondheim's scores are often deconstructionist, broken down to their most basic components). Eventually, special effects designer Bran Ferren came up with the idea of a laser sculpture, a "chromolume" (literally, "color-light"), a work that incorporates color and light just as

Seurat's painting did. This label is related to a term Seurat invented to describe the way the colors in his painting were blended by the eye: "chromo-luminarisme." The set around the device was entirely white to suggest Seurat's "blank page or canvas." Ferren actually created new technology to make the chromolume a reality, just as Seurat used science to create a new kind of painting.

## Dot by Dot

Sondheim seems to be fascinated by characters whose emotional growth has been stunted or who are terribly immature when it comes to love—both Fosca and Giorgio in *Passion*, Fay in *Anyone Can Whistle*, Johanna and Anthony in *Sweeney Todd*, Robert in *Company*, Hinckley and Fromme in *Assassins*, Frank in *Merrily We Roll Along*, most of the characters in *A Little Night Music*. In *Sunday*, Dot and George are both emotionally and socially immature (although we have to remember that George is only about twenty-four years old and we can assume Dot is about the same, even though they're often played by older actors). Dot seeks a thrilling love life rather than a satisfying or solid one. She likes bad boys. She tells George he's fixed and cold, but then admits she likes that in a man. She seeks out men who will treat her badly, then complains when they do. She enters into a relationship with a man obsessed with his work and incapable of expressing his emotion, and then pouts when he obsesses over his work and can't say he loves her. She lives with a man who never approves of her, yet she judges herself only by George's criteria: her concentration, her reading skills, the shape of her body. She's got some serious self-image issues that she's not addressing. We might well wonder what her relationship with her father was like.

She exists only in her relationship to George and his art. In the opening song, she says that she finds George physically attractive but the thing she loves most is his painting, his talent. After all, genuine talent can be extremely sexy. But what she loves most is the thing that will forever keep them apart emotionally. She wants to be the center of his universe, yet she can never be because his art will always come before her. She can only come close when she is the subject of his work.

In fact, we might well wonder if Dot is more in love with George's art than with him. When she fantasizes about being immortalized by an artist, she says "All it has to be is good," not a loving memorial, just good art. She speaks rapturously about his stroke and his touch, but she's talking about his *painting*! It's fair to suggest that maybe she's talking about both his art and his sexual prowess, but even then the art is as important as the love, if not more so. George demands that she understand him, his fits, his moods—his role as misunderstood genius—but he is not required to understand her at all. And she *accepts* this arrangement.

She finally leaves with Louis because he makes an effort to understand her, but he also does not have the talent and passion that she so loves in George. She will give up the thrill of loving George for the safety of loving Louis. She has no choice now; she has a child that needs security more than excitement.

## By George

No matter how much Stephen Sondheim may swear he's not George (the only Sondheim show in which people don't think the protagonist is really Sondheim is *Pacific Overtures*), it's not hard to see Sondheim's own artistic life mirrored in Seurat's. Like Seurat, Sondheim creates difficult, challenging, sometimes hard to understand art, work that is sometimes not very commercial, work that is sometimes derided even by others in his own field. Like Seurat, Sondheim has people constantly telling him to create something more commercial. Jules is a more sympathetic version of Broadway producer Joe Josephson ("There's not a tune you can hum. You need a tune to go bum bum bum di-dum . . .") in *Merrily We Roll Along*. After Sondheim had lampooned the commercial side of Broadway in *Merrily*—and it ran only nine performances—it's not hard to see his frustration come through in *Sunday*. This is undoubtedly one of the things that drew Sondheim to this material, but it would probably be going too far to suggest that any of the personal details of Seurat's (fictionalized) life parallel Sondheim's.

George literally is what he does. He does not exist outside his work. It defines him. He sees everything as his art, as color and light. In the song "Color and Light," he says to the figures in his painting: "It's getting hot . . . it's getting orange . . ." Heat immediately transfers for him into color, into the language of his art. He says "I am not hiding behind my canvas. I am living in it." How could he have a real life, too? And we have to remember the time in which Seurat lived and worked. Science and technology were moving ahead by leaps and bounds. Wagner was transforming music theatre.

There was a monologue written for George to go early in Act II, after the eulogies. It was cut from the original production, but it was included in some versions of the published script. In the speech, George talks about lying in bed at night as a child, watching the play of light through his bedroom window, observing the world through its light and shadows that played on his bedroom wall. Just as he would do as an adult, George would "watch the rest of the world through a window."

## Entering the World of the Hat

Many Sondheim fans see "Finishing the Hat" as a song about the creation of beauty, and about the too-often romanticized loneliness of artists. But if you look and listen carefully to the lyrics, it's doubtful that either of those things is really what this song is about. We're sucked in by the poetic lyrics, the soaring melody, just as George is sucked in by the seductive world of his obsession, but there is more going on here.

Perhaps the song is really about George justifying his unconscionable behavior toward Dot by hiding behind the Noble Beauty and Sacrifice of Art. He's telling himself (and us) that it's okay for him to be mean to Dot (and to others) because he has something more important to do than worry about people's feelings. He has art to create; he has to "finish the hat." And in that light, the song takes on a much darker tint, and also a much clearer purpose in the show. Throughout the song, the title phrase is always part of a larger thought, not standing alone by itself, and we can't ignore the context in which that phrase is used. Sondheim is telling us something very specific here about George, not about art. After all, this is *Sunday in the Park with George*, not *Sunday in the Park with Art*.

At the beginning of the song, George says:

*Let her look for me—good.*
*Let her look for me to tell me why she left me—*

George really believes that Dot is the one at fault here, not him. The main idea of this song is set up clearly here at the beginning (as it is

SUNDAY IN THE PARK WITH GEORGE ■ 161

with most Sondheim songs). This is not a song about art; it's a song about blame. George is deeply hurt, which means that he cares more for Dot than he admits, or the hurt wouldn't be as deep. George goes on to say that no one can possibly understand the reasons for his behavior. Maybe, he reasons, that's why people always think it's his fault, when he knows it's always someone else's fault.

The first time we hear the phrase "Finishing the Hat," it's not the beginning of a thought; it's the continuation of a thought. George is saying it would be nice if anybody *could* understand the act of finishing the hat, could understand his compulsion to put his work above all else, "how you have to finish the hat." In other words, it's not his fault he's inattentive, insulting, thoughtless, rude—it's his art's fault, because that's what forces him to be as he is. He justifies the fact that he watches the world rather than participating in it, which by implication justifies the fact that he refuses to play by the rules of the real world. After all, he's not a part of that world, so why should he live by its rules? And yet, we'll see at the end of Act I that he's not a part of the world of his art either; he is outside of it. He belongs nowhere.

George is aware of the real world, but only as "voices that come through the window . . . until they distance and die." It's interesting that the world of his art is a world of light, but he sees the real world as "the night." George sees the real world, and the people in the real world, as inferior (though we must remember that George's opinions aren't necessarily Sondheim's opinions). So George refuses to interact with the real world in any meaningful way. He must keep himself at a distance so he can fully observe it. He thinks "It's the only way to see." The only way to create art, he believes, is to remove himself from the real world—and thereby ignore its rules and conventions.

Late in the lyric, he says:

*When the woman that you wanted goes,*
*You can say to yourself, "Well, I give what I give."*

In other words, if she can't handle it, that's just tough. She knows George's rules coming in, and if she can't live by them, that's her problem and not George's. It doesn't even occur to him that he should change his behavior. That's not even an option. He knows that anyone who gets close to him figures out the most basic truth about him: no matter what he's doing, there's always a big part of him that is not there, not in the real world, not in the moment, a part of him who's standing back, watching, not interacting, not caring, just observing. And that's his justification for being the way he is. It's not because he's a jerk (he tells us); it's because he's a great artist. He really believes that he must submerge his emotions, that he must reject polite society, that he must ignore the complaints and needs of those who care about him, because if he gives in, if he allows himself to live in the real world instead of in the world of the hat, he will no longer be a great artist. He thinks his mission as an artist gives him universal absolution. But Dot blows a hole in his arrogance in the song "We Do Not Belong Together." She says to him, "You have a mission, a mission to see. Now I have one, too, George." (She's talking about raising a child, another act of creation.) Dot is saying to him that creating art may be important, but other things are important too. (Interestingly, their two missions are what Marie will sing about in Act II—"Children and Art"—the only two things worth leaving behind when you die.)

"Finishing the Hat" is not *about* the creation of art any more than *Fiddler on the Roof* is about the Russian Revolution. "Finishing the Hat" merely *uses* the creation of art as an excuse for George's behavior. His argument is an eloquent one, but it's pure bunk. And perhaps he doesn't even really buy it himself. Yes, some great artists were nasty people, and other great artists were friendly, kind, compassionate people. Creating art is not a legitimate excuse for being a heartless, cruel man. George is asking us to feel sorry for him, poor misunderstood, innocent artist that he is, but his argument is not compelling enough. And perhaps that's Sondheim's greatest achievement with this remarkable song—it is beautiful, even a little seductive, but we can't accept George's excuse. If we did, if George himself accepted it, then there would be nothing for him to learn, no reason for him to grow, and no reason for the story to continue. George must know, or at least suspect, that it's bunk.

But *could* this song just be about art, and not all this other stuff? Well, Sondheim doesn't just stop the story in the middle of a musical for meditations on related topics. Songs like "Finishing the Hat," "Beautiful," and "Lesson #8" let us see George trying to figure things out, trying to learn. To ignore that is to ignore the fundamental action and structure of the show, which is, after all, about George and his relationships—not the nature of art.

## Apples and Oranges

Jules and Louis exist as counterparts to George, as yardsticks against which to measure him. Both Jules and George are talented, serious painters, but Jules represents convention (in Act II, as well, in which the same actor plays the museum director) and George represents artistic defiance, aesthetic revolution, and the intellectualization of art. Jules believes that art should be somehow magical, that an artist should be inspired, touched by a muse—he says in "No Life" that George's "touch is too deliberate." Jules doesn't like art that has been planned out or *constructed*. He likes art that is utterly emotional. Jules' art is safe, commercial, palatable, *normal*. He tries to help George, encouraging him to paint more conventionally, recommending his work for art shows. He likes George, maybe even envies his freedom. He respects George and is happily surprised when George asks for his opinion. George is an artist's Don Quixote; Jules paints pictures that people buy. Maybe Jules is what Dot wishes George would be, an artist who also has a life. But then, he wouldn't be George.

Louis and George are paired up as rivals for Dot's affections. Like Jules, Louis is safe and conventional. George is passionate but Louis is dependable. Being with George is like living in a funhouse. Being with Louis is a life with signposts, easily discernible, a life in which one knows exactly what to expect. Dot is bored by Louis, but she can depend on the fact that he'll be there tomorrow.

## The Happy Villagers

In his book, *The Dramatist's Toolkit*, Jeffrey Sweet notes that in almost all musicals the central conflict comes down to whether or not the protagonist, who begins as an outsider, can assimilate into society or a particular social group. Either he assimilates or he must be removed. In Sondheim's *Company*, Robert stands outside the social norm when it comes to relationships. All his friends are in couples, but he is not. The show can't end until Robert assimilates, deciding he too wants to be in a couple. In *Sweeney Todd*, Sweeney cannot (or will not) assimilate, so he must die. In *The Music Man*, Harold Hill learns to accept the ways of River City when he falls in love with Marian, so he can stay.

In *Sunday in the Park with George*, the nineteenth-century George does not assimilate. He refuses to follow the agreed-upon rules of the society in which he lives, so he must be removed. He dies at age thirty-one. But the world into which he is expected to assimilate is incomplete. None of the people around him in Act I are fully drawn characters—because we only see them as *he* sees them, and as he says himself, he doesn't paint faces. In other words, he's only interested in their form, not their humanness. Their stories are begun—the affair between Franz and the Nurse, the affair between Jules and Frieda, Yvonne's suspicions, the Celestes and their soldiers—all interesting, funny stories worth exploring, and yet they are left unfinished, just glimpses, as if we're just eavesdropping. They are just raw material for George, not people he wants to know, definitely not people he wants to be like. He refuses to connect with these people—and this is his greatest problem—so he is removed.

In Act II, the twentieth-century George is dealing with a different social group. His conflict is not with society at large but with the artistic community. At the end of Act II, he learns to reclaim his artistic vision and impulse, and he is assimilated back into the art world as the characters from Seurat's painting, representing the world of art, gather around him and welcome him back. In Act I, Dot was a part of regular society (though only tenuously), but George was not. They could not be together. But in Act II, Dot is now a part of the world of art because she is now a figure in the painting. When the modern-day George joins that world at last, the two of them can finally be together.

## Into the Words

Of the many textual themes to watch for in the script and lyrics, the most prevalent is the theme of light. George is constantly talking and singing about light. Dot complains about light, about the heat of the sun in the first scene, about the glaring lights in her fantasy about the Follies Bergères. But George's work (in either century) doesn't exist without light. His medium is a visual one, and vision doesn't work without light.

Another theme deals with connecting. Dot says to George in her first song, "Before we get through, I'll get to you, too." And indeed she will. In the fantasy sequence in her first song, she implies that she wants not just love, but "connection." The show's climax in Act II is when George and Dot's love song finally blossoms fully. Sondheim says *Sunday in the Park with George* is a love song developing over two hours. Like many of Sondheim's shows, *Sunday* is about connecting—

in fact the word *connect* is peppered throughout the score—and it is only when Dot comes back to George (actually his great-grandson) at the end of the show that he can connect. Sondheim is making a statement about love and about artists building on that which has gone before them. And in a way, he's established that both Georges are, in a way, the same person, the Artist as icon.

George cannot connect. Even in his painting, there is no connection. No one is looking at anyone else. No one even looks at us (or at George as the artist). In the show's first scene when George is painting Dot, we see why this is so. George consciously avoids connecting. He tells Dot, "Look at the water, not at me." Dot sees this too, as she tells us that if you want to find "connection," you don't want to be a model (remember, George is the only painter she's ever modeled for).

At the beginning, George and Dot "do not belong together" as Dot sings in the third scene; they both have a great deal to learn before they will belong together. We see how far away they are from each other when Dot says she wouldn't like being in the Follies (could this be a conscious reference to Sondheim's earlier show?) because of "all that color and light"—the two things that most ignite George's passion for his art. And in rejecting color and light, she is implicitly rejecting George, who exists only for color and light. Their Act I song "We Do Not Belong Together" will, in fact, metamorphose into their song of connection in Act II, "Move On." The last line of "We Do Not Belong Together" is Dot singing "I have to move on." They both have to, but it will take one hundred years before they have learned enough to come back together.

The two instrumental chords that begin "Move On" have represented conflict in the relationship between George and Dot (and by extension, between George's art and his life) throughout the show, in "Color and Light," "Everybody Loves Louis," "Finishing the Hat," "We Do Not Belong Together," and elsewhere. This theme of conflict also accompanies Dot's wishing her body and her life were different in "Color and Light," and George wishing the dog was different in "The Day Off." But whereas Dot can't change her body, George *can* change the dog. He tells his mother in "Beautiful," "Watch while I revise the world." Unfortunately, he can only revise what the world *looks* like; he can't change what's underneath. When George sings, "Pretty is what changes. What the eye arranges is what is beautiful"— his belief (and Sondheim's) that art is making order out of chaos— we hear his humming/painting motif in the orchestra. He is explaining his art to his mother, and the music underscores this by connecting us back to the scene in which he's actually painting. But again, he can only make order out of chaos on the surface. It seems that he can never make order out of the chaos of his and Dot's emotions. We hear the humming motif again as he finishes the painting in the Act I finale, his final interaction with Dot (though she will later interact with the other George).

## Change

The main word in the duet between George and his mother ("Beautiful") is *changing,* another major theme of the show. In the song, they're talking about trees being cut down (interestingly, George has "cut down" his mother's favorite tree earlier in the act by erasing it from his sketch), and about technology taking over, a theme fully realized in the great-grandson George's chromolume light sculpture. But the Act I George sees beauty in change and in the advances of science; one can only assume he would approve of his great-grandson's chromolume.

Dot is also concerned with change. She's trying to change into what George wants her to be. She's learning to read and write; she's trying to learn to concentrate and be a better model. She's physically changing as she becomes pregnant. And the pregnancy changes her internally as well. She can no longer accept George's lack of commitment to her. Now that she will have a child, she needs stability. So she makes a huge choice: to marry Louis and move to America. As she says in Act II in "Move On,"

*I chose and my world was shaken—*
*So what?*
*The choice may have been mistaken,*
*The choosing was not.*
*You have to move on.*

She knows at this point that change is essential to ensure a future for her and her child. The only way George can make her stay is by changing himself, and he's not capable of doing that. George is unhappy because as he grows as an artist, he's not growing as a person. The situation has changed between them and his inability to grow and accommodate those changes destroys his relationship with Dot.

In the song "Beautiful," George's mother wants him to "draw it all" to preserve their world before it goes away, but George doesn't draw things as they are—he can't really preserve anything because he changes things the minute he draws them. To remind us of this after the line "pretty is what changes," we hear George's humming theme, the music that accompanies George's painting or drawing, high up in the accompaniment. To his mother, changing represents the destruction of things; but to George changing represents the idealization of things, which is the essence of his art ("If the tail were longer" and "So black to you, perhaps. So red to me.").

The George in Act II is unhappy because his work is stagnant; he has lost the ability to change, to grow artistically. Until he learns how, he can't resolve his conflicts. His resolution comes from returning to the island where his great-grandfather began the journey of self-discovery, the attempt to connect. Though Seurat never achieves his goal, his great-grandson does, with a little help from Seurat's own words (as transcribed by Dot in her grammar book) and from the ghost of Dot. Finally George and Dot do connect, across time, through art. We know that George will finally find a way out of his artistic stagnation. He will finally "move on."

## Seeing Green

Sondheim and Lapine play a lot with the theme of art versus commerce. George represents art; Jules represents commerce. The musical motif for "Finishing the Hat" represents the creation of art in Act I; the same motif represents the creation of funding in "Putting It Together" in Act II. In fact, the entire song, "Putting It Together" is about the friction between art and commerce. During that sequence, Charles Redman, a museum director, mentions a commission to George and then says, "Hope you don't mind me bringing up business at a social occasion." Of course, it's *not* a social occasion; it's a business occasion. Is Redman really not conscious of that? Is he just pretending not to know that? He's only there to scout George, and certainly George can't make another chromolume without another commission. In the original Broadway production, the use of cutouts of George made an interesting comment. In Act I, the cutouts are used to create the art, as elements in the painting (trees, the monkey, other people), but in Act II, the cutouts are used to help George raise money.

## Kids

One of the most emotional themes in the show is children. Sondheim has been quoted several times saying the greatest regret of his life is not having children. "Children and Art" is certainly a testament to his strong feelings on this subject. Children and references to children appear throughout the show: Dot and George's baby, which forces Dot to choose a dependable life with Louis; Jules and Yvonne's monster child, Louise; the song "Children and Art," the centerpiece of the second act; the baby in the painting (Marie). In Act I, George tells Dot that he's living in his painting; perhaps he put his child into the painting so that he could be with her. In Act II, Marie laments the fact that the modern-day George and his ex-wife Elaine never had children, that the family line will end with George. Of course it won't; their family line continues in Seurat's painting.

## The Score: Getting Through to Something New

This score was groundbreaking (as much of Sondheim's work has been) when *Sunday in the Park* opened in 1984. It was the first minimalist Broadway score, a score based on a very limited amount of thematic musical material, developed and mixed in endless variations. Just as Seurat used only a few colors in endlessly varied combinations to create a full world of color, Sondheim did the same with the score. Just as Seurat used only eleven colors, orchestrator Jonathan Tunick only used eleven instruments in the pit. (And let's not forget that Seurat's eleven colors—plus white—correspond in some way to the twelve half-steps in a musical octave.) Also, unlike most Broadway scores, it's packed with leitmotifs, short musical phrases that represent characters or ideas, a device Sondheim would continue to use in *Into the Woods* and *Passion* (he had used this device before but not to this extent). Very few of the numbers are easily discernible, traditionally structured songs. Apparently in early drafts for the show, Sondheim wrote that the score should be one long rhapsody, the label he later used to describe *Passion*.

Just as the real Seurat was a mysterious loner who did not interact much with those around him, so too the musical Seurat sings mostly in soliloquy. It is rare that George (in either period) sings to another character, and when he does, it's because Dot has pushed him so far and the stakes are so high that he has no choice. Consider the lengthy

"Color and Light" sequence (he does sing to the figures in his paint-ing, but that doesn't count), "Finishing the Hat," "Putting It Together," and "Lesson #8." He only sings to others in "We Do Not Belong To-gether," "Move On," and "Beautiful," and in all three songs he's only responding to another character who sings the bulk of the song. In contrast, most of Dot's songs are not soliloquies—her first song be-ing the major exception.

## Sunday in the Park

The show opens with a series of musical figures, arpeggiated chords, which will be a prominent leitmotif throughout the show. They rep-resent the creation of art. The stage is completely white and as these chords are played, George enters and the white stage becomes the park, and he brings Dot out. The creation of the famous painting has begun to the sound of these "creation of art" chords. On top of these chords, we hear the first quote of the "Sunday" theme, the melody of the first lines of the Act I finale, "Sunday." Not only is Sondheim es-tablishing this theme as important, he's also creating a framing device (appropriate for a musical about a painting), beginning and ending the act with the same music. It's interesting that there is no overture and the first music we hear is not a song.

The set, which is made of portals and cutouts, will eventually be-come a re-creation of Seurat's famous painting. In the original pro-duction, everything on stage (except the actors) was completely flat, like the painting. The use of cutouts popping up out of the floor, floating in and out of the wings, and flying in from above, was taken directly from the style of the baroque theatre; the difference is the amount of modern technology used to make it happen.

Dot begins her first song, "Sunday in the Park with George." The accompaniment figure for this song—the staccato bass note followed by a dissonant chord—will be used again later to represent how diffi-cult art can be. It will be used for "It's Hot Up Here" in Act II, among other things. Halfway through the song, Dot goes to George and sings about how much she loves his eyes, his beard, his body. The chords under this section are the "conflict" chords and will be extremely im-portant throughout the score. Dot ends this section by saying that more than anything else she loves George for his art—which will also cause her tremendous grief and destroy their relationship. When she gets to the word "painting," the music changes to the accompaniment figure we'll hear later in "Finishing the Hat," George's song about understanding an artist's passion.

Already within the first scene, Sondheim has established in our ears the main themes and motifs he'll use for the rest of the score. He's not only let us hear them, he's associated them very closely and clearly with certain ideas, conflicts, and characters. He's also established so many details about the world in which these characters live. The lyric of this first song tells us that Dot models for George a lot ("Why is it you always get to sit in the shade . . .") and that she doesn't like it; that George is a frequent topic of gossip, and that Dot is connected to the gossip circuit; that George paints animals as well as people; that George is emotionally distant and obsessed with his art; that Dot and George are sleeping together; that the location of this scene is an island in the middle of a river (the Seine); that a big part of Dot's attraction to George is his art and his talent, but also his physical looks; that Dot has been with other painters; that Dot and George get up very early when they come here to work; that they live in the city; and other more nebulous details about Dot's personality and temperament. That Sondheim manages to work in this much information, to give us some good laughs, to set up both main characters, and then to add important musical themes to the mix is a testament to his genius. There's not another theatre artist alive who could do the same.

## Back at the Studio

There is a brief inset scene in which Jules and his wife Yvonne make fun of one of George's paintings in the song, "No Life." At this point we find their derision arrogant and annoying. We already like George to an extent, and to see this pompous couple ridiculing his work is hard to take. Jules even compliments Yvonne on her more stinging put-downs: "It might be in some dreary socialistic periodical." (There's a wonderful moment of self-referral here because it almost seems as if Jules is complimenting her on her clever internal rhyme, even though within the context of the scene the two of them aren't aware they are singing or rhyming. In fact, the word "periodical" creates two rhymes, the first half making an internal rhyme with "dreary," and the second half making a rhyme with "methodical." Perhaps Jules is complimenting Sondheim.) What we don't yet know is that they are right about one thing—George does not have any "life in his life."

We will see as the show progresses that Jules and Yvonne are more right than we'd like them to be.

They are also correct in their assessment of George's work as more mechanical and methodical than the paintings they're used to; George is consciously employing scientific principles to his work, not relying solely on emotion. His work is not spontaneous, born out of some burst of inspiration; it is carefully planned and plotted, just like Sondheim's theatre scores. In John Russell's book, *Seurat*, he quotes a friend of Seurat's, the poet Verhaeren, who says that Seurat did not want to be "carried away" by his work, that he was obsessed with always trying something new, something unknown, something unproven, again, much like Sondheim. Who's to say if this is good or bad, but it was certainly a bit radical for 1884. As to Jules and Yvonne's observation that there is no life in George's art, they couldn't be farther off the mark; in fact, George has thrown his *entire* life into this art.

After this song, we go for the first time to George's studio as we hear the "Finishing the Hat" accompaniment figure again, the figure that represents George's feeling that others do not understand his work and his passions. This scene will set up the inherent conflicts between George and Dot both musically and textually, the fact that Dot really can't understand George.

"Color and Light, Part I" establishes a new motif, the staccato accompaniment figure that accompanies George's brush strokes on his canvas. This is the first time we've seen George paint (he was only sketching before) and this motif is the musical equivalent of George's physical brush strokes which create the pointillistic style he uses in his painting. There are two versions of this motif, the single-note version and a version that adds chords beneath the single notes. Both will be used again. This scene sets up the very different priorities that George and Dot have, which will eventually destroy their relationship. The song then sets up George's humming motif, which he hums while he paints. This will return in the Act I finale. Halfway through Part I of this song, we hear the "Finishing the Hat" accompaniment figure, as George explains to the people in the painting what he's doing. Even though real people can't understand him, he knows that the people he creates on his canvas will. This accompaniment figure is about people not understanding George; here, finally, are people who do.

Just as we heard the conflict chords under Dot's description of

George's body in the first song, now, in "Color and Light, Part II," they underscore the description of her own body, and the conflict between how she perceives her body and how she'd like it to be. Maybe she thinks if she were prettier, George would pay more attention to her. The end of this section of conflict chords intensifies the greatest conflict of all: Dot hates too much color and light, and yet color and light is all George lives for. That's why it's the title of this very lengthy musical scene. After the "Follies" interlude, "Color and Light, Part II" continues with these two motivic accompaniment figures alternating.

"Color and Light, Part III" continues the brush stroke motif and George's humming motif. The lyrics here ("Red, red, red, red, red, red orange . . .") are a stream of consciousness verbalization of George's immersion in his color and light as he paints. The line "yellow comma yellow comma" is interesting because it could be taken two ways. Is George aware of these words he's saying, and is the "comma" actually a grammatical pause, an acknowledgment of his mumbling? Or is the "comma" a reference to the brush strokes, which weren't dots at all but were little curved strokes in the shape of commas? It's interesting to note that he sings "num, num, num" here as he hums, while he rubs his *numb* wrist. In fact, the lyric to Part III of this song is full of George's subconscious ramblings about the things swimming around in his head: his numb wrist, Dot wanting to go out, Dot getting fat (she's really pregnant but he doesn't know that yet), and other things. Then we hear the conflict chords again, but this time they are interrupted. As Dot sings about why she loves George over the conflict chords, George's lines interrupt hers with completely different chords. Finally, George and Dot harmonize for the first time, because they are feeling the same thing for the first time, on the line, "I could look at her/him forever." Their love, their attraction is the one they share. It is the one time they can sing together in harmony. The "Finishing the Hat" accompaniment returns as Dot realizes that she cannot understand him.

After "Color and Light, Part III," the conflict between George's art and life is vividly demonstrated. Though he has promised to take Dot to the Follies Bergeres, his painting comes first. When she reminds him of his promise, he replies that he has to finish the hat. Nothing— literally nothing—is more important to him than his painting. And really, Dot is foolish to keep believing it can be otherwise. This is nothing new for her. "Color and Light, Part IV" wraps up with the brush stroke motif as George returns to his painting and the scene ends.

The first part of Act I has introduced George, Dot, and their conflict. Musically, the score has established important themes for George, Dot, and their relationship. The second part of Act I will focus on the other characters in the painting.

## A Little Gossip

The music taking us out of the studio scene is "Finishing the Hat" again, framing this scene as the creation of art chords frame the act. The bulk of the gossip music is full of dissonant chords and odd melodic intervals, musically creating the seeming randomness of George's pointillistic style and the completely unrelated people who will come together in George's great painting. The melody for the lines, "Artists are so crazy. Artists are so peculiar," is the same as the melody for the lines, "That is the state of the art, my friend, that is the state of the art," in Act II, in the song "Putting It Together." (In the later song, the phrase has added a few more notes, but it's still the same basic melody and outline.) In a way, the two statements are textually the same, too; in other words, you have to be nuts to make a career as an artist.

Back in the park, George gets into an argument with the Boatman, talks to the Celestes, and sees Louis bring pastries to his friends; and we hear the creation of art chords. Why? Because George is watching everyone, getting to know them, getting inside them so that he can bring them to life on his canvas. To make this point more overtly, Part I of "The Day Off" shows us George getting inside the mind of a dog he's drawing. The song starts with the conflict chords as George finds the differences between the reality of the dog and George's ideal of the dog. As George draws his ideal dog, he returns to his humming motif. Now he steps into the dog's head and becomes him. He sings a duet between two dogs, both given voice by George. At first glance, this may seem a bit slapstick for the style of this show, but it's an important moment. George doesn't only understand the people he draws; he understands every thing he draws as well. We get another pointillism joke as George obliges the first dog by adding some pointillistic ants.

The rest of "The Day Off" lets us get inside the heads of the people who populate George's world, for the most part using musical ideas established by the two dogs. This part of the show establishes the reasons each of these people have for being on this island on this Sunday, also setting up relationships, conflicts, and other information, which will help the final tableau make more sense than the audience thought possible. George sings, "Everyone's on display on Sunday," which will become literally true in Act II when they are all part of the painting, hung in a museum. It's even true here, on another level of reality, since they are all on stage in a musical in front of an audience. Sondheim has also snuck in another pointillism joke when the nurse refers to George's mother as "dotty."

Dot sings "Everybody Loves Louis," built initially on accompaniment figures from "The Day Off." But when Dot sings of her relationship with Louis, the music returns to the conflict chords that usually describe George and Dot's relationship. These chords return later in the song when Dot compares Louis to George, and the end of that section returns to the "Finishing the Hat" accompaniment. The song, "The One on the Left," finishes the section built around "The Day Off."

Now alone in the park, George sings "Finishing the Hat." The song starts with lines sung earlier by other characters as George flips through his sketch pad. As he looks through the sketches of the various characters, he gets inside their head and he sings their thoughts at the moment he captured them. Then the conflict chords return as Franz's line, "She looks for me," becomes George's line. For a moment, he has become one with Franz, finding a commonality between them. Franz was speaking of the Nurse, but George is speaking of Dot. He says he had thought that she had understood, but like other girlfriends, she had not. This is set to the brush stroke accompaniment, illustrating George's art, which is what Dot can't understand. When he gets to the line, "But if anybody could," the music turns to the main "Finishing the Hat" accompaniment figure, which we've already heard a lot. This is a figure that represents an understanding of George's work, and it underlines George's explanation of why his work has to dominate his life. George's great flaw, which is connected to one of the show's most prevalent musical themes, is that even though he knows why he screws up relationships, he still can't change. Usually, when a character figures out what's wrong, he can fix it. But here, understanding does not mean resolution.

## Hard to Say Good-bye

The third section of Act I begins as we return to the studio, using the main "Sunday in the Park with George" motif in the scene change. This scene introduces "We Do Not Belong Together," the moment when the conflict comes to a head, the moment when the tension in the relationship reaches critical mass. Something must happen. This is the same music that will be used at the end of the show to accompany the final resolution of this conflict. The scene begins with dialogue, Dot and George arguing, over the conflict chords. When George defends his work, the music changes to the brush stroke figure. The conflict chords return as we see that neither George nor Dot can deliver what the other wants. Dot wants George to talk about his feelings, but he can't ("Why do you insist you must hear the words when you know I cannot give you words?"). This is the meat of the conflict and the music reflects that. The main body of the song starts with a new accompaniment figure.

Interestingly, this new figure is built on the second arpeggiated chord from the beginning of the show, part of the creation of art motif. George and Dot's relationship has been built quite literally—emotionally and now musically—on George's work. George uses Dot as his model and Dot is attracted to George because of his painting and his talent. Here the music that signals the creation of art throughout the show (in the first studio scene, in the Act I finale, and elsewhere) becomes the accompaniment to the song that discusses how George's work keeps them apart. This is one of the many conflicts set up but not resolved in Act I. In Act II, this accompaniment will return for "Move On," a song in which George's work brings him and Dot back together again.

The problem George and Dot face here is that Dot's priorities have changed since she became pregnant. She can no longer afford to put up with George's crap. She has to think of her child and her child's future now. She sings to George, "You have a mission, a mission to see. Now I have one too, George. And we should have belonged together." George's mission is to create art. Dot's mission, now, is to build a future for her child. Dot and George should have belonged together because they should have been a family, raising their child together. George can't be part of a family, so Dot must create a new family for herself and her child. There are only two things worth leaving behind when we die, Marie will tell us in Act II: children and art. George will create the art and Dot will raise the child.

At the end of the song, there is an instrumental section, based on the conflict chords, which leads us back to the park for the last scene in the act. The melody over the chords is from the next song, "Beautiful." As George stands alone and abandoned, this snippet of melody in the flute is the music that will lead up to the word *solitude* in the next scene.

## The More Things Change

Back in the park now, George and his mother have their first real conversation, in the song "Beautiful." George's mother, alternately senile and lucid throughout the play, worries that the world is changing too quickly, that George must draw it all so that it can be remembered. Perhaps she sees her own mortality in the march of time, and she hopes that she might find some scrap of immortality as a part of George's art (another connection between children and art). The literal source of her worry is the erection of the Eiffel Tower in the distance, a structure many Parisians thought was ugly when it was built, a symbol of the destruction of nature by machines. This provides a wonderful link to Act II, when the other George's art will be made literally with machines. Even here in the 1880s, George is "modernizing" his art with his new scientific approach to painting. George's mother worries that her time—and she herself—will be forgotten, but we already know that she was not forgotten. She exists in the painting and here in the musical. Marie will pass on the family history to the modern George, and Sondheim and Lapine will preserve this moment (even though the details may be fictional) for us.

But the song raises lots of questions. What exactly is it about? It seems to touch on many things, some easy to discern, others less obvious. Is it about the difference between what things really are (pretty) and how George perceives and idealizes them (beautiful)? Notice the way George and his mother remember the events of his childhood so differently. Is the song more generally about point of view—George's versus his mother's; nature versus science; George's versus Dot's? Is it about science in the guise of the Eiffel Tower (and maybe also George's pointillism) encroaching on nature? Is in fact the Eiffel Tower a symbol of George's new "scientific" approach to painting? He calls the tower a "perfect tree" in the song. (Later in his career, Seurat did a painting of the Eiffel Tower.)

One passage in particular makes a thoughtful, if complicated, point. George sings:

> *Pretty isn't beautiful, mother.*
> *Pretty is what changes.*

*What the eye arranges*
*Is what is beautiful.*

George contrasts "pretty" and "beautiful," but what is his point? Does he (or Sondheim) think that beautiful is better than pretty in some way? Many artists would argue that pretty is only a surface quality, while beautiful goes much deeper, involving the mind and emotions, perhaps even changing the viewer in some way. Surely "what the eye arranges" refers to his practice of "drawing only what you want to see." Does it also apply to the idea that the viewer's eye mixes the colors of George's painting, literally arranging small brush strokes of color into recognizable forms and secondary colors? "Pretty," representing the actual state of things, is changeable. "Beautiful," representing the ideal state of things, does not change. The ideal always remains the same because it is never realized and therefore can't fade or age. George changes what is pretty when he draws it, but once he paints it, it no longer changes. It is frozen in time.

"Beautiful" is a perfect setup for the Act I finale, "Sunday," in which we leave the actual "pretty" park and enter George's "perfect," idealized park, in which he "arranges" reality, people, and objects into a park the way he sees it. Up until this point, we've seen George's mother as senile, maybe even a bit crazy; and yet she is like George in that she often sees what she wants. Is Sondheim underlining a comparison between these two with this song? In this too-brief moment, what can we see about George's relationship with his mother? Does he fail here just as he does with Dot? It seems that despite the way she avoids him earlier in the show, here his mother does acknowledge that his art is important, that it matters in the grand scheme of things, perhaps even that she is proud of him.

This song has tremendous import. Its position just before the Act I finale gives it great weight. The fact that it's George's only personal moment with his mother in the whole show means that this message is important to George and to Sondheim (whose relationship with his own mother was difficult and painful). There are many rich layers of meaning in this lyric, and perhaps the song will mean different things to different people, depending on whether or not they are artists or know artists, how they view their own landscape and its evolution, whether or not they fear death, what their relationship with their mother is like. More than most of Sondheim's lyrics, this one is closer to pure poetry, full of images, thoughts, philosophy that will fit differently on each person who hears it.

## Harmony

As Jules and Frieda enter, we hear "No Life" in the underscoring, illustrating the fact that while everyone else is living, taking chances, risking what is important to them, George just sits and draws. As much as we hated Jules and Yvonne for their comments when they sang "No Life" early in the show, we see now that they're right. George has forever lost Dot, as well as his child. Other people are falling in love, having sex, having affairs, and George, by his own admission, can't look up from his sketch pad.

At the end of the first act, all hell has broken loose. All the conflicts and tensions that have been set up during the act come to a boil, people fighting, yelling, the boatman chasing Louise, and all watched passively by George and his mother. But it's time for George to create art from the chaos of this world. We hear the creation of art motif from the first moments of the show. Everyone on stage freezes. George says "Order," and everyone turns to him. He in is control now. He will make art of this. As the motif continues, George recites the words that describe the creation of art: *order, design, tension, balance,* and *harmony.* As he does, the people in the park, the figures in the painting all go to a place and a pose that they held at some earlier point in the act, the point at which perhaps George first saw them or sketched them. When George finally says the word, *harmony,* the main accompaniment of the song begins, an accompaniment without the dissonance of the other songs. The people stroll through the park, singing. As they move, George directs them, arranges them. By the end of the song, as the melody and harmony build to a thrilling climax, each character finds his place in this space, in this "perfect park" that George has created, and for the first time in the show, they sing together in harmony.

It's important to note that this is no longer the park in which much of the Act I action has taken place. It is now George's park, the park in his painting which has only a passing connection to the real park. In this "perfect park," things are no longer as they were; now they are ideal. They are as George wants to see them. Bickering becomes merely visual tension. Attraction becomes balance. Sondheim and Lapine give us several clues that this has happened. This is the first time that George conducts and directs the characters. They no longer have independent minds; they are George's figures. This is the first time they all sing in (more or less) traditional harmony instead of the dissonant cacophony we've heard thus far. The descriptions of the park are of the elements of the painting. The water is no longer part of the Seine; it's now "blue, purple, yellow, red water." It's triangular. The grass is no longer covering the island; now it's elliptical. The shadows no longer fall naturally; now they are arranged. We hear George's humming motif, a motif we only hear when he is creating art. Most tellingly, they walk through the shadows, towards trees, "*forever*" [emphasis added]. This one word clues us in to the fact that this is George's painting, his masterpiece. This Sunday afternoon on the island of La Grande Jatte will not last just one afternoon.

It will last forever.

At the very end of the song, after the singing has stopped, we hear the creation of art motif and then the same three chords that opened the song, moving toward each other in great dissonance, until they meet in one final harmonious chord. Over the ringing of the last chord, we hear the two-note "Sunday" motif. The painting is complete. The act is over.

But it's important to remember that the many conflicts are not resolved. George has created his masterpiece, but he has not learned much yet, and he has not reconciled his real life with his artistic life. Perhaps the lessons he needs to learn can't be learned in just one lifetime. So his story and life, and his need to reunite with Dot, will be carried on in Act II by another George, his great-grandson, who in many ways is really the same George.

## Act II

Act II opens with the exact same image that closed Act I: the tableau of the painting. No one on stage moves. There is silence. The score says that the audience should feel the tension, waiting for something on stage to happen. But it doesn't. Finally, music starts. It's the accompaniment from the first song, "Sunday in the Park with George." In Act I, this was a song about how hard it is to pose for a painting. Now, reformed as "It's Hot Up Here," it's about how hard it is to be *in* the painting. These people are no longer real people in the park; they are now figures in a painting. In a way, this music has become a theme representing the old saying, "One must suffer for one's art."

The chorus uses new music, but the verses use the same music Dot did in the first song. The lyric goes for every possible laugh, describing in detail how awful it is to be stuck in a painting forever, unable to move, trapped with the same people for eternity. These people no longer live; they only exist as George perceived them, not as they really were. They cannot "run amok," they cannot make choices or do as they choose anymore. They're stuck there "in this gavotte," or in other words, in George's prearranged, carefully positioned tableau.

Once again, the show indulges in a "day in the life" perspective, only instead of observing the people whose images end up in a famous painting as we did in Act I, this time we're observing the images themselves. As much as these people hated each other in real life, they hate each other even more now, a hundred years later. Louise wants her glasses that George took from her. The boatman stinks. Jules is flirting with Dot and Yvonne can't do anything about it. People don't think George has captured their best side or that he painted them in proper proportion. And they don't like now being controlled completely by George, their free will forever usurped. Everyone's a critic (and in fact, several of them *will* be critics in the next scene).

In fact, the things they're complaining about are precisely the things Seurat was most careful about: light, design, composition, and balance. The tension among these characters is more profound than ever. They complain that "the outward show of bliss up here is disappearing dot by dot," in other words, Seurat's careful creation of tension among the elements in his painting is still going strong. We wonder if Seurat really can have both tension and harmony at the same time. But that's exactly where the magic lies. Just as he has taken separate independent colors and put them next to each other for the eye to blend—"divided, not mixed on the palette, mixed by the eye"—he has done the same thing with the people. He has taken independent figures, all drawn at different times on different days in different spots, and arranged them next to each other on the canvas. They are separate, not interacting, and yet when we step back they do blend, becoming a full, integrated work of art. And Sondheim and Lapine have done the same thing, by creating these many disparate characters and then bringing them together this way.

Though time continues for us, it doesn't for them. They still want the same things they wanted a hundred years ago—the soldier wants the girls, Jules still wants a romp in the tall grass. They haven't changed because they're stuck in this one moment forever, just as the modern-day George is stuck artistically and personally. Their stagnation is like his, but they have an excuse. There's an old dramatic device playwrights use to maintain dramatic tension in a scene; for each character on stage, they ask why doesn't that character leave, what keeps him there, what does he want? In this case, the answer is a joke: they don't leave because they're stuck in a painting. Time has stopped and yet they have an awareness that time continues outside their world.

The similarities between the two acts is almost overwhelming. The music in Act II is directly based on the music in the first act, even presented in the same order for the most part. The modern-day George's worry that his chromolumes have become perhaps nothing more than repetition is echoed in Sondheim's score, which includes lots of musical repetition, but only in the interest of minimalist development; he rarely uses exact repetition. Sondheim is in control of repetition; George is not. And it's this minimalist repetition that helps binds the two acts together, making each one incomplete by itself.

After the song, the characters come forward one by one and talk about George—in the past tense. He died at age thirty-one. Up until this moment, we've mostly seen things only through George's eyes. But now we get an interesting view into the opinions of others about George. We find out that Jules did indeed respect him and considered him a friend, that the women found him sexy and mysterious, that they all wanted to be in his painting for their own shot at immortality.

## Back to the Future

The story flashes forward one hundred years to 1984. The scene is the auditorium of the Art Institute of Chicago, where the Seurat painting hangs. Seurat's great-grandson, also named George, enters pushing a wheelchair containing Marie, the modern George's grandmother and Seurat's daughter, now ninety-eight years old. The modern-day George (from here on out, I'll refer to the Act I George as Seurat) is an inventor/sculptor and we are the audience for his latest work, a light sculpture called Chromolume #7. After a slide show about Seurat and his work, narrated by George and Marie, they turn on the chromolume, accompanied by a synthesized, sequenced musical score. Hidden inside the fast complicated music are the brush stroke motif, the creation of art motif, and the "Sunday" bugle call motif, all from Act I.

Midway through the presentation, the chromolume shorts out.

George has to explain and apologize while the machine is fixed. He says to us (as we, the audience, play the role of the audience at the museum), "No electricity, no art." Perhaps Seurat's mother was right; perhaps science and technology are taking over and becoming too important. This sets up for us the notion that George has lost his way, that he's no longer in control of his art or his artistic vision. While they're trying to fix the chromolume, museum director Bob Greenberg steps forward to entertain the audience. He mentions the fact that the museum has sold its air rights to raise money and that tours are available after the presentation of the new condominiums above them. (We laugh at this monologue, but the Museum of Modern Art in New York actually did this.) This is a great setup for "Putting It Together" and the theme of commerce versus art.

The next scene is a reception after the presentation, in the room where the Seurat painting hangs. This is a musical scene, incorporating singing, spoken dialogue, and underscoring, called "Putting It Together." Much of this piece consists of cocktail chatter about George and his work (and, just for fun, a number of French words thrown in here and there). Appropriately, it is set to the same music as the gossip scenes from Act I, when the denizens of the park gossiped about Seurat. There's a wonderful connection between the two Georges in this piece, because the melody set to the words, "putting it together," is the same melody (minus one note) that Seurat sings to the words, "finishing the hat." They share the same creation music; significantly though, the nineteenth-century George is actually creating the art while the twentieth-century George is working to finance it. Our century, Sondheim seems to say, has corrupted the artist and his art; the creation isn't possible anymore without the schmoozing. And who better would know that than a Broadway composer and lyricist who has spent a career going through the torture of backers' auditions, *New York Times* reviews, and other fiscally necessary evils?

The connection between art and science is presented as both awful and funny, as George's technician tells him he's leaving the art world to go back to NASA, where there's less pressure. We laugh at the unintentionally awkward comments made, at the tensions between certain people or over certain topics, at the degree to which George must schmooze people he obviously can't stand. But even as we laugh, we also understand how difficult it is for George to be not only artist, but also marketing expert, fundraiser, and celebrity. Certainly George understands how to promote himself and his art better than Seurat did, but the relationship between art and the real world is still an uneasy one.

George's conversation with art critic Blair Daniels underlines two threads running through the show. First, she says she liked seeing Marie on stage with George at the presentation of the chromolume because it added a necessary humanity that she apparently think has been lacking in his work. Like his great-grandfather, George is accused of creating work that is too cold, too mechanical, devoid of human emotion. The other thread is the acknowledgment of the show's stage tricks. In the original production, there are jokes throughout Act I about the stand-ups that fly in from above, pop up from below, sail in from the sides. Seurat's mother complains of the tree that disappeared when George decided he didn't like it there. The soldier talks to a cardboard companion. Here in Act II, George has been making his way through this reception bringing up cutouts of himself to schmooze with people as he makes his escape. Yet here as he talks to Blair Daniels, he keeps trying to pull a new one up but it never appears. Finally after several tries, he runs into the wings, and returns with a portable cutout, which he slams down in front of Blair. Unlike the rich folks and jealous artists, George can't escape an art critic; she has too much power, too much influence.

The bugle call motif, the humming motif, and other motifs from Act I show up in the accompaniment. Part XVII of the piece uses an unusual chord we heard earlier in "Finishing the Hat," just as art critic Blair Daniels finds George. There are seventeen discrete parts to this musical scene, each one a mini-scene of its own, each related musically to the others. The scene is almost a one-act musical.

After the reception, we hear the relationship/conflict chords as George speaks to his ex-wife Elaine. Marie knows she won't be alive much longer, and she has to impart an important lesson to George before she goes, but she doesn't know how to get through to him. When George is left alone with Marie, sitting in front of their family tree on canvas, the time seems right. She sings "Children and Art." Aside from another instance of the conflict chords, and an accompaniment figure related to "Finishing the Hat" in the middle, this is all new music. Before the song, Marie tells Blair Daniels that there are only two worthwhile things to leave behind when you die: children and art. The painting is both a family tree and a great work of art. Marie knows that George is the last of their family line; George has inherited his great-grandfather's talent and passion, but he won't be passing those things on. George needs a connection to the past, to those who've gone before him. We all stand on the shoulders of those who've gone before us; but to do that, we have to have some connection to them. If George could learn from the past, he might not be doomed to repeat the difficulties Seurat faced. If each generation is condemned to start from scratch, we'll never get anywhere. At the end of the song, George begins to understand. He says to himself "Connect, George, connect."

## Once on This Island

A short instrumental reprise of "Children and Art" returns us to the island for the last scene. George is there to present the chromolume in tribute to the island where his grandfather worked, in a kind of collaboration through time, even though that island is forever changed. It is a Sunday afternoon.

George has come full circle, returning to the exact spot where this musical began, on the island where his great-grandfather, his other self, did his greatest work, and George has with him the red book connecting him to Dot as well. George reads/sings "Lesson #8" from Dot's red grammar book, reading sentences about Marie, the fictional Marie after whom his grandmother was named. He begins for the first time to find a real connection to Seurat, to put himself in Seurat's place. This is the beginning of the most important sequence in the show, the time when George will finally learn what he needs to learn. He speaks of himself/Seurat in the third person, putting himself in Marie's place, objectifying himself, making himself someone who is acted upon instead of someone who acts. He finally realizes that he must connect to his past, to his great-grandfather. But has his metaphorical family tree on this island been cut down? Was Seurat's "cutting down" of his mother's tree at the beginning of the show a portent of things to come (even though he did put it back, in the Act I finale), of George's cutting himself off from his family tree in Act II?

Dot appears, to sing "Move On." She is the conduit through which the two Georges can connect. She learned so much from Seurat—some of which she wrote in the red book that George now holds—and Dot will now pass on what she learned from the George in 1884 to the George in 1984. Just as in *Assassins*, when Sondheim and John Weidman represented the assassins' influence on each other by actually physically placing them in each other's presence, here Dot's physical presence represents her influence through the red book. As is already more than evident, this show does not pretend to historical or physical reality; it is about spiritual and emotional reality. What's really happening is that George is reading Seurat's words, written down by Dot, given to Marie, then passed on to George. Here he stands, where his great-grandfather once sketched, and at last he can connect. For dramatic purposes, we actually see Dot on stage, and we hear her sing.

George is having an artistic crisis as well as a personal one. Seurat did not have artistic crises. He had an unshakable belief in his work, even when no one else did, a belief in the importance of an artist's vision, in the singular artistic perspective that an artist brings to his work when he perceives the world through the prism of his own personality. When Seurat sang, "There's nothing to say," it meant that he was unable to verbalize the feelings Dot needed to hear. Here in Act II, when George sings (to the same music), "I've nothing to say," he means as an artist. Seurat's main block was personal communication, but George's is artistic communication. Perhaps together, the two Georges almost make one healthy man.

Dot must instill (or re-instill) Seurat's artistic conviction, the courage to risk, in the modern-day George. The music of "Move On" is the same as "We Do Not Belong Together" in Act I, and the two songs even share bits of lyrics. Ironically, though in Act I Dot accuses Seurat—accompanied by this music—of not having any feelings, here in Act II, George sees—in the same music—the feelings Seurat had but could not verbalize. When he looks at Dot, he sees "the care and the feeling." Seurat expressed his love through his work, not through words. But the Act I song doesn't end; the music slowly segues into "Beautiful." It doesn't end because the problem is left unresolved. But here in Act II, the conflict established in Act I, in 1884, is finally resolved, and here the song can end. The true resolution comes in the wisdom of Seurat now passed on to George through Dot:

*Anything you do,*
*Let it come from you.*
*Then it will be new.*
*Give us more to see . . .*

Apparently, Dot has gained a great deal of wisdom herself during her hundred years in the next world. She is a confident, intelligent, articulate woman, a woman who has grown emotionally and intellectually since we saw her last. She is now the woman George Seurat wanted. He's dead, but in his place the modern-day George can reconcile with Dot. As in most Sondheim shows, these two characters don't get to harmonize musically until they have reconciled. Aside from one moment in "Color and Light" when they sing of their incredible mutual attraction, Dot and George don't harmonize until this song, when they are finally in emotional harmony as well as musical harmony.

The theme of making a choice, whatever the consequences, is a thread throughout many of Sondheim's musicals. Here in *Sunday*, Dot sings:

> *I chose and my world was shaken—*
> *So what?*
> *The choice may have been mistaken,*
> *The choosing was not.*

We have to make choices without knowing where they may lead, she's telling George. To stand paralyzed at the fork in the road, or to live in regret over the choices you've made, is not to have lived. Yet in *Merrily We Roll Along*, we watch as Frank makes innocent choice after innocent choice without thinking of the consequences, exactly as Dot suggests, and his life ends up in ruins. In *Follies*, Ben looks back with barely hidden bitterness over the roads he didn't choose and the life they might have led to. In *Company*, Robert doesn't want to make any major life decisions without some guarantees as to the outcome; so his life becomes stagnated and empty. The central concept of *Into the Woods* is making choices and suffering the consequences, both for the chooser and for others. In *A Little Night Music*, almost every character has made the wrong choice of a mate and are living in relative unhappiness, but here, they all get a second chance.

## Connect the Dots

Finally George recites the magic words that Seurat began the show with, the words Dot recorded faithfully in the red book. And as the characters in the painting return, as the painting comes to life in front of George, as they reprise the Act I finale, "Sunday," he recaptures the beauty of his great-grandfather's work. As implied in the song "Beautiful," there is a difference between what is pleasant to look at and what stirs the emotions. George is no longer just looking at his great-grandfather's painting; it has come alive for him and, we can assume, so has his artistic vision. We can also assume that Dot appears to George now because he now believes, for the first time, that Marie was right, that the painting is his family tree. When the characters all bow to him, and he to them, we know that he has finally connected to his past, to his family, and to the island. They bow to him on the word "forever," because that's what art is about, after all, saying something that lasts long after we're gone. Through the painting, Seurat lives "forever," just as the people in the painting do, and just as the modern-day George can if he can find his way artistically again. When the figures in the painting sing of strolling "on an ordinary Sunday," two things race to mind: that this is certainly no ordinary Sunday, or that perhaps this is an ordinary Sunday and that there is magic even in the most ordinary of times and places, if only you know how to see it.

But perhaps this is not the real Dot who appears before the twentieth-century George. Perhaps this is the Dot of the painting, a perfect Dot who lives only in Seurat's "perfect park," a Dot infused with Seurat's calm and resolve, his clear understanding of art, his deep love for her (as observed by the modern-day George), and also Dot's rich emotions, her love, her enthusiasm for living and experiencing the world. Certainly her manner is different, her speech more eloquent, and she has an inner peace and wisdom the real Dot never had. All the good things from both Seurat and the real Dot have come together in this Perfect Dot; she is the consummation of their love. She is a combination of a real person (or two real people) and a work of art; perhaps her name has even foreshadowed this moment for us (which might placate the critics who think her name is too obvious). Like Marie, the Perfect Dot is the product of the coupling of Seurat and the real Dot, and so perhaps she represents Marie, and the passing to George through the family tree the accumulated wisdom of this family. This Perfect Dot is, in a way, a stand-in for Marie, finishing the job Marie began, setting George back on the right track.

This is certainly not the only reading of this scene, but it's well supported by the text and by the original Broadway performance of the scene (which gives us some strong insight into what the show's creators intended). Remember that at the end of the first act, we've clearly left the real park for the "Perfect Park," as evidenced by the

song lyric and the choreographed behavior of the characters as conducted by George. Here in Act II, the real park no longer exists the
way it once did (it's been commercially "developed"), so it's safe to assume that when we see the empty park again, the buildings gone, it
must be the "Perfect Park," and within it, the Perfect Dot, the Dot not
only created by Seurat in his painting but also the Dot created by
modern-day George in his head, knowing only as much as Marie told
him (particularly in "Children and Art") and he observed in the
painting. George's image of Dot is the quiet, peaceful woman in the
painting, no expression on her face, no conflict, no sorrow, just a
woman looking out at the water.

There is certainly an argument to be made that the real Dot matured—was forced to mature—when she moved to a new country
and raised a daughter. But a more practical than romantic marriage
to Louis and the challenges of adapting to an entirely new country
and society probably wouldn't have given her the profound sense of
inner peace she has at the end. And she probably hasn't matured
while being stuck in the painting, with no outside forces or events
acting on her, with nothing at all to effect change in her. And we have
to acknowledge that once George finished the painting, there were
two Dots ever after: the real Dot who moved to America and raised
Marie, and the Perfect Dot who lived on in the painting. This peaceful,
wise Dot at the end is not just an older Dot; it's a special Dot, a different but parallel Dot, one created by Seurat, by Marie, and by George.

Finally, we see that Seurat's magic words, the words Dot transcribed in her book, don't apply just to painting; they also apply to this
musical. Order, design, composition, tension, balance, and harmony
also describe Sondheim's score, Lapine's book, the sets, the special effects, and the lighting. These words also apply to life. George has to
learn to infuse his life and his work with a clearer design, with a healthy
tension, with a more thoughtful composition, with genuine balance,
with light and harmony. Like Sondheim's *Company*, this show does
not spell out for us explicitly what will happen to our protagonist after the curtain goes down. It's enough that we know he understands,
that he's made some decisions, that he will move on. George is ready
to begin anew. He has returned to the "so many possibilities" of the
"blank page or canvas." Perhaps he will try again with Elaine. Perhaps
he'll find someone new and build a life with her. Maybe he'll even
have children.

Or maybe he won't.

## Other Resources

Vocal selections, the full piano-vocal score, and the script for *Sunday in the Park with George* have all been published and are easily found. There are 250 numbered, first-edition copies of the published script signed by Sondheim and Lapine, and as of this writing, some copies are still available in a New York bookstore called Richard Stoddard Performing Arts Books. These first editions include some material that was later cut from the production and from subsequent printings of the script. A videotape of the original Broadway cast is commercially available as well. The painting is on display at the Art Institute in Chicago and is truly breathtaking to see. Music Theatre International also has a great teacher study guide available.